TOTAL WAR AND THE LAW

TOTAL WAR AND THE LAW

THE AMERICAN HOME FRONT IN WORLD WAR II

Edited by Daniel R. Ernst and Victor Jew

PRAEGER

Westport, Connecticut
London

Library of Congress Cataloging-in-Publication Data

Total war and the law : the American home front in World War II / edited by Daniel R. Ernst and Victor Jew.
p. cm.
Includes bibliographical references and index.
ISBN 0–275–97598–3 (alk. paper)
1. War and emergency powers—United States—History—20th century. 2. World War, 1939–1945—Law and legislation—United States. I. Ernst, Daniel R. II. Jew, Victor.
KF5060.T68 2002
342.73'0412—dc21 2002067940

British Library Cataloguing in Publication Data is available.

Library of Congress Catalog Card Number: 2002067940
ISBN: 0–275–97598–3

First published in 2002

Praeger Publishers, 88 Post Road West, Westport, CT 06881
An imprint of Greenwood Publishing Group, Inc.
www.praeger.com

Printed in the United States of America

The paper used in this book complies with the Permanent Paper Standard issued by the National Information Standards Organization (Z39.48–1984).

10 9 8 7 6 5 4 3 2 1

Copyright Acknowledgments

The editors and publisher gratefully acknowledge permission for use of the following material:

Excerpts from the papers of Harold Burton, William O. Douglas, Felix Frankfurter, Robert Jackson, Joseph Rauh, Jr., Wiley Rutledge, Harlan Stone, and Earl Warren courtesy of the Library of Congress.

Excerpts from the papers of Hugo L. Black courtesy of Hugo L. Black, Jr.

Excerpts from the Earl Warren letter to Jerome B. Kavanaugh, March 6, 1942, and from the oral histories of Earl Warren, Carey McWilliams, Warren Olney, Tom Clark, and Percy Heckendorf courtesy of The Bancroft Library, University of California, Berkeley.

Excerpts from the Earl Warren Papers courtesy of the California State Archives, Earl Warren Papers.

Excerpts from the FDR Office Files, the Morgenthau Papers, the Morgenthau Diaries, and the FDR Personal Secretary Files courtesy of the FDR Presidential Library.

Excerpts from the papers of Louis Brandeis, Raoul Burger, Felix Frankfurter, Lloyd Garrison, and Mark deWolfe Howe courtesy of Harvard Law School Library.

Excerpts from the papers of Herbert Hoover, Bourke Hickenlooper, and Westbrook Pegler are used with the permission of the Herbert Hoover Presidential Library, West Branch, Iowa.

Excerpts from the papers of Lucille Cardin Crain and Polly Ruhtenberg courtesy of the University of Oregon.

Excerpts from the Rosenthal oral history courtesy of the Columbia University Oral History Research Office.

Excerpts from J. Willard Hurst, oral history interview, 1981, and the Willard Hurst Papers courtesy of the University of Wisconsin-Madison Archives.

Excerpts from the Marvin B. Rosenberry Papers 1845–1956, Archives, courtesy of the Wisconsin Historical Society.

Excerpts from Gunnar Myrdal, *An American Dilemma: The Negro Problem and Modern Democracy*. Copyright © 1944, 1962 by Harper & Row, Publishers, Inc. Reprinted by permission of HarperCollins Publishers, Inc.

Every reasonable effort has been made to trace the owners of copyright materials in this book, but in some instances this has proven impossible. The author and publisher will be glad to receive information leading to more complete acknowledgments in subsequent printings of the book and in the meantime extend their apologies for any omissions.

Contents

Introduction

Daniel R. Ernst and Victor Jew

For much of the past decade, many Americans have seemed obsessed with a war fought fifty years earlier. A large number consumed and were sometimes consumed by memories of World War II. That war—more precisely, the forty-four months of U.S. participation in the conflict—reappeared in memory and merchandise, in books, television, and film. Stephen Spielberg's *Saving Private Ryan* grossed nearly $200,000,000 within the United States just months after its opening in 1998.[1] The film also inspired an outpouring of curiosity, honorifics, and memorializations, including small, face-to-face encounters with D-Day veterans that were perhaps more moving than the official fiftieth anniversary observances held several years earlier. More generally, the men and women who fought the war abroad and on the home front have been hailed as the "greatest generation" for their many acts of courage, sacrifice, and patriotism.[2] Particularly when contrasted with the divided nation that fought the Vietnam War, the home front during the "Good War" sometimes seemed like the spontaneous crusade of a united people convinced of the justice of their cause.

If the collective memory of 1941–45 remains a comforting recollection of a consensual and unfailingly heroic time, it has not been for lack of attempts by professional historians to complicate the matter. Long before the commemorations of the 1990s, Richard Polenberg's *War and Society* (1972) and John Morton Blum's *V Was for Victory* (1976) fully explored the social and political conflicts of the home front. "World War II freed both unifying and disunifying forces in American society; in some ways it made for cohesion, in others for fragmentation," Polenberg wrote. "The war years were a time when many people freely made sacrifices of the most generous sort and when others callously sought to benefit from those sacrifices, a time when many Americans experienced a sense of true community and when others succumbed to virulent racial, religious and class hatreds."[3]

Many historians have followed Polenberg's and Blum's lead. For example, they have probed the multiple contradictions of the class-directed and gendered recruitment of women workers into the factories, explored conflict between white and black Americans, discovered new levels of government duplicity in the Japanese American internment episode, and recovered the record of military service forged by gays and lesbians.[4] Americans may have remembered the war as a time when "a spirit of cooperation, unity, and generosity impelled [them] to work long hours, purchase large numbers of war bonds, and good-naturedly endure sharp restrictions on [their] freedom to consume and spend."[5] The social and political conflict that actually transpired is better captured in the title of the historian David M. Kennedy's recent synthesis of the literature, "The Caldron of the Home Front."[6]

Dispelling popular nostalgia has been only one aim of the professional historians. They have also tried to show the ways in which the war years permanently transformed American politics and society. In this they have been joined by a number of historically minded social scientists, some of whom have portrayed the 1940s as a decisive moment in the development of American politics. During the New Deal, they argue, a new political regime, the "Democratic order," emerged. Its disparate elements often clashed in the 1930s, but during the war years they were consolidated into a stable if heterogeneous system. Thus the political scientists Karen Orren and Stephen Skowronek consider the 1940s "the decade in which modern liberal reform moved beyond political and group confrontation to insinuate itself into the basic arrangements and routine operations of the national state."[7]

Developments in constitutional and legal history might not, at first, seem a promising vantage point from which to view the place of World War II in American political development. After all (and as the ancient maxim holds), *inter arma silent leges*: in wartime the laws are silent. The silences of the law during World War II—especially the U.S. Supreme Court's acquiescence in the internment of Japanese Americans—have been thoroughly documented, initially by the political scientist Edward Corwin in his penetrating lectures, *Total War and the Constitution* (1947), and subsequently by scores of scholars.[8]

Even considered as a check on government, however, the law did speak up; in fact, as William M. Wiecek writes in his contribution to this volume, it sometimes spoke eloquently. When one considers the law's role as an affirmative agent of government, its voice can be heard everywhere in wartime America. For the war effort was not (or not simply) a spontaneous social movement, as nostalgic celebrations have sometimes implied. It was also an astounding act of governance by a state that was poorly prepared for the task. The European belligerents entered the war with well-established, centralized, locality-penetrating bureaucracies staffed by professional civil servants. In the United States the public sector lacked such an "autonomous bureaucratic core."[9] Federal commissions and administrative agencies were more recent in origin than their European counterparts, national administrators were more often obliged to share power with state and local officials, and the national government still lacked a broadly based tax on personal income. Existing public bodies had to be strengthened or streamlined, new ones built, and private entities coordinated. To a remarkable extent, the learning and expertise needed to perform these tasks were the possessions of American lawyers.

The point was obvious to a foundation officer who introduced a conference on law and the war in 1943. "The contemporary struggle necessarily enlarges the sphere of law and creates the need for its amendment in many ways."[10] At some points the expanded legal sphere receded after 1945, although rarely to the status quo ante bellum. At others, the institutions, practices, and ideas were extended still further and became permanent components of American governance.

The essays in this volume thus join the larger historical literature of World War II and its place in American political development. Although each may be read for the particular concerns that animate its author, each also contributes to an emerging understanding of how law helped shape a distinctive period in American political development. To make that contribution clearer, we will first summarize recent works on the political history of the 1940s and then relate each essay to the themes found in that literature.

THE NEW POLITICAL HISTORY OF WORLD WAR II

When the United States joined the global conflict of the 1940s it set itself the task of fighting a war that was at once total, democratic, and hegemonic. As a total war, it required (in Corwin's words) "the politically ordered participation . . . of all personal and social forces, the scientific, the mechanical, the commercial, and the economic, the moral, the literary and artistic, and the psychological."[11] For the United States and many of its allies, it was also a democratic war, requiring the support of public opinion and the private owners of labor, capital, and wealth. As the political scientist Bartholomew Sparrow has observed, the federal government had "to reach out for resources owned or controlled by societal actors in order to survive." Finally, World War II was a hegemonic war, in that it elevated the United States into a dominant role in international affairs. As Sparrow again writes, "Just as the end of the Punic Wars marked the fall of Rome, and as the end of the Napoleonic Wars marked the beginning of British hegemony, so did the Second World War mark the start of American international dominance."[12]

In peacetime the U.S. Constitution presented considerable barriers to so great and sustained a mobilization of social resources. The principles of separation of powers and federalism adopted in the first American constitutions certainly made it impossible for some new George III to rise up in the land, but they also hampered those who would use the state to direct or control the social and economic forces of a modern, industrial nation. Gradual changes in the first decades of the twentieth century, brought to a sudden crisis in the Court-packing plan of 1937, improved matters considerably. Commencing in the spring of that year, the U.S. Supreme Court generally upheld regulation of the national economy, vast schemes of public investment and expenditure, and a luxuriant growth of agencies and commissions. Congress proved more jealous of FDR's attempts to bring the fractious federal executive under his control, but even its refusal to enact the president's most ambitious proposals for reorganizing the executive was offset by the transfer of the Bureau of the Budget from the Treasury Department to the Executive Office of the President in 1939. The war powers acts opened the doors to a more extensive, if presumably temporary, expansion and restructuring of the executive branch. Indeed, the wartime state far exceeded its New Deal precursor. The federal bureaucracy grew from one to almost four million persons, new or sharply intensified relations between the state and civil society emerged, and great innovations in administrative methods were introduced.[13]

The constraints on the war mobilization lay not so much in the formal commands of the U.S. Constitution as in the system of politics it had engendered. Foremost on the political landscape, thanks to its continuing dominance in Congress, was the national political party. In contrast with the issue-oriented, centrally controlled parties that emerged elsewhere in the industrialized West, American political parties developed in a polity structured by federalism, single-member congressional districts, and winner-take-all elections. They organized constituencies from the locality upward, binding the heterogeneous parts into a working whole through the generous distribution of public offices, grants, and other kinds of patronage.[14]

After his landslide election of 1936, FDR attempted to remake the Democratic Party with a purge of its most conservative elements. Southern Democrats, who opposed any federal programs that might upset the "racial civilization" of their region, were his special targets.[15] When the purge failed, the outraged survivors joined with Republicans in opposing the New Deal. Bolstered by the backlash over FDR's Court-packing plan, his tacit support of the sit-down strikes of industrial unions, and the recession of 1937, the new conservative coalition obtained enough clout by 1938 to block further expansions of the New Deal state. After the 1942 elections, a solid congressional majority set out to "protect white supremacy, reduce federal spending except on the war, eradicate various New Deal agencies, and challenge the authority of the White House." With Southern Democrats controlling congressional committees charged with oversight of the military and with Republican congressmen pressing the demands of defense contractors, the prospects for social reform through the extensive command-and-control regulation of business were slight indeed.[16]

Yet other kinds of state-building continued at an accelerated pace, thanks to the efforts of a different set of political actors. Since the turn of the twentieth century, the growth of state and federal bureaucracies held out the promise of creating "an executive-centered political system," in which middle-class professionals successfully contested party regulars for control of policy-making.[17] The National Labor Relations Act, massive public works projects, social insurance programs, and other initiatives of FDR's legislative program of 1935 gave him an unprecedented opportunity to circumvent hostile political machines by creating "pro-New Deal networks that were not controlled by local Democratic powers." Every favorable ruling of the National Labor Relations Board, every award of a government contract, every Social Security check received was a new point of contact between the state and the citizenry, and each class of beneficiary potentially a new component of a "progressive liberal bloc."[18] Thus, as the political scientist Martin Shefter has observed, the new bureaucracies promised to "perform for the administration precisely those functions served by party organizations in cities and states governed by centralized political machines."[19]

During much of FDR's presidency, the most prominent advocates of an executive-centered polity were "the New Dealers," a collection of lawyers, social workers, academics, and regional planners who shuttled between the private sector and government and had scant regard for the party regulars. Their power lay not in their electoral clout (which was negligible) but in their continued usefulness to the president as administrators and experts.[20] Those who entered government in the 1930s usually did so as champions of command-and-control regulation, publicly owned utilities, state-sponsored collective bargaining, and comprehensive, federally funded social insurance.

After the outbreak of war in Europe and still more after Pearl Harbor, the New Dealers found themselves on the defensive as their social aims ran headlong into the need for the active participation of businessmen in mobilizing American industry. Subject to regular harrying by conservative congressmen during the appropriations process, challenged within their own agencies by "dollar-a-year" businessmen, and circumvented by a general shift in effective decision-making from civilian agencies to the armed services, the New Dealers' authority ebbed away during the course of the war.[21]

As it did, the most ambitious goals of the most visionary New Dealers fell by the wayside.[22] The war effectively foreclosed the possibility that the federal government might develop the capacity to direct the details of industrial production, to serve as an employer of last resort, or to fund universal, noncontributory systems of social insurance and social provision from general revenues.[23] Before the war, for example, Thurman Arnold had turned "the graveyard of the Justice Department," the Antitrust Division, into an effective guardian of the consumer interest. But with the coming of World War II, Arnold's repeated clashes with war agencies over contracts with industrialists disrupted the administration's efforts to pacify an often turbulent home front. When Arnold took on the railroad industry, cartelized under the aegis of the Interstate Commerce Commission, FDR finally "benched" his antitruster in 1943 by appointing him to the federal judiciary.[24]

If, then, the war years saw a retreat by liberals from an ambitious New Deal agenda, they also put beyond serious question the legitimacy of "a powerful and active administrative arm in Washington."[25] During the war the federal income tax was established as "the dominant source of federal revenue, as virtually all working Americans started to pay federal income taxes." Further, the Treasury Department's Bureau of Public Debt engaged in an extensive and sophisticated marketing of government securities. These innovations financed lasting postwar growth in federal expenditures and civilian employment.[26]

The strengthening of the federal government's power to tax and borrow also heralded a new kind of liberal reform, the use of fiscal planning to suppress unemployment, stabilize prices, and steady economic growth without the divisiveness of direct controls like those employed by the Office of Price Administration.[27] Targeted public investment, tax deductions and credits, and other budgetary measures gave quite disparate groups of Southerners, industrialists, and trade unionists common cause to support the new political order. As Orren and Skowronek write, a "peculiarly American brand of Keynesian economics" held "together in the same orbit interests and ambitions that in other circumstances could be expected to be regularly at loggerheads." The federal bureaucracy survived, albeit at the cost of accommodating the "least liberal, indeed avowedly antiliberal, elements" of the Democratic Party.[28]

Fiscal planning was not the only "policy instrument" to survive the war.[29] In the 1930s, New Dealers pioneered the use of government contracts as a planning tool by imposing minimum labor standards on contractors and creating a bureaucracy to enforce them within the Department of Labor. When federal expenditures on materials ballooned during the war, so did the opportunities for policy-making. Had the New Dealers been able to control the terms of this "contractual planning," they might have turned it to socially progressive ends. Instead, it became the instrument of the corporate professionals who staffed new procurement divisions within the armed services and were more concerned with rationalizing production than promoting social reform. Particularly in sectors that were heavily dependent on government expenditures, such as aircraft production and microelectronics, wartime contracting laid the foundation for the "military-industrial complex" of the postwar era.[30]

The war also helped entrench an "associative" approach to governance in some fields of public policy. Well before the war, some progressives had hoped to avoid the evils of a politicized bureaucracy by organizing voluntary associations that could take the initiative in regulating broad realms of economic life. They believed that the state should help organize these associations, present alternatives for their consideration, and promote bargaining within their ranks and with other groups, but then defer to whatever decisions emerged from the process as much as possible.[31] In the area of social security, a "private welfare state" emerged from the collective bargaining agreements of trade unionists and employers with only a slight increase in the related federal bureaucracy.[32] In contrast, another field of associative governance, wartime labor policy, was implemented by a small army of arbitrators who enforced the collective bargains of employers and unions when they could agree and imposed "the best practices of employers and unions" when they could not.[33]

In whatever form, wartime state-building acquired added significance from the hegemonic nature of U.S. participation in the global conflict. The political coalitions and innovations in statecraft that permitted the United States to acquire a dominant role during the conflict often proved serviceable in promoting American economic and military interests in the Cold War that followed.[34] "Security" had been a watchword for domestic policy-making during the New Deal; in the late 1940s the term acquired new connotations in light of the United States' leading role in international affairs, assumed with the active support of many of the corporate professionals who had managed the war effort.[35] Domestic and international concerns intertwined as never before. As the political scientist Brian Waddell writes, "National security became wedded to economic security: the ideology of national security made it possible to combine Keynesianism, corporate internationalism, and militarization into a governing consensus."[36]

TOTAL WAR AND THE LAW

The chapters published here significantly advance our understanding of how the law constrained and how it advanced the growth of the American state during a total, democratic, and hegemonic war. The law joined in the fighting of a total war when judicial and law enforcement personnel took on unexpected, war-related tasks; Supreme Court justices loosened important constitutional restraints on the executive branch; Treasury lawyers and officials protected the federal government's vastly expanded power to tax; other lawyers used government contracts to intrude far into the sphere of labor-management relations; and labor and military policy conflicted with racial supremacy in the South. The law helped keep the war democratic by refusing to surrender the ideals of an independent judiciary, the rule of law, and a limited administrative state and by reaching an accommodation with the American party system. And the law prepared the United States for its dominant global role after the war. Law and lawyers pioneered methods of policy-making through government contracts and fiscal control that flourished in the postwar national security state. Conflicts between individual liberty and military necessity, made salient in Supreme Court cases during the war, reappeared during the McCarthy era. The Japanese American internment decisions and sadly ineffective efforts to enforce race-blind labor and military policies revealed the hypocrisy of fighting a war for freedom abroad while denying it at home, much as the civil rights movement would during the Cold War.

The first two chapters, by Melvin I. Urofsky and William M. Wiecek, view the subject from the pinnacle of the American judiciary, the U.S. Supreme Court. The Court emerged from the constitutional travails of the Great Depression and New Deal as a potent symbol of Americans' commitment to "government under law." Whether it could continue to play that in wartime—whether it could ensure that the American war effort would be democratic as well as total—was a question of great moment and some anxiety when the war came. "We may well wonder in view of the precedents now established whether constitutional government as hitherto maintained in this Republic could survive another great war even victoriously waged," Charles Evans Hughes had warned in the wake of World War I.[37] As Hughes stepped down from the Chief Justiceship in the summer of 1941, Americans were about to learn whether his fears were well founded.

By Pearl Harbor, seven of the Court's nine justices were FDR's appointees. Their nominations had been inextricably linked to the party transformations and state-building of his administration. Hugo Black and James Byrnes had been heavyweights within the Democratic Party and were rewarded for their support of the administration in the Senate. William O. Douglas, Felix Frankfurter, Robert Jackson, Frank Murphy, and Stanley Reed were New Dealers who had either served within the federal bureaucracy or (in Frankfurter's case) staffed it with protégés. After Pearl Harbor several justices wanted to leave the Court, but, with the exception of Byrnes, FDR felt that his appointees could better help the war effort by staying where they were. There they could continue to interpret New Deal legislation sympathetically, and some could continue to assist him in the ad hoc and informal ways they had before their appointment.

Urofsky's findings suggest that the extrajudicial activities of the justices did not, in themselves, subordinate the Court to the presidency in the consolidating Democratic political order. Justice Murphy, for example, obtained a commission as lieutenant colonel in the army reserves, and

Jackson played poker with FDR and wrote speeches for him, but both voted against the administration in *Korematsu*, the landmark case reviewing the relocation of Japanese Americans. On the other hand, Chief Justice Harlan Fiske Stone scrupulously rejected extrajudicial assignments from FDR, but he pushed his Court to back the administration in the Nazi Saboteurs' case.[38] Frankfurter's extrajudicial work for Roosevelt was extensive, even outrageous. Yet Urofsky believes that the justice's intensely felt love of country was more important than his allegiance to FDR. On balance, Urofsky concludes, "the rule of law was not silenced, but it was often threatened by the patriotic excesses of some justices."

A greater threat than the president's requests for help was the government's demand that the justices defer to its claim of military necessity. A crucial element in the Anglo-American notion of the rule of law was, as the Oxford law don Albert Venn Dicey put it, that citizens be able to have the actions of public officials reviewed "in the ordinary legal manner before the ordinary Courts of the land."[39] Dicey acknowledged that courts could be closed and martial law established in dire emergencies, but he interpreted this exception quite narrowly. In *Ex parte Milligan* (1866), the U.S. Supreme Court similarly asserted the supremacy of common-law courts wherever they could be held. But was *Milligan* still good law in an age of total war? If it were not, Wiecek observes, the Court would have been free to indulge in "an unhealthy deference to military judgment and military views of necessity" during the war. Given the hegemonic nature of the conflict for the United States, the justices might have remained deferential to the Cold War that followed, and Hughes's fears would have been realized. Civilian control of the military and the new intelligence community, a crucial precondition of "government under law," would have been seriously diminished.

Wiecek shows that the justices gave up much of the high ground taken by *Milligan*. In four dramatic cases, involving the legitimacy of military commissions that tried German saboteurs and Japanese war criminals, procedural and evidentiary safeguards in treason trials, and the establishment of martial law in Hawaii, they compromised civil liberty in order to avoid a standoff with the executive branch. In the Nazi Saboteurs' case and *Yamashita* (which involved the trial of a Japanese officer under harsh terms set by the "American Caesar," General Douglas MacArthur), the majority conceded what Wiecek terms "a broad, potentially illimitable power in military courts."[40] The Court did reassert the supremacy of the courts after the war in *Duncan v. Kahanamoku*, which condemned the continuation of martial law in Hawaii long after any credible threat of invasion had passed. Still, Wiecek concludes, the damage had been done. The Court had shown itself to be willing to "mute" the voice of the laws when a majority shared "the general anxiety induced by enemy threat."

For Urofsky and Wiecek, the Court's greatest failure to protect the rule of law in wartime was its acquiescence, in the *Hirabayashi* and *Korematsu* decisions, in the mass internment of Japanese Americans, two-thirds of whom were U.S. citizens. Sumi Cho's essay on Earl Warren's role in the internment shows what can happen when state officials, freed from the strict scrutiny of the courts and heedless of the liberties of a politically vulnerable minority, try to do their part in a total war. She shows us Warren not in his familiar guise as U.S. Chief Justice but as California's attorney general, well along in his steady climb from legislative clerk to governor of the state. Although Cho is interested in Warren's war years primarily for what they and *Brown v. Board of Education* (1954) tell us about the civil rights jurisprudence of today, her narrative also reveals much about the law and politics of wartime America.

First, Warren's activities in 1942 illustrate the unexpected ways in which law could affirmatively contribute to state-building during the war. When the Democratic governor assigned Warren, a Republican, no meaningful role in the civil defense of the state, he resolved to create one for himself. His principal tool was the state's Alien Land Law of 1920, which authorized him to file suit on behalf of the state to reclaim land held by aliens ineligible for citizenship. These "escheat" actions had rarely been brought before the war, but in 1942, at Warren's instigation, they came in a flurry. Of even greater significance, Warren used the statutes as grounds for compiling maps showing the land ownership of the state's Japanese Americans. Although methodologically flawed, Warren's maps helped convince national policy-makers that Japanese Americans were plotting a campaign of sabotage and had to be interned.

Warren later protested that he had only been trying to discharge his "responsibility for public security," but it is also true that a legal campaign against Japanese Californians was good politics in 1942. Cho shows that California's Progressive Republicans resorted to anti-Asian appeals long before Pearl Harbor. Warren's hero, Hiram Johnson, had made anti-Asian appeals as a governor and U.S. senator, and Warren himself had found it useful to join a nativist group as he campaigned for district attorney in 1926. In 1942 Warren and his fellow Republicans recognized the "anti-Jap" card for the winner it was, and they played it for all it was worth. In seeking the governorship, Warren and his associates carefully cultivated the nativist American Legion and blasted the Democratic incumbent for being overly solicitous of the "Japs." Through such instances of political calculation and racial insensitivity, the politics of race survived the war.

Like Cho, Daniel Kryder seeks to explain the survival of "resistant strains of racial prejudice" after the collapse of "a formal system of race caste." African Americans realized that the federal government's need for their labor in industry and the military could be turned to their advantage in their struggle against white supremacy. Many embraced a "Double V" campaign: victory at home, as well as abroad. Their efforts did produce a favorable response, including the creation of the Fair Employment Practices

Committee and an official, if inconsistently enforced, policy of integrated public facilities on Army bases.[41] Yet, as Kryder has elsewhere written, too often federal officials "not only absorbed pre-existing civilian race tension, but fueled black-white animosity through the federal sponsorship of caste."[42]

Gunnar Myrdal's *An American Dilemma* (1944) provides the point of departure in Kryder's attempt to explain why Jim Crow survived the war. The Swedish sociologist argued that the conflict would revolutionize the racial treatment of African Americans by confronting white Americans with a contradiction between their beliefs and their behavior. They believed and fought for "the American creed" of equal opportunity, yet they also embraced a system of segregation that denied that opportunity to their black counterparts. Wartime investigations of Southern industry and military operations would make the contradiction painfully obvious to all Americans, Myrdal argued. They would have to resolve it in favor of racial equality if the United States was to assume its likely postwar role as an exponent of freedom throughout the world.[43]

While appreciative of Myrdal's argument, Kryder maintains that his explanation of the relationship between wartime state-building and race relations was incomplete. First, Myrdal did not foresee that FDR would sacrifice racial reform for the sake of social peace and the continued support of racist Southerners for the administration's war efforts. Political necessity drove the race policy of the Democratic president, just as it did that of the Republican governor Earl Warren. Second, Myrdal attributed too much weight to the mental anguish of white Americans and not enough to the militancy of African Americans. If presidential calculations of political necessity were the key, then they had to be changed in favor of racial equality. Only after African Americans mounted sustained, militant protest in the 1960s did the view from the White House change. Only then did racial equality become a war aim, rather than, as FDR put it, a matter of "long-range planning" to be postponed indefinitely.

What was urgent for FDR was revenue. Total war required a vast expansion of the federal government's revenues, attained in large part through the transformation of the personal income tax from a "class tax" to a "mass tax." The wartime builders of the new tax regime met many administrative challenges with innovations such as withholding from wages and salaries. They also needed to persuade American workers that their taxes were vital to the war effort. Government officials did not count on patriotism alone to ensure the compliance of taxpayers. Rather, they engaged in a "politics of sacrifice" by commissioning Irving Berlin songs and Walt Disney cartoons to affirm and applaud those Americans who willingly paid their taxes and by questioning the loyalty of those who prominently objected to the new tax regime.[44]

Carolyn C. Jones shows just how effective the politicians of sacrifice were in her case study of the female industrialist and tax resister Vivien Kellems. Kellems raised real and persistent problems in the administration of the federal income tax, such as fairness in the treatment of married and single persons. Yet what made her "Public Enemy Number One" in the eyes of Treasury officials was her frontal assault on the new tax regime. Her call in 1944 for employers to refuse to pay taxes and build up their own capital reserves threatened both the war effort and an emerging tool of fiscal planning. Kellems claimed that she only wanted to end the "boondoggling" of "a little group of Communists in the White House." This was, on its face, a plausible appeal to a growing body of anti-New Deal sentiment, but it failed utterly when the administration revealed Kellems's romance with a Nazi agent and her surprising tolerance of "boondoggling" when it took the form of war contracts with her own company. Even the industrialists and libertarians who shared her dim view of "the gangster Truman administration" kept their distance. After the war she mounted several Quixotic campaigns of tax resistance, including a constitutional challenge to the withholding mechanism, but she did so largely on her own.

The volume's final two chapters, by Daniel R. Ernst and Reuel E. Schiller, return readers to wartime Washington but stray from the "Marble Palace" of the U.S. Supreme Court to the less exalted domiciles of the federal bureaucracy. Both authors view the war as a period in the long-term development of the administrative state; both investigate how the great expansion of the executive branch during the war forced American lawyers to revise their understanding of "government under law." The wartime consolidation of the Democratic order was not just the emergence of a durable political equilibrium in Congress and the presidency. It was also a process of institutional and intellectual accommodation, in which courts and a court-centered notion of the rule of law gave ground to administrative agencies, boards, bureaus, and commissions, acting on their own calculations of the public interest.

The backdrop for Ernst's chapter is, for political historians at least, a familiar event: the fall of Vice President Henry A. Wallace's Board of Economic Warfare (BEW). During its short life, the BEW was home to some of the New Dealers Wallace had come to rely on during his tenure as Secretary of Agriculture and to younger figures, such as Willard Wirtz, a future U.S. Secretary of Labor. The agency's most controversial job was the overseas procurement and development of commodities to replace those cut off by the Pacific war. Critics charged that Wallace was more interested in improving the welfare of peasants than winning the war. After a spectacular public quarrel between Wallace and the conservative Secretary of Commerce Jesse Jones, the BEW was abolished and, with it, Wallace's chance to remain on the presidential ticket in 1944.

Ernst views the rise and fall of the BEW from the perspective of Willard Hurst, a protégé of Felix Frankfurter and, later in his career, the leading American legal historian of his generation. Hurst arrived at the BEW convinced that administrative agencies were needed to deal with social problems that were too complicated to be solved through market transactions or private lawsuits. He soon acted on those beliefs by writing clauses into procurement contracts that obligated sellers to observe certain minimum health, safety, and wage standards in their dealings with their employees. These "labor clauses" made the most of the BEW's narrow mandate, but they also embroiled the agency in quarrels with the State Department, the Reconstruction Finance Corporation, and congressional opponents of the New Deal. In the end, Hurst saw the clauses fall prey to divisions within the executive branch and the requirements of party politics.

Hurst returned to academia after the war convinced that the principal culprit had been the shortsightedness of businessmen and party politicians like Jones and his congressional allies. The divided, party-directed American state, he learned, was not a machine that would go of itself; to run properly it needed the close attention of lawyers trained to discern and act on "the immanent rationality of the social order."[45] Like the political scientist Stephen Skowronek, who has more recently argued that lawyers have constituted "a special intellectual cadre that maintains an underlying continuity in governmental activity through social and political changes," Hurst believed that the legal profession performed a distinctly political function, the organization of the fractious American state.[46]

If Hurst trusted practicing lawyers to protect a new, policy-oriented version of the rule of law, a more common approach after the war was to entrust that role to a revitalized judiciary. Reuel Schiller argues that in the 1930s and during much of the war most American judges were quite deferential to administrative agencies, which therefore enjoyed "an exceptional amount of independence and flexibility." This "era of judicial deference" ended as a direct result of the war. The rise of totalitarianism in Italy, Germany, the Soviet Union, and Japan gave new force to the old argument that centralized bureaucracies were incompatible with democracy in America. Americans' experience with such vast, intrusive wartime agencies as the War Production Board and the Office of Price Administration did nothing to dissuade them of their views. Even liberal New Dealers learned that agencies could be "inefficient, incompetent, bullying, and perhaps even captured by the interests they were supposed to regulate." Like other policy-makers, they increasingly looked to the new tools of fiscal planning to promote economic prosperity without the inefficiencies and abuses of command-and-control regulation.

Ultimately, Schiller argues, support grew for a "new judicial ascendancy" over the administrative process. Even former New Dealers on the Court insisted that administrators be checked by the judiciary. The Administrative Procedure Act of 1946 and the justices' own reformation of administrative law required federal agencies to adopt norms of procedural fairness borrowed from the courts.[47] The new measures were not intended to roll back the administrative state, but to specify the terms upon which administrators would play a still greater role in the governance of postwar America.[48]

The contribution of law to American political development during World War II was too large and complex to be surveyed in a single collection of writings. This one neglects such important topics as labor policy, propaganda and censorship, the draft, military justice, and international law. Yet the chapters published here advance our appreciation of the law's role in the consolidation of the political regime that emerged in the New Deal and persisted into the 1960s. They show that the United States emerged from total war with its ideal of government under law intact, if tarnished by its treatment of Japanese and African Americans and susceptible to new assertions of military necessity in a national security state. Taken together, the chapters suggest that World War II was not the "Good War" of popular legend, but that its consequences for law and political development were as great as any military conflict in America's past.

We have incurred many debts in completing this volume. Most of the chapters appearing here were first presented at a conference in November 1998, hosted by the Department of History of Michigan State University. We are grateful to Maureen Flanagan, Michael Lewis, Mark L. Kornbluh, and Thomas Summerhill of Michigan State's History Department and Richard D. Friedman of the University of Michigan Law School for their comments at the symposium and to Stanley I. Kutler for concluding remarks that placed the war in the context of a larger political era.

Several members of the Michigan State Department of History helped make the symposium and this volume possible by their role in establishing or overseeing the Sweet program, including John W. Eadie, David Lo Romer, Leslie Page Moch, and Henry Silverman. Anne Forrester Barker, a doctoral candidate at Michigan State, was a tireless, dedicated, and thoughtful research assistant during the planning of the conference. Her (and her husband's) efforts ensured that the symposium itself went off without a hitch. Margaret A. Jeffrey, assistant to the department chair, helped with patience and much sage advice.

We are grateful to Mark Tushnet for advice during the editing of the volume and to Laura Kalman for her comments on this introduction. Kevin Vincent and Heather Waldbeser, students at the Georgetown University Law Center, provided invaluable assistance in the preparation of the bibliography and index, respectively.

Finally, we thank Jack and Margaret Sweet, whose generous gift to the Department of History at Michigan State University funded the symposium whose results appear here. Gratitude for his encounter with the world of ideas while an undergraduate was one reason why Jack Sweet and his wife established the Sweet program at Michigan State. We planned the symposium and have edited this volume with the hope of stimulating further such exchanges between scholars and an engaged and thoughtful public.

NOTES

1. John Gregory Dunne, "Virtual Patriotism: Feeling Good About War," *New Yorker*, November 16, 1998, 98; Louis Menand, "Jerry Don't Surf," *New York Review of Books*, September 24, 1998, 7–8.
2. Brokaw, *The Greatest Generation*.
3. Polenberg, *War and Society*, 153; Blum, *V Was for Victory*.
4. Adams, *Best War Ever*; Adams, "'Good War' Myth," 59; Blum, "Unity and Stability during World War II"; Fussell, *Wartime*; Polenberg, "Good War?"; Erenberg and Hirsch, *War in American Culture*.
5. Gerstle, "The Working Class Goes to War," 105.
6. Kennedy, *Freedom from Fear*, 746–97.
7. Orren and Skowronek, "Regimes and Regime Building," 692. See also Sparrow, *From the Outside In*, 7. In terming this period the "Democratic" order, we follow Plotke, *Building a Democratic Order*.
8. Corwin, *Total War and the Constitution*. See also Polenberg, "World War II and the Bill of Rights"; Rehnquist, *All the Laws But One*, 184–225; and Peter Irons's landmark study of the internment, *Justice at War*.
9. Hawley, "Social Policy and the Liberal State."
10. William T. Hutchinson, "Foreword," in Puttkammer, *War and the Law*, iii.
11. Corwin, *Total War and the Constitution*, 4.
12. Sparrow, *From the Outside In*, 8, 30. Sparrow credits Gilpin, *War and Change in World Politics*, for his notion of hegemonic wars.
13. Hooks, *Forging the Military-Industrial Complex*, 43–49, 85; Adams, "'Good War' Myth," 67; Orren and Skowronek, "Regimes and Regime Building," 692.
14. Shefter, *Political Parties and the State*, 283 n. 3; see also Skowronek, *Building a New American State*, 24–26; Skocpol, *Protecting Soldiers and Mothers*, 71–76.
15. Katznelson and Pietrykowski, "Rebuilding the American State," 334. See also Katznelson, Geiger, and Kryder, "Limiting Liberalism."
16. Polenberg, "Decline of the New Deal," 246–66; Blum, *V Was for Victory*, 222; Orren and Skowronek, "Regimes and Regime Building," 695–96; Leuchtenburg, *Supreme Court Reborn*, 157–58.
17. Shefter, *Political Parties and the State*, 75. See also Hawley, "Social Policy and the Liberal State," 119–20; James, *Presidents, Parties, and the State*, 268–71; Balogh, "Reorganizing the Organizational Synthesis."
18. Plotke, *Building a Democratic Order*, 137, 157.
19. Shefter, *Political Parties and the State*, 82–83.
20. Plotke, *Building a Democratic Order*, 110–11; Hooks, *Forging the Military-Industrial Complex*, 217.
21. Waddell, "Corporate Influence and World War II," 233–37.
22. Compare Brinkley, *End of Reform*, 4, with Plotke, *Building a Democratic Order*, 192.

23. Clark, "Limits of State Autonomy"; Lichtenstein, *Labor's War at Home;* Atleson, *Labor and the Wartime State;* Sparrow, *From the Outside In,* 33–96. Edwin Amenta sees the years 1942–45 as decisively altering the course of American social policy, because of the importance he attributes to the abolition of the Works Progress Administration and other means-tested work programs that targeted able-bodied men. Amenta, *Bold Relief,* 191–230.

24. Brinkley, *End of Reform,* 106–36; Miscamble, "Thurman Arnold Goes to Washington."

25. Orren and Skowronek, "Regimes and Regime Building," 693.

26. Sparrow, *From the Outside In,* 275–76.

27. Ibid., 98; Katznelson and Pietrykowski, "Rebuilding the American State," 306; Brinkley, *Liberalism and Its Discontents,* 37–62. To a certain extent, the statism of the OPA was offset by the widespread participation of volunteers in the enforcement process. See Jacobs, "*'How About Some Meat?'*"

28. Orren and Skowronek, "Regimes and Regime Building," 695, 696, 701.

29. Not discussed here, because of its absence from the existing literature on state-building during World War II, was the government corporation or public authority. At the federal level the government corporation was pioneered during the Progressive Era and was prominently employed during the Depression (notably, in the form of the Reconstruction Finance Corporation and Tennessee Valley Authority). Radford, "William Gibbs McAdoo"; Walsh, *Public's Business,* 26–29; Evans, "Federal Corporations."

30. Hooks, *Forging the Military-Industrial Complex,* 93–98, 125–62; Sparrow, *From the Outside In,* 161–257; Nagle, *History of Government Contracting,* 427–64. The degree to which the corporate professionals acted "as agents of the state" (Gregory Hooks's view) or as "a front for extensive corporate discretion" (Brian Waddell's estimation) remains unresolved in the existing literature. However, after his study of Navy procurement, Sparrow concluded that "public service and professional integrity" better characterized their conduct than subservience to corporate interests. Hooks, *Forging the Military-Industrial Complex,* 147; Waddell, "Economic Mobilization," 182–83; Sparrow, *From the Outside In,* 248–49.

31. Hawley, "Herbert Hoover"; Hart, "Herbert Hoover's Last Laugh."

32. Sparrow, *From the Outside In,* 33–66; Amenta, *Bold Relief.*

33. Lloyd K. Garrison (1944), quoted in Atleson, *Labor and the Wartime State,* 55. See also Dubofsky, *State and Labor,* 182– 88; Sparrow, *From the Outside In,* 67–96.

34. Sherry, *In the Shadow of War;* Hogan, *Cross of Iron.*

35. Kennedy, *Freedom from Fear,* 363–80. A remarkable percentage of these were Wall Street or Washington lawyers who, in the "Wise Man" tradition of Elihu Root, Theodore Roosevelt's Secretary of War and Secretary of State, played prominent roles in defense or foreign policy establishments. They included Dean Acheson, Thomas Finletter, Struve Hensel, John J. McCloy, Robert Patterson, and Henry Stimson. Brinkley, *Liberalism and Its Discontents,* 164–209; Sparrow, *From the Outside In,* 168, 174–75; Eiler, *Mobilizing America.*

36. Waddell, "Corporate Influence and World War II," 248–49. Compare Blum, *V Was for Victory,* 120.

37. *New York Times,* June 22, 1920, quoted in Corwin, *Total War and the Constitution,* 3.

38. For further insight into the Court's decision, see Bittker, "World War II German Saboteurs' Case."

39. Dicey, *Law of the Constitution*, 110. On Dicey and his influential definition of the rule of law, see Cosgrove, *Rule of Law*, 79–87.

40. Wiecek's narrative also suggests that a majority of the justices felt the case for deference all the more strongly after their deference to the agencies and commissions of the New Deal. As Justice Black recorded in his notes of the justices' deliberations in the Nazi Saboteurs' case (quoted by Urofsky), the Court was "bound to give some play to Executive [as Commander-in-Chief] as to an administrative agency."

41. The total desegregation of the military came only after the war.

42. Kryder, "Race Policy," 166. For the analogous case of the Civil Rights Division of the Department of Justice, see Goluboff, " 'Won't You Please Help Me Get My Son Home.' "

43. On the relationship between desegregation and American foreign policy after the war, see Dudziak, *Cold War Civil Rights*.

44. Leff, "Politics of Sacrifice"; Jones, "Class Tax to Mass Tax."

45. The phrase is the legal historian Robert W. Gordon's, who used it to describe "Progressive" lawyers (like Hurst). Gordon, "Legal Thought and Legal Practice," 95. See also Gordon, "Hurst Recaptured," 171–72.

46. Skowronek, *Building a New American State*, 31. See also Halliday and Karpik, "Politics Matter"; Rueschemeyer, "Comparing Legal Professions."

47. Schiller discusses these changes at greater length in "Enlarging the Administrative Polity."

48. Ernst's study of Willard Hurst suggests that Schiller's claim that "academic defenders of administrative discretion . . . were nowhere to be seen by 1946" may need qualifying. Although Hurst's continued sympathy for the administrative "prerogative" would seem to put him at odds with the new judicial supremacists, perhaps the two positions were reconcilable. Hurst assumed that lawyers would guide administrators in the exercise of their discretion. Judicial review strengthened the lawyers' hand within the agency and gave some force to their claim to be the "guardian of the statute" that created the agency. For an example from the New Deal, see Glennon, *Iconoclast as Reformer*, 98–100.

Chapter 1

Inter Arma Silent Leges: Extrajudicial Activity, Patriotism, and the Rule of Law

Melvin I. Urofsky

The day after Pearl Harbor, Felix Frankfurter banged his fist on his desk and told his startled law clerk, Philip Elman, "Everything has changed, and I am going to war."[1] Other justices shared this desire to get involved, to help their country even if they could not actually join the military; some even wanted to resign from the Court. Robert H. Jackson later recalled that while there were "occasional cases of importance involving the war power," such cases were "peaks of interest in a rather dreary sea of briefs and arguments, many of which seemed to have little relationship to the realities of what was going on about us."[2] In the end, only James Byrnes actually stepped down to play a key role in the Roosevelt wartime administration. William O. Douglas, Frank Murphy, and Robert H. Jackson desperately wanted to return to the executive branch, but Roosevelt thought they would be more useful to the nation on the bench.[3] Felix Frankfurter, as always claiming that he would never soil the silk robe by extrajudicial activities, in fact behaved as if he were a member of the wartime cabinet.[4] Even Owen Roberts got involved, and headed the initial investigation into Pearl Harbor. Only Chief Justice Harlan Fiske Stone steadfastly opposed administration requests that he take on extrajudicial duties. When Congress proposed a War Ballot Commission to be chaired by the chief justice, Stone objected that it was improper for a justice to administer the law, an executive function.[5] Even when President Roosevelt personally asked Stone to head an investigation of rubber supply problems, Stone declined.[6]

In this chapter, I want to detail some of the justices' extrajudicial activities immediately preceding and during the Second World War, and then examine the proprieties of such conduct, and whether it impacted on the primary responsibility of the Court—the impartial interpretation of law and the Constitution.

The most theatrical, probably the most personally satisfying, and undoubtedly the most ludicrous effort by a judge to get into the war effort involved Frank Murphy of Michigan, a man with a temperament more suited to the executive than to the judicial branch. Roosevelt had named Murphy to the Court in January 1940, and almost from the day he took his seat Murphy wanted to leave. On several occasions he made it quite clear to Roosevelt that he would be glad to abandon the bench for a more active role in the nation's defense. Felix Frankfurter, who detested Murphy's judicial liberalism, wanted him off the Court as well, and apparently with Roosevelt's blessing, offered Murphy several positions, including the ambassadorship to Mexico. Murphy would not bite, and insisted that he would resign only in return for the War Department. But Henry Stimson held that post, and Roosevelt had no intention of getting rid of the highly respected Republican. It is also likely that Roosevelt had no desire to further Murphy's presidential ambitions. The president offered to send Murphy back to the Philippines in his old post as governor-general, with a hint that he would be Stimson's eventual successor, but Murphy showed no interest.[7]

When Roosevelt wanted to extend aid to the Soviet Union and feared that American Catholics would react negatively, the administration asked the Catholic Murphy if he would present the case for aid at the annual convention of the Knights of Columbus. Murphy agreed, and according to historian George Herring, he made "the most effective presentation" of the case up to that time.[8]

Following Pearl Harbor Murphy grew even more restless and tried unsuccessfully to secure a commission in the army, but legislation prohibited him from going on active status unless he resigned from the Court. Army Chief of Staff George C. Marshall, probably to get Murphy off his back, suggested that the justice be commissioned a lieutenant colonel in the infantry and placed in an inactive status during Court recess. Marshall also advised Murphy he could begin his service by attending officers' training school at Fort Benning, Georgia. Two days after the Court recessed on June 8, 1942, Frank Murphy accepted a commission as a lieutenant colonel, and took a train down to Fort Benning.

Popular approval greeted Murphy's histrionic gesture, but Chief Justice Stone was furious. When Congressman Emanuel Celler of New York wrote to Stone questioning whether Murphy could be both a justice and a member of the armed forces, the chief had to admit that Murphy had not discussed the matter with him, and in fact his first knowledge of what Murphy had done came to him in the newspapers.[9]

The only other visible action by a member of the Court involved Owen Roberts, and the Roberts Commission became the first of eight groups to investigate what had happened at Pearl Harbor. It met from December 18, 1941, to January 23, 1942, and, among other things, found no evidence of espionage either in Hawaii or on the American West Coast.[10] Justices William O. Douglas and Robert H. Jackson were frequent, if nonpublicized, visitors to the White House, and in addition to their participation in FDR's poker games, also counseled the president, and on occasion wrote speeches for him.

The most active member of the Court, however, was the diminutive Frankfurter, whose immigrant origins had imparted a fiercely burning patriotism. Throughout his life Frankfurter never made a secret of his enormous love of America or his gratitude at what it had allowed an immigrant to achieve. His law clerks recalled the justice bouncing down the halls of the Supreme Court whistling "Stars and Stripes Forever," albeit off-key, and on his deathbed he told his chosen biographer, "Let people see . . . how much I loved my country."[11]

Two sets of cases illustrate Frankfurter's burning passion for his adoptive country and how this influenced his judicial behavior—the flag salute cases and revocation of citizenship. Prior to *Minersville School District v. Gobitis* (1940),[12] the high court had four times upheld state court decisions validating compulsory flag salute laws. Jehovah's Witnesses, however, objected to the salute because of their literal reading of Exodus 20:4–5, and equated the salute to bowing down before graven images. Frankfurter, who took the ideals of patriotism and the responsibilities of citizenship very seriously, had little patience with those who, as he saw it, refused to meet their civic obligations. During oral argument on the case, he passed a note to Frank Murphy questioning whether the framers of the Bill of Rights "would have thought that a requirement to salute the flag violates the protection of 'the free exercise of religion'?"[13]

Chief Justice Hughes assigned the opinion to Frankfurter, who framed the "precise" issue in terms of judicial restraint, and called upon the Court to defer to the wisdom and prerogatives of local school authorities. "To the legislature no less than to courts is committed the guardianship of deeply cherished liberties."[14] Privately, Frankfurter took great pride in the opinion, and predicted it would preach "the true democratic faith of not relying on the Court for the impossible task of assuring a . . . tolerant democracy."[15]

As is well known, within a short time the Court reversed itself. Appalled at the attacks upon Witnesses that followed in the wake of the *Gobitis* opinion, and perhaps coming to a greater appreciation of what free exercise of religion meant, the Court agreed to hear a new challenge to the compulsory flag salute in the October 1942 term. Two new appointees to the Court, Wiley Rutledge and Robert H. Jackson, gave the dissenters their majority.

Jackson, who rarely voted for minority rights against a public interest argument, wrote one of the most eloquent opinions of his career. "If there is any fixed star in our constitutional constellation, it is that no official, high or petty, can prescribe what shall be orthodox in politics, nationalism, religion or other matters of opinion or force citizens to confess by word or act their faith therein."[16]

A furious Frankfurter penned an impassioned dissent, noting that he belonged to "the most vilified and persecuted minority in history," but he nonetheless recognized that "minorities may disrupt society." Minorities, in the name of rights, could not ride roughshod over social order and civic obligations. He had had a difficult time writing the dissent, he explained to Jackson, "because it is credo and not research."[17] Frankfurter then sent literally dozens of copies of his dissent around to his friends. He suggested to Franklin Roosevelt that a copy be placed in the Hyde Park library, since it would "furnish to the future historian food for thought on the scope and meaning of some of the Four Freedoms—their use and misuse."[18] As Robert Burt has suggested, Frankfurter in effect was telling the Witnesses to give up their absurd practices and become full-fledged Americans, just as he had done.[19]

The second set of cases involved revocation of citizenship, and we will look at one in particular, that of William Schneiderman. The justices all remembered quite vividly the excesses of the Wilson administration during World War I and some, such as Frank Murphy and Robert Jackson, had, in their terms as attorneys general, taken steps to make sure that such excesses would not be repeated should the United States enter this conflict.[20] Nonetheless, the Court still recognized the need of the government to protect itself.

Under this rationale, the Justice Department sought to revoke the citizenship of naturalized citizens of German and Italian origin who either displayed disloyal behavior or who had secured their citizenship illegally or under false pretenses. Within a year after American entry into the war, the government had initiated over two thousand investigations and had secured the denaturalization of forty-two people. The case testing this campaign, however, did not involve a Nazi or a fascist sympathizer, but a communist.

Born in Russia in 1905, William Schneiderman had come with his parents to the United States in 1908; he applied for citizenship in 1927, and by then had already joined several communist groups. In 1932 he ran for governor of Minnesota as the Communist Party candidate. In 1939, the government moved to strip Schneiderman of his citizenship on the grounds that his communist activities in the five years prior to the naturalization process showed that he had not been truly "attached" to the principles of the U.S. Constitution. Schneiderman, in turn, argued that he did not believe in using force or violence and that, in fact, he had been a good citizen; he had never been arrested and had used his rights as a citizen to advocate change and greater social justice.

Schneiderman's case came before the Court in early 1942, by which time the United States had entered the war and had publicly acknowledged the Soviet Union as an ally. Wendell Willkie, the Republican candidate for president in 1940, represented Schneiderman and eloquently pleaded with the Court not to establish a legal rule that a person could be punished for alleged adherence to abstract principles. The government, recognizing how embarrassing a victory might be, privately suggested to Chief Justice Stone that the Court delay its decision. Although Stone understood the Justice Department's quandary, he believed more important issues were at stake, namely, that the political branches should not interfere in the business of the Court. Moreover, Stone, a fervent patriot, believed that people like Schneiderman who did not support American institutions ought not to avail themselves of American citizenship. At the conference on December 5, 1942, Stone led off discussion of the case with a forceful statement that the government ought to have the power to rid the nation of agitators who not only did not believe in the Constitution, but worked actively to overthrow the government.[21]

Given his idolization of Holmes and Brandeis, Frankfurter might have been expected to speak in defense of Schneiderman, as Holmes had done so eloquently in defense of Rosika Schwimmer, another immigrant who held unpopular views.[22] But Frankfurter supported Stone's view, and he explained his position in conference at length and with great emotion. This case, he began, "arouses in me feelings that could not be entertained by anyone else around this table. It is well-known that a convert is more zealous than one born to the faith. None of you has had the experience that I have had with reference to American citizenship." He had been in college when his father received his naturalization papers, "and I can assure you that for months preceding, it was a matter of moment in our family life." For Frankfurter, "American citizenship implies entering upon a fellowship which binds people together by devotion to certain feelings and ideas and ideals summarized as a requirement that they be attached to the principles of the Constitution." While mere membership in the Communist Party did not constitute grounds for either denying or revoking citizenship, Frankfurter believed that Schneiderman's actions went far beyond paying dues. Schneiderman had committed himself to the "holy cause," and "no man can serve two masters when two masters represent not only different, but in this case, mutually exclusive ideas."[23] Frankfurter voted to affirm the conviction, but only he, Roberts, and Stone did so.[24]

After several delays, the Court finally handed down its decision in the spring of 1943. Frank Murphy's opinion for the majority conceded that naturalization constituted a privilege granted by Congress, but once that privilege had been granted, a person became a citizen and enjoyed all the rights guaranteed by the Constitution, including freedom of thought and expression. Membership in the Communist Party had not been illegal at the time Schneiderman had taken out his papers, and the government had not proven current membership "absolutely incompatible" with loyalty to the Constitution.[25]

Frankfurter gave Murphy a hard time during the circulations of the majority opinion. One day he suggested that Murphy might want to add to his opinion the statement that "Uncle Joe Stalin was at least a spiritual co-author with Jefferson of the Virginia Statute for Religious Freedom." A few days later Frankfurter sent a note, signed "F.F. Knaebel," offering Murphy the following as a headnote for the decision: "The American Constitution ain't got no principles. The Communist Party don't stand for nuthin'. The Soopreme Court don't mean nuthin', and ter Hell with the U.S.A. so long as a guy is attached to the principles of the U.S.S.R."[26]

Stone, joined by Frankfurter and Roberts, entered a vigorous dissent that seemed strange coming from the man who had stood alone in the first flag salute case. "My brethren of the majority," he said, "do not deny that there are principles of the Constitution . . . civil rights and . . . life, liberty and property, the principle of representative government, and the principle that constitutional laws are not to be broken down by planned disobedience. I assume also that all the principles of the Constitution are hostile to dictatorship and minority rule."[27]

Shortly after Murphy circulated his draft opinion, he stopped to talk with Frankfurter, and confessed that while everybody should have freedom of opinion, Congress did have the right to set conditions for citizenship. He conceded that the opinion "skates on the thinnest possible ice—awfully thin," but Murphy did not like the idea of canceling a person's citizenship ten years after it had been conferred. Frankfurter casually dismissed the issue as none of the Court's business. If Congress had set conditions, "then it is our business to enforce what Congress has commanded and not overrule the legislative power."[28]

But if citizenship could be canceled because of strong—or weak—beliefs held by an individual, then no naturalized citizen could be secure in his or her rights. As a naturalized citizen himself, Frankfurter believed he owed full and complete loyalty to the United States, and so did every other naturalized citizen—and with no less passion. Communists could not share that love of country that true patriots had, and therefore could be stripped of their citizenship. The notion of full freedom of belief, it would seem, did not apply in this case.

It is not surprising, therefore, that Frankfurter's strong patriotic feelings would lead him to do all he could in the aid of his country, even if he had to do it covertly so as to preclude any hint of judicial propriety. (Franklin Roosevelt, it should be noted, appeared to have had no qualms about Frankfurter, Douglas, Murphy, and Jackson advising and helping him out, even to drafting legislation or political speeches.[29]) One of Frankfurter's greatest assets was his wide array of friends and acquaintances. If the president needed to find out about something or someone, he could always ask Felix; if Roosevelt needed to fill a position, Felix usually knew just the right person. Justice Frankfurter came to the president's aid in the spring of 1940 when Roosevelt badly needed to replace the isolationist Harry Woodring, the secretary of war who not only opposed preparedness but had proven an incompetent administrator.

At lunch in the White House in April 1940, Roosevelt could hardly wait to talk about conditions in the War Department, and informed Frankfurter that he had been considering former New York City mayor Fiorello H. LaGuardia, Secretary of the Interior Harold Ickes, and New York governor Herbert Lehman. Frankfurter raised objections to all three, and then came up with a solution—named Henry L. Stimson, who had served as secretary of war under Taft and as secretary of state in the Hoover administration. Stimson had ability and experience, and the fact that he was a Republican would underscore Roosevelt's oft-stated belief that the current crisis transcended partisan differences. But could Stimson, at the age of seventy-three, take on the enormous physical and mental demands of putting the nation on a war footing? Frankfurter thought it could be done, and with typical resourcefulness set about to implement the plan.

First he arranged for Stimson to lunch at the White House so that Roosevelt could personally gauge the older man's physical and mental condition and sound him out on his interest. Then Frankfurter suggested that if named, Stimson should devote his energies to shaping policy, and leave the burden of daily administration to a former Frankfurter student, Robert Patterson, whom Roosevelt had recently appointed to the federal bench. Gaining Roosevelt's approval for the plan, Frankfurter dispatched Grenville Clark to see if Stimson and Patterson would be amenable. Both men agreed, Clark reported back to Frankfurter, and the justice went to the White House on June 3, 1940. Roosevelt told Frankfurter he had "struck fire," and only wished he knew more about Patterson. Anticipating that, Frankfurter had already asked Clark to draft a memo detailing Patterson's career and abilities. Less than three weeks later Roosevelt named Stimson and Patterson to head the War Department.[30]

The appointment of the two men gave Frankfurter access to one of the most important departments of the government, a fact to keep in mind when discussing the wartime cases. He met with Stimson often, mediated between the cold, formal war secretary and the ebullient president, and recommended names for key positions. When the administration needed to calm the black community during the 1940 election, Frankfurter arranged for William L. Hastie, another of his former students, to be appointed an aide to Stimson.

One might argue that suggesting names to the president is hardly a breach of judicial ethics, even if it does blur the line of separated powers. But in 1940 Frankfurter helped draft the lend-lease bill, which allowed the United States to supply ships and war materials to Great Britain. While isolationists never challenged the constitutionality of the measure, Roosevelt, beset by so many pressures at the time, might have felt some relief that a justice of the Supreme Court had vetted it. Frankfurter not only helped Benjamin Cohen with the technical details, but drawing on his vast political knowledge of Congress, spent many hours advising the president's staff on how to put the measure across. It was he who suggested that the bill be numbered H.R. 1776. America had once gained her independence by fighting Great Britain; now, according to Frankfurter, we have "to seek independence through interdependence," a phrase Roosevelt relished and used often. Immediately after the bill's passage in late February 1941, Frankfurter sat down and wrote a lengthy memorandum outlining what American industry would have to do to help achieve the goals of the program.[31]

Despite a constant disavowal of any extrajudicial activity throughout the war,[32] Frankfurter responded to requests from the White House and just as often put forward ideas of his own. The dinner-seminars at his Georgetown apartment, 1511 30th Street, N.W., brought together high officials from different departments who discussed common problems while their host moderated, listened, and then suggested solutions.

Frankfurter sanctimoniously preached that "when a priest enters a monastery, he must leave—or ought to leave—all sorts of worldly desires behind him. And this Court has no excuse for being unless it's a monastery."[33] Neither Frankfurter nor his colleagues—Murphy, Douglas and Jackson—seemed able to renounce the world of high politics. If Frankfurter had indeed entered a monastery, he might well have called himself Brother Richelieu.

The critical question, of course, is did these extrajudicial activities, these burning passions of patriotism, affect how the justices decided specific cases? Or, to put it another way, did it affect decision-making more than the individual prejudices and assumptions of justices usually do? I would like to suggest that in some of the important wartime cases, the patriotism of the justices did in fact affect the decisions they reached.

In June 1942, German submarines put eight operatives ashore on Long Island and Florida with orders to sabotage bridges, industrial plants, and military installations. The scheme failed completely, and authorities quickly apprehended the saboteurs and their few American confederates. Roosevelt immediately named a special military tribunal of seven generals to try the saboteurs, with orders to transmit the record of the trial directly to him. In the same proclamation, he closed the civilian courts to "all persons who are subjects, citizens, or residents of any nation at war with the United States . . . and are charged with committing or attempting . . . to commit sabotage."[34]

Secretary of War Stimson almost immediately turned to his old protégé for advice, and Justice Frankfurter was glad to assist. Frankfurter recommended that the panel be composed solely of regular military officers and not include any civilians, even high-ranking civilians in the War Department. Frankfurter also backed Stimson when the war secretary and Attorney General Francis Biddle clashed over whether to permit press coverage, with the War Department insisting on secret trials.[35] (Frankfurter, it might be noted, was the only member of the Supreme Court with any experience in military justice, having served briefly with the army judge advocate general's office at the end of World War I.[36])

According to Michael Parrish, the Stimson diary entries "probably reveal only a fraction" of Frankfurter's extrajudicial involvement.[37] The justice most likely discussed the issues on a regular basis with John McCloy, his confidant in the War Department, who lived near Frankfurter in Georgetown and often walked with him in the evenings. Given this participation in developing the government's framework for trying the saboteurs, it might have been expected, given Frankfurter's constant preaching on judicial ethics, that he would have recused himself when the issue reached the Supreme Court. To the contrary, he became the administration's most ardent supporter,[38] while failing to inform either the Chief Justice or any of his colleagues about his role as advisor to the War Department.

The military panel commenced the trial in secret, but the two army colonels appointed to defend the Germans, Kenneth C. Royall and Cassius M. Dowell, tried to get their clients a civilian trial based on the Civil War precedent of *Ex parte Milligan*.[39] In that decision, the Court had held that in areas apart from battle zones in which the civilian courts remained open, the government could not preempt the civil judiciary through military tribunals.

Colonel Royall went to see Justice Owen Roberts, who immediately recognized that a constitutional question existed. A few days later Justice Hugo Black, Colonels Royall and Dowell, Attorney General Francis Biddle, and Judge Advocate General Myron C. Cramer met at Roberts's farm in Pennsylvania. Prior to the meeting Roberts had conferred with the chief justice, who had authorized Black and Roberts to bring the matter to the entire court if they believed it appropriate. Before the meeting ended, Black and Roberts agreed that the whole court should convene to hear the appeal the following week.[40]

For the first time in more than two decades, the Court interrupted its summer recess to hear a case. When the Court convened on July 29, 1942, Douglas had not yet arrived from the West Coast, and Murphy, attired in his army uniform, decided to recuse himself. When oral argument began, Frankfurter immediately began peppering Colonel Royall, another one of his former students, as to why the defendants had appealed directly to the

Supreme Court and not gone through the traditional appeals route. After several minutes of debate on questions of procedure, Royall got to the heart of the matter: the presidential order establishing the military tribunal did not provide for "review in the ordinary sense." Moreover, since the commission reported its findings directly to the president, he was not even sure the defendants and their lawyers would be informed of the findings; executions might be carried out before counsel could appeal. Royall's sense that only Supreme Court review of the process could ensure that justice prevailed; the Court accepted the case and began to hear arguments on the legitimacy of the panel.[41]

In conference, Frankfurter questioned whether proper procedures had been followed, but it appears he did this as much to establish the semblance of impartiality as to satisfy his usual craving for nit-picking. He backed the chief justice's decision that the Court had to hand down a decision, and quickly. Moreover, Stone believed it had to be unanimous to demonstrate that the Court had absolutely no reservations about the government's conduct in wartime. In fact, some of the justices did have questions, but for political reasons agreed to go along with Stone's proposal that they limit their decision to two very narrow issues—whether the Court had jurisdiction to hear the petition for habeas corpus and whether the president had authority to order the saboteurs tried by a military panel.

Even deciding these questions required extensive debate, since no one had defined the saboteurs' status. Were they spies or prisoners of war? If the latter, Congress had specifically provided for their treatment in the Articles of War, a body of law that rarely came before the Supreme Court. The justices also briefly discussed a question they really did not want to answer, namely, the extent of the president's war powers. Hugo Black's notes summed up the consensus: "Constitution makes President Supreme Commander and Congress can carry on war. Time out of mind it is within the power of the Commander-in-Chief to hang a spy. Articles of War recognize that there is a law of war. . . . By all usages they were not prisoners of war. Bound to give some play to Executive as to an administrative agency."[42] On July 31, 1942, less than forty-eight hours after hearing the case, the Supreme Court issued a brief per curiam opinion upholding the power of the military commission to try the saboteurs and announcing that a formal opinion would be filed later.[43]

The reason for the unusual procedure was simple. While all eight of the justices who sat on the case agreed that the president had the authority, they disagreed on the jurisprudential support of that authority. Stone, as noted, wanted a unanimous opinion for political reasons, but at the same time he did not want to delay the results lest the Court be seen as hampering the administration's conduct of the war. He went back to his summer home in New Hampshire and there hammered out an opinion which he presented to his fellow justices when the Court convened in October.

Stone's opinion can be seen not only as a statement of law—there never really was any question that the president had the power and that the Court would confirm his actions—but as a statement of the Court's full-hearted support of the war effort. Stone went well beyond the truism that the president had the power to establish military commissions to try spies. He took pains to rebut each and every point raised by the defense, pointing to thirteen separate clauses in the Constitution supporting the presidential war powers. In addition, the chief justice ruled that the constitutional guarantee of grand jury indictment and petit jury trial did not apply to defendants appearing before a military tribunal on charges arising under the laws of war. In sum, the president had acted lawfully, and so had the military commission.[44]

For all the unanimity shown in the opinion, the justices did harbor doubts about that part of the presidential proclamation closing the civilian courts to this type of case. As Stone told his friend John Bassett Moore, the case "presented a great many legal puzzles which had never been ironed out or considered by the courts." And, in case Moore missed it, Stone pointed out that the opinion did not mention the validity of the presidential proclamation or a number of other questions regarding interpretation of the Articles of War.[45]

As the justices had hoped, the press and the public greeted the decision with overwhelming approval, claiming that even in the middle of a great war, the American traditions of liberty had been preserved. While a few law journals noted the procedural irregularities, the writers dismissed these concerns on the ground that "in wartime quick justice and absence of delay are essential."[46] Approval of *Quirin* has remained constant, and as recently as 1990 David Currie hailed the decision as "a salutary reminder that it is not the courts alone that have a responsibility to see that those charged with offenses are afforded appropriate protections."[47]

There is little doubt that the Court reached the right decision in *Quirin*, given the state of military law at that time; in fact, it is likely that had the current code existed the same result would have been reached. But the internal memoranda, the discussions, the rush to judgment indicate that the justices saw their job less as dispensing justice than as validating the decision of the executive branch. Moreover, Felix Frankfurter's role in the case is, to say the least, irregular. Frank Murphy had the decency to recuse himself because at the time he was wearing the uniform of the U.S. Army. Frankfurter, who had advised the War Department on how to set up the whole arrangement, could hardly have voted any way but to sustain the procedure. But, as usual, Frankfurter talked one game of judicial restraint, of the judicial monastery, and played another.

The facts of the Japanese relocation cases are well-known, and need little more than a brief outline here.[48] Following the attack on Pearl Harbor, a combination of military officials, West Coast government leaders, and xenophobic newspaper writers like Westbrook Pegler led Roosevelt to agree to a plan to relocate all Japanese Americans from the West Coast to inland centers, thus removing an alleged threat of fifth-column activity should there be a Japanese invasion. Roosevelt authorized the plan on February 19, 1942, in Executive Order 9066; Congress ratified it in early March, and General John L. DeWitt began to implement the relocation at the beginning of March. All told, some 110,000 men, women, and children were uprooted from their homes and placed in concentration camps for the duration of the war. The entire plan had been conceived and proceeded on highly racist assumptions.

The constitutional issues were clear. On the one hand, those affected by the plan had never been charged with any crimes; they had never had any administrative hearings; there was absolutely no proof that they posed any threat to national security. They were essentially found guilty of being Japanese by birth or ancestry. Under any circumstances, the plan clearly violated the Fifth Amendment's due process clause.[49] In contrast stood the war powers of the president and Congress and the issue of how much deference the courts should pay to the policy decisions of the political branches. The three internment cases that reached the high court caused the brethren much anguish, but the majority stood solidly behind the administration plan.

The first case to reach the Court involved Gordon Hirabayashi, who had been arrested for failing to report to a control center and for violating the curfew. He had been convicted, sentenced to two three-month prison terms, and then had appealed his conviction on the grounds that the military had exceeded its constitutional authority. Both the federal district and appeals courts upheld the conviction, and the case came to the Supreme Court in the spring of 1943.[50]

Chief Justice Stone may not have been willing to act extrajudicially on behalf of the administration, but he was determined to support the war effort down the line within the Marble Palace. Stone strongly endorsed the army's actions, and he used all his persuasive powers to mass the Court in back of the government. On May 30, he circulated the first draft of his opinion which centered around a truly awesome reading of the war powers. Such authority went far beyond purely military matters on the battlefield, and could be directed at any and all "evils that attend the rise and progress of the war." Black and Douglas immediately endorsed Stone's views, but made significant suggestions to emphasize what they considered a key element in the Court's decision, judicial deference. Black urged Stone to include a statement making explicit that the Court had no business second-guessing the military, and Stone gladly obliged: "It is not for any court to sit in review of the wisdom of their [the military commanders'] action or substitute its judgment for theirs."[51]

The chief wanted a united Court on this issue, but at least two members had grave doubts. William O. Douglas had grown up in the Pacific Northwest with Japanese American friends, and knew that not all of them, as Stone had insisted in his draft, had strong racial attachments to Japan. The lack of due process also troubled Douglas, but he would be willing to concur in an opinion that approved the military orders as a temporary expedient, and urged Stone to limit the Court's decision to that holding. Moreover, he wanted the Court to issue a requirement that individuals had to have an opportunity to be classified as loyal citizens.[52]

Douglas circulated a concurring opinion incorporating his views, and Frankfurter exploded. He urged the chief to send at once "for Brother Douglas and talk him out of his opinion by making him see the dangers that he is inviting." The Douglas view would unleash thousands of habeas corpus proceedings, and "it would be for me deplorable beyond words to hold out hopes by any language that we use . . . hopes, which to put it very mildly, are not likely to be fulfilled." Douglas ought to be pulling along with everyone else instead of acting as if he were "in a rival grocery business." Trying to get Douglas to change his mind would probably be useless, Frankfurter concluded, because Douglas "will want to make the spread eagle speech."[53]

Frank Murphy alone on the Court seemed willing to face head-on the issue of racism. He termed the discrimination "so utterly inconsistent with our ideals and traditions, and in my judgment so contrary to constitutional requirements, that I cannot lend my assent." Frankfurter pleaded with Murphy not to dissent, for the sake of the Court. As opinion day approached, Frankfurter wrote:

> Do you think it is conducive to the things you care about, including the great reputation of this Court, to suggest that everybody is out of step except Johnny, and more particularly that the Chief Justice and seven other Justices of this Court are behaving like the enemy and thereby playing into the hands of the enemy. Compassion is, I believe, a virtue enjoined by Christ. Well, tolerance is a long, long way from compassion—and can't you write your views with such expressed tolerance that you won't make people think that when eight others disagree with you, you think their view means that they want to destroy the liberties of the United States and "lose the war" at home?[54]

The appeal succeeded, and on June 21, Chief Justice Stone was able to announce an opinion upholding the curfew, in which all the members of the Court supported the result. He had labored on it through four drafts, and had spent endless hours trying to assuage the doubts of at least five members of the Court about the legality of the detention program. The final opinion evaded all of the hard issues that the doubters had raised, and when Stone circulated his final draft, Frankfurter gave it his blessing: "You have labored with great forbearance and with concentration to produce something worthy of the Torah."[55]

But not all of the brethren agreed with Stone's broad enunciation of the war powers or his cavalier attitude toward the labeling of all Japanese Americans as potentially disloyal. Douglas, Murphy, and Wiley Rutledge entered concurring opinions that came close to dissents; all indicated that they had agreed to what they considered an unconstitutional program because of the allegedly critical military situation. The tone of their opinions indicated that it would be far more difficult to get unanimity if another challenge reached the Court.[56]

Sixteen months later that challenge came, and this time the Court would not be able to evade the larger constitutional issues. Fred Korematsu had been charged with failing to report to an assembly center for relocation. His attorneys claimed that the entire exclusion order violated the Constitution by depriving citizens of their freedom without trial or other guarantees of due process. Moreover, the mass expulsion of an entire group based solely on a racial classification constituted a cruel and unusual punishment forbidden by the Eighth Amendment.[57]

At the Justices' conference on October 16, 1944, Stone tried to limit the discussion to a narrow technical question. Korematsu had been convicted of violating the exclusion order, designed to keep Japanese out of certain militarily designated areas. The only question the Court had to answer, according to the chief justice, was the constitutionality of that exclusion order. Framed this way, the case could be decided on narrow grounds similar to that in *Hirabayashi*.[58]

Stone turned to the senior justice, Owen J. Roberts, who had endorsed the earlier opinion, only to find Roberts dead set against the chief's plan. The combination of exclusion and prohibition orders gave Japanese Americans a cruel choice—defy the order and be imprisoned, or report to an assembly point, and be relocated to a concentration camp. Black and Frankfurter supported the chief, as did Rutledge and Reed. But four justices, Roberts, Murphy, Jackson, and Douglas planned to dissent on grounds that the military had overstepped its constitutional bounds of authority. Jackson, normally a supporter of strong government, declared, "I stop at *Hirabayashi*."[59]

Stone assigned the opinion to Black, who tried to follow the chief's lead in describing the case in the narrowest possible terms. When Black circulated his draft, Frankfurter responded the same day: "I am ready to join in your opinion without the change of a word." However, Frankfurter suggested, the elimination of one sentence would make even stronger the deference shown by the Court to congressional authority to prosecute the war. Black deleted the sentence.[60] However, Black concluded his opinion in a semi-apologetic manner: "We cannot—by availing ourselves of the calm perspective of hindsight—now say that at that time these actions were unjustified."[61]

This, however, struck Frankfurter as irrelevant; the Court owed deference not to the military but to the Congress. He dashed off a brief concurrence declaring that he found "nothing in the Constitution which denies to Congress the power to enforce a military order by making its violation an offense triable in civil courts." Then he saw the draft of Jackson's dissent, which included the phrase "Our forefathers were practical men, and they had no delusions about war being a lawless business." As Peter Irons notes, Frankfurter wasted no time responding to this "sacrilege." He called in the wife of his law clerk, Harry Mansfield, who was completing a graduate degree in history, and put her to work tracking down the Revolutionary War records of each member of the Constitutional Convention. Although Jackson deleted the offending sentence in his final draft, Frankfurter kept in his sentence lauding the Framers and their actual knowledge of what war meant, since "a majority had had actual participation in war." Frankfurter concluded his brief concurrence declaring that DeWitt's exclusion orders could not "be stigmatized as lawless because like actions in times of peace would be lawless." As for Congress endorsing those orders, "That is their business, not ours."[62]

In the end, only three justices dissented—Roberts, Murphy, and Jackson. Murphy had always been unhappy about the relocation, and Roberts, from his work heading the first Pearl Harbor commission, knew that there had been absolutely no evidence of Japanese sabotage on the West Coast. Jackson, whatever his personal feelings about the relocation, took the most lawyerly approach, worrying what the decision would mean in the future if the Court approved a policy based entirely on racial classification. Whatever the military necessity may be, Jackson warned, once the Court approved that action it became a precedent ready to be used—and abused—in the future:

The principle then lies about like a loaded weapon ready for the hand of any authority that can bring forward a plausible claim of an urgent need. . . . All who observe the work of the courts are familiar with what Judge Cardozo described as "the tendency of a principle to expand itself to the limit of its logic." A military commander may overstep the bound of constitutionality, and it is an incident. But if we review and approve, that passing incident has become the doctrine of the Constitution.[63]

Douglas swallowed his dissent when Black agreed to add a paragraph noting that the minority viewed the issues of evacuation and detention as inseparable, and therefore raising additional constitutional issues.[64] *Korematsu*, according to one of Black's biographers:

was the worst judicial opinion that Justice Hugo Black wrote in his thirty-four years on the Court. It was devoid of meaningful analysis of the underpinnings of military

> policy. It was deceptive in its strained narrowing of the constitutional issues that had been presented by Korematsu's attorneys. And it was a philosophically incoherent defense of broad government power by one of the most influential civil libertarians in the Court's history. . . . Although Black did not say so, he had given the military a license to trample on individual rights at will during wartime.[65]

And Frankfurter, who had opposed just this sort of trammeling in his days as a reformer, not only went along, but encouraged Black and Stone in their views, and denigrated the dissenters as unpatriotic! Black never regretted these decisions; years later he said that if he had been president, he would have done exactly the same thing, and he continued to justify it on grounds of military necessity.[66]

Recent evidence indicates that the Solicitor General knew there was no military necessity and deliberately misled the Court in this area.[67] Frankfurter, however, should have known better, if for no other reason than from his frequent meetings with the men he had helped place in the War Department, including John J. McCloy, one of the officials responsible for implementation of the internment program. By the time the cases came to the Court, the threat of a Japanese invasion of the Pacific Coast had evaporated, and the only questions the War Relocation Authority had to answer involved political, not military, risks. But Frankfurter said nothing. He condemned Douglas for the "spread eagle speech" in opposition to the internment; he, in turn, willingly abdicated judicial responsibility in the name of patriotism.

The divisions in the *Korematsu* case indicated that several of the justices felt it no longer appropriate to defer to government claims of military expediency. On December 18, 1944, the same day the Court handed down its decision in *Korematsu*, the justices unanimously authorized a writ of habeas corpus for Mitsuye Endo, a citizen whose loyalty had been clearly established.[68] Although the American Civil Liberties Union had hoped to use *Endo* to challenge the entire detention program, Justice Douglas carefully skirted that issue, and confined his ruling to the single question of whether the War Relocation Authority could detain persons whose loyalty had been confirmed. He held that it could not, but he had difficulty with his opinion, since this case came perilously close to the larger issue raised in the *Korematsu* dissents—whether a person accused of no crime could be detained by military officials outside a combat zone.

In the *Milligan* case, decided *after* the Civil War had ended, the Supreme Court had said no, but Douglas now tried to distinguish between the two situations. Milligan had been held by the army, whereas Endo had been detained by a civilian agency. Douglas ignored the fact that the War Relocation Authority had been created for no other purpose than to assist the military in carrying out the evacuations. In their concurrences with the result, Justices Murphy and Roberts attacked the Court's refusal to resolve an important constitutional issue that had properly come before it—whether a loyal citizen who had committed no crime could be deprived of her liberty.[69] Ironically, Chief Justice Stone, who always emphasized the independence of the judiciary from political affairs, held up announcement of the decision until after the 1944 presidential election, eliciting a threat from Douglas to make the results known on his own.[70]

What are we to make of these cases, and of the actions of Frankfurter, Stone, and others in deciding them? It is hardly surprising that judges are patriotic, and that in wartime they would want to do everything they could to help their nation in its struggle. We have known for over a century that the prejudices of judges are as important as legal syllogisms in deciding cases; they may be even more important if the Legal Realists were right. But did patriotism and related judicial prejudices distort the rule of law? Was the old Latin maxim, *inter arma silent leges,* proven correct: in the clash of arms, was the law silent? Did the justices exceed the bounds of judicial propriety in the name of patriotism? Did they decide incorrectly because the nation was at war?

For the most part, scholars have given the wartime Court relatively high marks in the area of civil liberties. Alpheus Mason, in his biography of Chief Justice Stone, concedes that war often abridges individual liberty, but concludes that "the amazing thing is not that so much freedom was sacrificed on the altar of military necessity . . . but that more was not. Even in the time of greatest stress, the Justices upheld the citizen's liberty to think, speak, and act to an extent that the nation at peace has sometimes felt it could ill afford to maintain. In this realm Stone's Court almost brought a miracle to pass."[71] Paul Murphy also notes that the "Court's favorable civil liberties record was in some ways one of the most remarkable aspects of the war period, particularly when one compares it with the black picture of World War I."[72] Other scholars have been less charitable. John Frank claimed that "the dominant lesson of our history in the relation of the judiciary to repression is that the courts love liberty most when it is under pressure least."[73]

The truth is somewhere between Mason's near miracle and condemnations of the Court as repressive. Certainly some of the justices who later—and rightly—earned reputations as ardent defenders of individual liberty seemed all too willing to look the other way when the government claimed military necessity. One wonders if Black and Douglas would have voted as they did if the war had come later in their judicial careers, after they had reached their mature views on the extensive reach of the Bill of Rights. Frank Murphy and Robert Jackson intuitively opposed many of the measures undertaken in the name of the common defense, yet they too recognized that in a nation at war there would have to be sacrifices, and at times these might entail restrictions on individual liberties.

There is no question that the Court was wrong on the Japanese internment cases, but correct in those cases involving denaturalization, the definition of treason, the precedence of civilian courts, and freedom from an imposed flag salute. These have all become staples of American constitutional law.[74]

Yet Felix Frankfurter was on the wrong side of nearly all these cases, as was Harlan Fiske Stone, and I would suggest that the reason for their vote can be found in their intense patriotism coupled with their view of judicial deference to the political branches, a deference which in Frankfurter's long career often amounted to abdication of judicial responsibility. It was Stone who, in the minds of many scholars, fathered the modern era of judicial protection of individual liberties in his famous *Carolene Products* footnote.[75] It was Stone who alone dissented in the first flag salute case. Yet Stone's intense patriotism led him to place naturalized citizens in a second-class status and to demand a uniformity of viewpoint totally at odds with the protections of the First Amendment.

In Frankfurter's case, hypocrisy compounded patriotism. Frankfurter engaged in certain activities that might be excused on the grounds that in wartime each citizen must do what the country demands. The president needed Frankfurter's help in several instances, and I do not fault the justice for recommending particular people to the executive. In fact, prior to 1971 many justices continued to advise members of Congress and the executive branch after going on the bench on matters of appointment.[76] But drafting legislation and then guiding the political efforts to secure its passage surely violates the rule of separation of powers. While it is true that the lend-lease law never faced a challenge in the courts, it is hard to believe that Frankfurter would have recused had such a challenge come before the high court.

I find his actions in the saboteur and internment cases even more reprehensible. Felix Frankfurter took an active role in framing the government's procedures in the saboteur cases. Not only did he not recuse; he failed even to inform the brethren of his actions. Frankfurter was in a position to know exactly how minimal a threat Japanese Americans posed to American security, yet he did nothing to stop the forced evacuation of 110,000 innocent civilians. And this from a man who lamented in the second flag salute case that he belonged to the most vilified minority in history!

In the end we were lucky that, except in the internment cases, a majority of the Court did stick to the fundamentals. And even in the most difficult cases, where the justices faced enormous pressure to endorse the administration's actions, there were always dissenting voices reminding the majority of the rule of law. In World War II, the rule of law was not silenced, but it was often threatened by the patriotic excesses of some justices.

NOTES

1. Simon, *Antagonists*, 133.

2. "The Reminiscences of Robert H. Jackson," Columbia Oral History Collection (Columbia University 1952–53), 1135, 1136, box 259, Robert H. Jackson Papers, Manuscript Division, Library of Congress, Washington, D.C.

3. Roosevelt evidently asked Douglas to head what would become the War Production Board but then changed his mind. Douglas to Hugo Black, September 8, 1941, Hugo L. Black Papers, Manuscript Division, Library of Congress, Washington, D.C.

4. For a fuller discussion of Frankfurter's wartime activities, see Murphy, *Brandeis/Frankfurter Connection*, chs. 6–7.

5. Mason, *Harlan Fiske Stone*, 713–14. Stone also managed, a few years later, to prevent Congress from naming the chief justice to the Atomic Energy Commission.

6. Franklin D. Roosevelt to Stone, July 17, 1942; Stone to Roosevelt, July 20, 1942; Stone to John Bassett Moore, December 31, 1942, all in Harlan Fiske Stone Papers, Manuscript Division, Library of Congress, Washington, D.C.

7. Fine, *Murphy*, 206–12.

8. Herring, *Aid to Russia*, 7.

9. Fine, *Murphy*, 216–20; Celler to Stone, August 13, 1942: Stone to Celler, August 15, 1942, in Jackson Papers.

10. The Roberts Commission published no separate report at the time, but the Joint Congressional Committee on the Investigation of the Pearl Harbor Attack, the last of the eight groups, included not only its records but those of the other investigating bodies as well. See *Pearl Harbor Attack, Hearings* (Washington, D.C.: Government Printing Office, 1946).

11. Freedman, *Roosevelt & Frankfurter*, 744.

12. 310 U.S. 586 (1940); for a fuller discussion of the cases, see Manwaring, *Render Unto Caesar*.

13. Fine, *Murphy*, 185.

14. 310 U.S. at 600. Only Harlan Fiske Stone dissented (310 U.S. at 601), and had he circulated his draft earlier it is likely he would have picked up the votes of Black, Douglas, and Murphy, who expressly recanted their *Gobitis* vote in *Jones v. Opelika*, 316 U.S. 584, 623–24 (1942).

15. Quoted in Mason, *Security through Freedom*, 217.

16. *West Virginia Board of Education v. Barnette*, 319 U.S. 624, 642 (1943).

17. Ibid., 653; Frankfurter to Jackson, June 4, 1943, reel 1, part 3, Felix Frankfurter Papers, Harvard Law School, Cambridge, Mass. (hereafter FF-HLS).

18. Frankfurter to Roosevelt, May 3, 1943, in Freedman, *Roosevelt & Frankfurter*, 699.

19. Burt, *Two Jewish Justices*, 44–45. A more subtle psychological reading of the Frankfurter opinions in the two cases, but which also emphasizes his strong patriotic feelings, is Danzig, "Justice Frankfurter's Opinions," 675.

20. Murphy, *Constitution in Crisis Times*, 176–78; Frank Murphy's tenure as attorney general is detailed in Fine, *Murphy*, chs. 1–7.

21. "Summary of discussion at Conference on Saturday, December 5, 1942," reel 7, part 1, FF-HLS.

22. Schwimmer, a Quaker, had been denied citizenship because in the application form she had resolutely responded "No" to the question, "If necessary, are you willing to take up arms in defense of this country?" even though women normally were excused from answering that item. "If there is any principle of the Constitution that more imperatively calls for attachment than any other," Holmes had written in a dissent joined by Brandeis, "it is the principle of free thought—not free thought for those who agree with us but freedom for the thought we

hate." *United States v. Schwimmer*, 279 U.S. 644, 653, 654–55 (1929) (Holmes, dissenting).

23. "Summary of discussion," FF-HLS.

24. Douglas evidently believed at first that Schneiderman's petition ought to be dismissed on the grounds that there was sufficient evidence he had sworn allegiance falsely at the time of naturalization. During the conference, however, he changed his mind. Conference notes re: *Schneiderman* [n.d.], William O. Douglas Papers, Manuscript Division, Library of Congress, Washington, D.C.

25. *Schneiderman v. United States*, 320 U.S. 119 (1943).

26. Frankfurter to Murphy, May 31, 1943, Stone Papers; Frankfurter to Murphy, June 2, 1943, Jackson Papers. Murphy wrote back in the same vein, "My dear F.F.: Many thanks for your original and revised headnotes in the *Schneiderman* case. Not only do they reveal long and arduous preparation, but best of all, they are done with commendable English understatement and characteristic New England reserve." Murphy to Frankfurter, June 2, 1943, reel 2, part 3, FF-HLS.

27. 320 U.S. at 181.

28. "Notes on the Schneiderman case," June 1, 1943, reel 7, part 1, FF-HLS.

29. All four were frequent visitors at the White House, and for more than the weekly poker games. Tully, *F.D.R.*, 290.

30. Freedman, *Roosevelt & Frankfurter*, 521–30; Murphy, *Brandeis/Frankfurter Connection*, 197–200.

31. Simon, *Antagonists*, 133; Freedman, *Roosevelt & Frankfurter*, 582–86; Murphy, *Brandeis/Frankfurter Connection*, 216–20.

32. When a former colleague, John Maguire, wrote to Frankfurter asking his assistance in getting a death sentence commuted, the justice declined. "You above all ought not to be surprised that since I have been down here I have kept within the orbit of my judicial job with finicky scrupulousness; that on no matter even remotely connected with law or politics would I dream of making any suggestion to the President. . . . You see, I take the tripartite separation of our Government seriously." Frankfurter to Maguire, June 5, 1943, reel 10, part 3, FF-HLS

33. Lash, *Frankfurter*, 155.

34. Presidential Proclamation No. 2561, *Federal Register* 7 (July 2, 1942): 5101. The history of events connected with the case is well drawn in Bernstein, "Saboteur Trial," 131.

35. Henry Stimson Diary, entries for June 29 and July 6, 1942, quoted in Parrish, "Justice Frankfurter," 65.

36. Lurie, *Arming Military Justice*, 46.

37. Parrish, "Justice Frankfurter and the Supreme Court," 66.

38. See, for example, Frankfurter to Stone, August 3, 1942, box 69, Stone Papers; Stone to Frankfurter, August 29, 1942, reel 4, part 3, FF-HLS.

39. 1 Wall. 2 (1866). Ironically, Stone's son Lauson, then an army major, had been assigned to help with the defense and came up with the idea of using *Milligan*; when it appeared as if the appeal to the Supreme Court might be heard, the army took Lauson Stone off the case. The chief justice thought briefly about recusing himself, but both the government and defense counsel urged him to remain on the bench and hear the case.

40. Mason, *Harlan Fiske Stone*, 654.

41. The Court's decision to hear the case should be seen as highly unusual, since the existing rules of military justice, adopted in the so-called Chamberlain reforms of 1920, did not mention appeal to civilian courts. Not until the 1984 revision of the Uniform Code of Military Justice did Congress provide for direct appeal to the high court from the United States Court of Military Appeals, and then under very limited circumstances.

42. Black, memorandum on *Ex parte Quirin,* July 29, 1942, in Douglas Papers.

43. *Ex parte Quirin,* 317 U.S. 1, 18 (1942). Within a few days the military tribunal found the eight men guilty, and sentenced six of them to die, one to life imprisonment, and one to thirty years at hard labor. As defense counsel had feared, they learned of the execution of their clients through the press. Military law at the time did not require review by higher authority such as the president or the secretary of war (although both approved the sentence); Congress did not establish a military appeals court until 1951.

44. For Stone's labors on drafting the opinion, see Mason, *Harlan Fiske Stone,* 658–64. A good discussion of the opinion is Cushman, "Nazi Saboteurs," 1082.

45. Stone to Moore, December 31, 1942, Stone Papers; see also Stone to Roger Nelson, November 30, 1942, ibid. For different views within the Court, see two memoranda by Stone, both dated September 25, 1942, Douglas Papers.

46. "Federal Military Commission," *Harvard Law Review* 56 (1943): 642; see also Schilling, "Saboteurs," 481.

47. Currie, *Constitution,* 281.

48. The full story is well-told in Irons, *Justice at War,* and U.S. Commission on Wartime Relocation and Internment of Civilians, *Personal Justice Denied.* For an interpretation more sympathetic to the administration policy, see Smith, *Democracy on Trial.*

49. The judgment of history has been almost universal in condemning the policy and the Court's decision. Two early and still powerful critiques have set the tone for all that followed: Rostow, "The Japanese-American Cases," and Dembitz, "Racial Discrimination."

50. *Hirabayashi v. United States,* 320 U.S. 81 (1943).

51. Ibid., 93. Frankfurter, working as Black's ally, picked up on a second theme of judicial deference, and urged Stone to amend the opinion in a manner to make clear to the country that "we decide nothing that is not before us." The Hirabayashi case dealt only with the curfew, and so should the Court's opinion; it should not address the more controversial aspects of the relocation plan. In his memo, Frankfurter wrote: "We decide the issue only as we have defined it—we decide that the curfew order as applied, and at the time it was applied, was within the boundaries of the war power." Stone recirculated the opinion with Frankfurter's language added, word for word. Ibid., 102.

52. Douglas to Stone, May 31, 1943, Douglas Papers, and June 7, 1943, Stone Papers; see also the discussion of Douglas's conflicting views in Irons, *Justice at War,* 237–39.

53. Frankfurter to Stone, June 4, 1943, Stone Papers. That same day, Frankfurter sent another memorandum to Stone, suggesting a revision in the Chief's draft that would close off the habeas corpus option Douglas had suggested.

54. Frankfurter to Murphy, June 10, 1943, reel 2, part 3, FF-HLS.

55. Frankfurter to Stone, [n.d.], Stone Papers.

56. The concurrences are at 320 U.S. at 105, 109, and 114 respectively. Rutledge wrote to the chief justice that "I have had more anguish over this case than any I have decided, save possibly one death case in the Ct. of Appeals." Rutledge to Stone, August 12, 1943, Stone Papers.

57. *Korematsu v. United States*, 323 U.S. 214 (1944).

58. Conference notes, October 16, 1944, Jackson Papers.

59. Murphy, Minutes of Conference, October 16, 1944, in Irons, *Justice at War*, 322.

60. Frankfurter to Black, November 9, 1944, reel 1, part 3, FF-HLS. Stone to Black, November 9, 1944, Stone Papers, also approving the draft but suggesting minor changes.

61. 323 U.S. at 230.

62. Ibid., 224–25; Irons, *Justice at War*, 340–41. Given the criticism that he had received from civil libertarians for his earlier opinions, Frankfurter must have welcomed the letter that the noted philosopher and advocate of free speech, Alexander Meiklejohn, wrote him following this decision. Although Meiklejohn had been asked by the American Civil Liberties Union to keep a watching brief in Washington during the war, he wanted Frankfurter and Black to know that he disagreed with the ACLU's condemnation of the *Korematsu* holding. A grateful Frankfurter responded that "even a judge gets comfort in finding agreement in those very few whose judgment one really values." Meiklejohn to Frankfurter, January 3, 1945; Frankfurter to Meiklejohn, January 8, 1945, reel 12, part 1, FF-HLS.

63. 323 U.S. at 246 (Jackson, J., dissenting).

64. Douglas wrote in his memoirs that he always regretted not dissenting in the relocation cases, which were "ever on my conscience." *Court Years*, 279–80. For a scathing critique of the majority's constitutional analysis, see Jacobus tenBroek's section, "Leviticus," in tenBroek, Barnhart, and Matson, *Prejudice*.

65. Simon, *Antagonists*, 155.

66. Dunne, *Black*, 213; see also Yarbrough, *Mr. Justice Black*, 232–36.

67. Irons, "Fancy Dancing."

68. *Ex parte Endo*, 323 U.S. 283 (1944); for details, see Irons, *Justice at War*, 99–103, 307 ff.

69. Murphy's concurrence is at 323 U.S. 307, and that of Roberts at 308.

70. Douglas to Stone, November 23, 1944, Douglas Papers.

71. Mason, *Harlan Fiske Stone*, 698.

72. Murphy, *Constitution in Crisis Times*, 247. Murphy does add, however, that this was the most popular war in the nation's history, and thus the type of challenges to civil liberties undertaken during the Civil War, World War I, and Vietnam were absent.

73. Frank, "Review and Basic Liberties," 114. For an immediate postwar view, see Fraenkel, "War, Civil Liberties," 717.

74. These cases are discussed at length in Urofsky, *Division and Discord*, ch. 2.

75. *United States v. Carolene Products Co.*, 304 U.S. 144, 152–53 n. 4 (1938). David P. Currie writes that "In his twenty years on the Bench, Harlan F. Stone had done more perhaps than any other Justice to bring constitutional law into the twentieth century. We are indebted to him for one of the most effective protests against the old order and for the authoritative program of the new." Currie, *Constitution*, 334.

76. In that year Richard Nixon accused Abe Fortas of violating the separation of powers and the independence of the judiciary by advising President Lyndon Johnson, a practice that Fortas had engaged in before he became a justice and that he continued after his appointment to the Court. See Kalman, *Fortas*, ch. 10. After that justices have been extremely careful not to engage in this type of activity.

CHAPTER 2

Sabotage, Treason, and Military Tribunals in World War II

William M. Wiecek

Silent enim leges inter arma, declared Cicero two millennia ago.[1] American historical experience suggests that there is some truth in his observation. Law as a constraint on war in the United States has never severely hampered military operations. In the two major wars the United States fought between 1789 and 1940, the relative position of the Supreme Court vis-à-vis the other branches receded during hostilities, while the powers of the president increased dramatically, though temporarily.

In the Civil War, President Lincoln ignored Chief Justice Taney's command that the army release John Merryman, a Maryland secessionist who was being held for guerilla recruitment and paramilitary operations.[2] The Peace Democrat Clement Vallandigham found that the First Amendment availed him little in a trial before a military commission, and the Supreme Court refused to accept jurisdiction of his appeal.[3] A bare 5–4 majority of the Court sustained the Lincoln administration's strategy and rationale for the president's response to secession and war.[4] It is a canard, exploded a generation ago,[5] that the Court was cowed and abject in the face of Congress' wrath during the Civil War, but it is nevertheless true that the judiciary did not oppose its power to that of the executive and the military in any significant constitutional confrontation. Similarly, during the Great War and after, the Court readily upheld the military draft,[6] and sustained numerous convictions of the war's opponents under the Espionage and Sedition Acts.

Some idea of the almost limitless potential of the *silent leges* idea can be glimpsed in a dictum of Justice George Sutherland in an interwar conscientious-objector case:

From its very nature, the war power, when necessity calls for its exercise, tolerates no qualifications or limitations, unless found in the Constitution or in applicable principles of international law. . . . To the end that war may not result in defeat, freedom of speech may, by act of Congress, be curtailed or denied so that the morale of the people and the spirit of the army may not be broken by seditious utterances; freedom of the press curtailed to preserve our military plans and movements from the knowledge of the enemy; deserters and spies put to death without indictment or trial by jury; ships and supplies requisitioned; property of alien enemies, theretofore under the protection of the Constitution, seized without process and converted to the public use without compensation and without due process of law in the ordinary sense of that term; prices of food and other necessities of life fixed or regulated; railways taken over and operated by the Government; and other drastic powers, wholly inadmissible in time of peace, exercised to meet the emergencies of war.[7]

Such a breathtaking vision of governmental power was all the more remarkable in a jurist who was otherwise ungenerous in his concessions to federal and state authority.

On the other hand, though, the United States has never experienced a wholesale abeyance of civil liberties or constitutional constraints during wartime, such as might be done (at least theoretically) under the civil-law doctrines of *kriegzustand* or *état du siège*.[8] Justice David Davis forcefully extolled that achievement in *Ex parte Milligan* (1866):

No doctrine, involving more pernicious consequences, was ever invented by the wit of man than that any of its provisions can be suspended during any of the great exigencies of government. Such a doctrine leads directly to anarchy or despotism, but the theory of necessity on which it is based is false; for the government, within the Constitution, has all the powers granted to it, which are necessary to preserve its existence.[9]

Although partisan critics vociferously argued to the contrary, the civilian and military arms of the national government were extraordinarily respectful of the people's civil liberties throughout the Civil War.[10] American jurists and commentators congratulated themselves for preserving constitutional constraints on presidential and military authority in the crisis of war. Meanwhile, the powerful and unblemished American tradition of military subordination to civilian authority that Davis celebrated in *Milligan* was reaffirmed in all successive wars.

On balance, then, Cicero's pessimistic observation does not apply to the United States. The Constitution retains its force unabated in wartime; the state and federal courts do not shutter their doors; no American Cincinnatus is called from his plow; the civilian population is usually unmolested, not only by military operations, but by the military itself. But would this experience continue through a total war in which all the resources of the state were mobilized to defeat powerful totalitarian enemies leagued in a globe-encircling military alliance?

With one major, egregious exception—the internment of Japanese Americans—the answer given by the Supreme Court was mixed. The World War II Court strove to balance liberty and authority, right and power, so that for much of the period Cicero's aphorism may be reversed: in the clash of arms, the laws often speak out eloquently.[11] In confronting questions of First Amendment speech and associational liberties, the rights of naturalized citizens with obnoxious views, the position of conscientious objectors, and the definition of treason, the Court preserved the rule of law, maintaining the judiciary's role as a guardian of popular liberty.[12] The major tragic exception to this generally benign picture was the race-driven plight of Japanese Americans in the nation's only experience with concentration camps. But in other cases, reviewed below, the Court sometimes faltered in its role as guarantor of individual and collective liberty in the face of governmental power.

During and after the war, the Court found itself revisiting issues that it had not encountered in almost a century, involving treason, military commissions, and courts-martial. The results were uneven: the Court repeatedly deferred to the authority of military courts, yet maintained the stringent substantive and evidentiary requirements for treason mandated by the Framers and affirmed by John Marshall.

THE CASE OF THE NAZI SABOTEURS

These issues were first raised dramatically when eight German saboteurs were rounded up by the FBI in the summer of 1942. The whole episode seems hare-brained in retrospect, but it provided the occasion for two major treason trials and the Court's most serious confrontation with military justice since the Civil War.

Early in the war, the German *Abwehr* (Military Intelligence) developed plans to sabotage defense plants and infrastructure in the United States. It recruited eight German nationals who had resided in the United States and become acculturated to varying degrees before returning around 1939 to aid the Reich. The army trained them as saboteurs and the navy transported them to American shores in U-boats (not too difficult a challenge in the early phase of the Battle of the Atlantic, when the wolfpacks roamed underseas almost at will). The eight were a mixed lot.[13] Two, Herman Haupt and Ernst Burger, were naturalized American citizens, although Burger had forfeited his citizenship by service as a conscript in the *Wehrmacht*. (He was the only soldier among them; the rest were civilians.) Only two, Burger and Edward Kerling, were active and dedicated Party members. Burger had been in the Munich beer hall putsch of 1923, had been an associate of Ernst Roehm but survived the purge, and had later been arrested by the Gestapo for forgery. Four others had been members of the Bund during their American sojourn.

The saboteurs landed in two groups: four under the leadership of George Dasch at Amagansett, Long Island; the others under the command of Kerling near Jacksonville, Florida. They promptly doffed their German Marine fatigues, changed to mufti, buried their explosives in the sand, and dispersed, with plans to rendezvous in Cincinnati in six weeks. But their plans miscarried immediately. Dasch ran into an unarmed Coast Guardsman on patrol on the beach and offered him $260 for his silence. The young seaman took the money, then returned to his station and reported what had happened. After a delay of twelve hours, the Coast Guard reported the incident to the FBI.

Dasch seems to have been unnerved by the encounter, though, and he decided to betray his comrades and turn himself in to the FBI. He persuaded Burger to join him. After Dasch confessed to the FBI in Washington, its agents promptly rounded up the remaining seven. (Haupt made it easier for them by brazenly walking into their Chicago office to try to talk his way out of pending draft-evasion charges!) J. Edgar Hoover orchestrated the release of information about the sensational event to hog credit for the capture for the FBI and himself and to assure the American people that any potential espionage or subversion would be readily contained.

From the first disclosure of the saboteurs' capture, President Franklin D. Roosevelt took an unwholesome and aggressively proactive interest in the case. The president demanded the death penalty for all: "offenses such as these are probably more serious than any offense in criminal law. The death penalty is called for by usage and by the extreme gravity of the war aim and the very existence of our American Government."[14] He suggested a court-martial for all the saboteurs, whatever their citizenship or civilian status. FDR was determined that the Germans not seek the succor of civilian courts. Perhaps dimly recalling the Lincoln-Taney confrontation over the imprisoned Confederate irregular John Merryman,[15] the president insisted, "I won't give them up. . . . I won't hand them over to any United States marshal armed with a writ of habeas corpus."[16]

FDR's demands raised grave legal problems, however.[17] A trial in civil courts would not satisfy the president's demand for death: only two (the American citizens) could be tried for a capital offense, treason. The others, being civilian citizens of a foreign power, could be tried only for sabotage under the Espionage Act of 1917, a noncapital offense. Treason convictions of the two American citizens would be difficult to obtain, given the stringent requirements for treason set by the Framers and by Chief Justice John Marshall. Courts-martial were available only for members of the American armed forces.

Thus Attorney General Francis Biddle, with the concurrence of Secretary of War Henry Stimson, recommended trial by a military commission, an extraordinary wartime tribunal composed of military officers convened to try individuals not in the military service for offenses against the laws of war.

Stimson conferred twice at social occasions with Justice Felix Frankfurter about the composition of the military commission. (Frankfurter recommended an all-military membership.)[18] But a military commission raised a complex of constitutional issues, the most fundamental being whether the luckless saboteurs could be tried by a military tribunal of any sort.

One of the earliest and most important precedents dealing with civil liberties in wartime was the case of *Ex parte Milligan* (1866), where the Court held that Congress could not authorize the trial of civilians by a military commission where the civil courts were open and functioning.[19] Lambdin Milligan, a civilian Copperhead in Indiana, had allegedly engaged in a variety of treasonable activities there. For these, he was tried by a military commission in Indianapolis and sentenced to be hanged. In vacating this sentence, Justice David Davis unequivocally condemned the use of military courts to displace the authority of civil courts:

> Martial rule can never exist where the courts are open, and in the proper and unobstructed exercise of their jurisdiction. It is also confined to the locality of actual war. Martial law cannot arise from a threatened invasion. The necessity must be actual and present; the invasion real, such as effectually closes the courts and deposes the civil administration.

He held martial law to be inapplicable to civilians where civil authority was undisturbed; were it otherwise, "republican government is a failure, and there is an end of liberty regulated by law. Martial law, established on such a basis, destroys every guarantee of the Constitution, and effectually renders the 'military independent of and superior to the civil power.' " "Civil liberty and this kind of martial law cannot endure together; the antagonism is irreconcilable; and, in the conflict, one or the other must perish." Strong words, unqualified by concessions to the urgency of the moment, Davis's ringing dicta would seem to preclude the Biddle proposal.

Undeterred, the president enthusiastically adopted his Attorney General's advice and appointed a military commission consisting of seven army generals to try the Germans for violating the uncodified international laws of war and the Articles of War: (1) appearing in civilian dress behind the lines to commit sabotage or espionage; (2) aiding the enemy; (3) spying; and (4) conspiracy to commit the substantive offenses. Biddle pointed out that these charges, all of which were capital, would be easier to prove than the statutory offense of violation of the Espionage Act or the constitutional offense of treason. He also observed that hearings on these charges would be far more speedy and expeditious than a trial before a civil court and that a military commission could provide secrecy, as a criminal trial could not. A military commission could "proceed without being bound by the technical rules of evidence or procedure."[20]

FDR's order was extraordinary (and constitutionally vulnerable) in several respects.[21] It provided a relaxed standard of evidence: "probative value to a reasonable man" in the opinion of the commission's president. Conviction and sentence required only a two-thirds vote of the tribunal—five members, rather than unanimity (for sentence of death). The judgment of the tribunal was to be sent directly to the president for review, rather than to the Judge-Advocate General of the Army and a review board, as required by the Articles of War.[22]

Biddle also recommended a special proclamation declaring the saboteurs subject to the laws of war and the jurisdiction of military tribunals. It also closed all civilian courts to the saboteurs. He was particularly concerned to shut off any avenue of recourse by habeas corpus. This would effectively deny habeas relief to these particular defendants without the constitutional complications that would be presented by a general suspension of the writ of habeas corpus, which had caused Abraham Lincoln so much difficulty.[23] The president gladly complied.[24] To cap his hawkish course, Biddle insisted that he himself present the government's case before the military commission. Stimson reluctantly agreed.

The president appointed two army attorneys, Cassius Dowell, a career J.A.G. officer, and Kenneth Royall, who was to become Secretary of the Army in the Truman administration, as defense counsel. (They were later joined by another army lawyer, Carl Ristine, who represented Dasch exclusively because of his unique situation.) Royall and Dowell determined to challenge the legality of the entire proceeding. They conferred with Justices Owen Roberts and Hugo Black at Roberts's farm outside Philadelphia, along with Army Judge-Advocate General Myron Cramer and Attorney General Biddle, and urged the justices to hear their challenge. Black and Roberts phoned Chief Justice Harlan Fiske Stone, vacationing in New Hampshire, who agreed to convene the Court in special session immediately.

The hearing before the military commission began on July 6 and concluded on July 27. The next day, after a finding of guilty, Royall and Dowell sought to obtain a Supreme Court hearing through two separate routes, a petition for a writ of habeas corpus from the Court itself and a petition for certiorari from affirmance of denial of habeas corpus by the U.S. District Court for the District of Columbia.[25] The Court granted certiorari and thereby agreed to review the constitutional challenges posed by the defense lawyers. It was symptomatic of the eleventh-hour haste that characterized the entire proceedings before the Supreme Court that the justices managed to grant certiorari only minutes before rendering their opinion in the case.

Defense counsel posed five powerful constitutional challenges:[26]

1. All eight petitioners had a right to seek habeas corpus from the Supreme Court: Haupt because he was an American citizen, the rest simply because no statute or valid executive proclamation forbade them from doing so. This was the only one of the petitioners' arguments that the Court accepted.
2. The presidential proclamation foreclosing access to civil courts was unconstitutional for a variety of reasons. FDR lacked power to issue it under either the Con-

stitution or statutes. (This raised the problem of the scope of executive power under *United States v. Curtiss-Wright Export Corporation* (1936), which had conceded dangerously expansive powers to the president as "the sole organ of the federal government in the field of international relations—a power which does not require as a basis for its exercise an act of Congress."[27]) It violated the ex post facto clause because it increased penalties after the commission of the offense.[28] It deprived the defendants of the procedural guarantees enumerated in the Fifth and Sixth Amendments, as well as the privilege of the writ of habeas corpus. Finally, the proclamation ignored the grant of judicial power to federal courts in Article III, bypassing them for an ad hoc tribunal transparently created for the sole purpose of convicting the saboteurs.

3. The military commission had no power to try the defendants for any of the charges. The charge of violating the laws of war amounted to the equivalent of inventing a common-law crime, a criminal offense unknown to the existing, written laws. The charges based on the Articles of War could be prosecuted only in courts martial for "cases arising in the land or naval forces" (Fifth Amendment).
4. The president's order creating the commission ignored various procedural guarantees provided in the Articles of War. These included the rules of evidence, investigatory matters, requirements for unanimity in voting, and review. It constituted an improper delegation of authority to the commission.
5. Most trenchant of all, defense counsel insisted that military trials for individuals who were not members of the American armed forces violated *Milligan*'s prohibition against military trials when civil courts were open and functioning. Neither Congress nor the president could bypass civil courts.

Attorney General Biddle, arguing for the United States, responded in the alternative either that *Milligan* did not apply because the factual circumstances of the two cases were so different, or that, if it did, it should be overruled in whole or in part.[29] He assumed, with reason, that rules based on the technology of warfare of *Milligan*'s era, particularly its concept of lines and fronts, had become partially obsolete in the era of "total and global war." This view was not unrealistic: the Battle of the Atlantic raged as he spoke; U-boats prowled daily within sight of the Atlantic coast; enemy personnel like the saboteurs could be landed almost at will; American naval and merchant seamen were dying in American territorial waters.[30] The New York and Florida coasts were realistically within the theater of operations; the Germans had penetrated coastal defenses with hostile intent; FDR's intuition that they were in the position of Nathan Hale and Major Andre was not unreasonable. None of this justified unlimited presidential authority to displace civil courts or the procedures specified in the Articles of War, but it did caution the Court that *Milligan* might rest on antiquated assumptions. Yet Biddle's position potentially plowed wide inroads into traditional concepts of American civil liberties, particularly those identified in *Milligan*. He dismissed the case as a relic, but it was no more a relic than was jury trial. Unlimited presidential power of the appalling sort authorized by *Curtiss-Wright* was the dangerous and anomalous innovation.

These arguments left the Court exposed in a precarious position. The justices were aware of FDR's almost bloodthirsty determination to put the saboteurs to death: Biddle had told Roberts that he was "apprehensive" that the president was going to order the prisoners shot no matter what the Court might do.[31] Congressman Emanuel Celler opined that "the eight Nazi saboteurs should be executed with all possible dispatch. . . . [The American people] are confident that the military tribunal will decree their death. Any interference with that trial by civil court would strike a severe blow to public morale."[32] A *New York Times* dispatch of July 28, datelined Washington, reported that "there is great dissatisfaction here with the length to which the trial has already proceeded. . . . On all sides hope was expressed that the Supreme Court would make short work of the move," that is, the habeas petition.[33]

When the justices assembled for argument on July 29, it immediately became apparent that they were divided in their attitudes. First, there was the matter of recusals. Lieutenant Colonel Frank Murphy, U.S.A.R., had just arrived from his training duties at Fort Benning, in full uniform. Felix Frankfurter insisted that he recuse himself because of his military status, and Murphy reluctantly complied. What his recusal meant for the outcome of the case must remain speculative, but Murphy was the foremost spokesman on the Court for the cause of civil liberties, and if he had delivered one of his fervid appeals for restraint of authority to preserve liberty, he might have deflected the position of some of his brethren. Frankfurter's fastidious concern for appearances did not suggest to him that he should recuse himself because of his previous discussions with Stimson, or because he, too, held an (inactive) military commission (Major, U.S.A.R.).[34] The Chief Justice was more scrupulous, however. His son Lauson Stone, as an Army J.A.G. reserve Major, had participated in the hearings before the military commission, and Stone asked both counsel and colleagues whether he ought to recuse himself. All insisted that Stone sit. He did, and lent a hawkish emphasis to deliberations.

On substantive questions, too, the justices were conflicted. They resented FDR's high-handed attempt by mere proclamation to oust the civil-courts of any role in considering the civil-liberties issues the case posed, and they were resolved to rebuff this dangerous overture. Though half the justices of the Stone Court could not be considered ardent civil libertarians, all shared an institutional concern for judicial power. All were troubled by the unseemly haste and secrecy of the proceedings, and they sensed that a lethal result was foreordained.

Yet none of the sitting judges had any stomach to challenge the president and the army, not from any squeamish poltroonery, but from motives of sincere patriotism. For six months American armed forces had been suffering serious losses and reversals, beginning with Pearl Harbor and the Philippines. Domestic anxieties ran high: the seeming ease with which enemy saboteurs could penetrate American defenses was unnerving and worrisome to the American people. They shared the president's indignation about the cheekiness of the sabotage attempt. Who could foretell whether more such attempts were in the offing? None of the justices wanted to impede defense efforts in a total, global war.

Hearings before the military commission suspended on July 28 to permit counsel to argue the habeas petitions before the Supreme Court. The Court heard oral arguments on the two succeeding days and announced its decision in a brief per curiam on July 31. The per curiam opinion stated that the charges against the saboteurs alleged an offense that the president could order tried before a military commission, that the commission was lawfully constituted, and that the Germans' detention under military authority was lawful. It dismissed their petition and denied certiorari.[35] Stone, who read the per curiam opinion, announced that the Court would file a full opinion later.

Hearings promptly resumed before the military commission, and on August 3, it sentenced the defendants to death by electrocution. FDR reviewed the sentences, commuted those of Burger and Dasch to prison terms on the recommendation of Biddle, and authorized a medal for J. Edgar Hoover. Six of the defendants were put to death on August 8. Burger and Dasch were imprisoned and eventually repatriated in 1948.

With the saboteurs dead or imprisoned, any opinion the Court might deliver would be anticlimactic. Yet that opinion posed formidable challenges to the integrity, ingenuity, and principles of the Court. If nothing else, the justices at least had to preserve the appearance of legitimacy. With only an occasional dissenting voice,[36] contemporary press and scholarly commentary effused fulsome self-congratulations about the fairness of the American judicial system, as contrasted with those of its enemies,[37] and the Court at least had to keep up appearances. The need for producing a result that at least *seemed* just was never far from the justices' minds as they struggled into the autumn to craft an opinion for the Court that would appear to preserve justice, legitimacy, judicial authority, and the subordination of the military to civil power, yet at the same time justify the result. The Chief Justice expressed this concern in a draft opinion circulated as a memorandum to the brethren in September. The Court must not be seen in the position "of having stood by and allowed six men to go to their death without making it plain to all concerned—including the president—that it had left undecided a question on which counsel strongly relied to secure petitioners' liberty," Stone cautioned.[38] The result of such attitudes, however, was the preservation of appearances by the sacrifice of the substance.

All the justices wanted to present a unanimous front; to uphold the result, to preserve judicial power (perhaps to fight another day), and to incorporate the entire proceeding, military commission and all, within the framework of a judicial system that preserves a decent concern for individual liberties. But beyond that, cohesion among them dissolved.

Stone, like most of his colleagues, was divided within himself. He did not share Robert H. Jackson's and Felix Frankfurter's breezy willingness to subordinate judicial power to executive and military authority in wartime, yet he was committed to justifying the result. How could he do otherwise, with the bodies of six Germans moldering in a potter's field? Moreover, he had to shepherd his discordant colleagues to a single opinion, despite the fact that he and most of them recognized the cogency of the arguments that Royall had made for the defense.

Stone undertook the task of drafting the opinion for the Court. In this, he was hampered not only by his own uncertainties about each of the major legal issues in the case, but also by the fact that he was working from his Franconia, New Hampshire, summer residence, and had to depend on his law clerks in distant Washington for research substantiating the issues he wanted to reach.[39] His correspondence directing their labors amply supports Michal Belknap's conclusion that he and his colleagues "had started with a conclusion and worked backward to find reasons justifying it."[40] Writing to Bennett Boskey about the Fifth and Sixth Amendment challenge, for example, he admitted that "I think [my statement in the draft opinion] is right but my authorities are meager."[41]

Once back in Washington after his summer break, Stone circulated a draft opinion. The brethren immediately wrangled over its substance. Jackson adopted the extreme position of wanting to validate anything the president did—in effect declaring civil courts to be hors de combat. "We have no more important duty than to keep clear and separate the lines of responsibility and duty of the judicial and of the executive-military arms of government," he argued. "Merger of the two is the end of liberty as we in this country have known it." In drafts, Jackson would have gone so far as to exempt courts from dealing with any "cases which relate to foreign relations."[42]

Frankfurter came close to the same position. In a peculiar, emotional memorandum to the Court, composed as an imaginary dialogue first between himself and the defendants, then between his former law clerks in military service and the Court, Frankfurter poured out his strongly-held feelings on the issues raised in the Germans' appeal. Frankfurter to the Germans: "You damned scoundrels have a helluvacheek to ask for a writ that would take you out of the hands of the Military Commission and give you the right to be tried, if at all, in a federal district court. You are just low-down, ordinary, enemy spies who, as enemy soldiers, have invaded our country and therefore could immediately have been shot by the military. . . . You've done enough mischief already without leaving the seeds of a bitter conflict involving the President, the courts and Congress after your bodies will be rotting in lime. . . . The Articles of War don't apply to you. And so you will remain in your present custody and be damned."

Lawyer-soldiers to the Court: "What in hell do you fellows think you are doing? Haven't we got enough of a job trying to lick the Japs and the Nazis without having you fellows on the Supreme Court dissipate the thoughts and feelings and energies of the folks at home by stirring up a nice row as to who has what power . . . ? Haven't you got any more sense than to get people by the ear on one of the favorite American pastimes—abstract constitutional discussion."[43] A lawyer reading this strange dialogue might have thought that "abstract constitutional discussion," especially where lives were at stake, would be appropriate in the circumstances. But this revealing plea at least had the useful effect of preserving unanimity by deterring Jackson from submitting a concurrence.

Stone conceded the weakness of the government's position and the difficulty that he would have in supporting it. His job was not made any easier by the fact that, as he put it the next summer, "I have had much difficulty herding my collection of fleas."[44] Stone therefore resorted to a strategy of simply evading the more serious constitutional challenges. He accomplished this in several ways. He began with a concession to the linked causes of judicial power and individual freedom, citing "the duty which rests on the courts, in time of war as well as in time of peace, to preserve unimpaired the constitutional safeguards of liberty."[45] He then made a nominal gesture in that direction by holding, disingenuously, that the presidential proclamation did not "preclude access to the courts for determining its applicability to the particular case." The court, he maintained, could pass on constitutional issues posed by the military commission. But since he used the opportunity he thus claimed for the courts to uphold a constitutionally dubious procedure, this blow for liberty was feeble.

Turning to the substantive points, Stone backed up to the most troublesome difficulty, *Milligan*, indirectly. To sustain denial of the writ of habeas corpus, he thought it sufficient to demonstrate that "Congress has authorized trial of offenses against the law of war before [military] commissions." Therefore, all eight Germans, including the American citizen, Haupt, were "belligerent enemies" triable as such by a military commission. The right to trial in civilian courts, as well as the protections of the Fifth and Sixth Amendments, had never historically been extended to persons tried by military commissions.

The trouble with this position, as Stone uneasily recognized, was that the only authorities for it were executive and military, not judicial; moreover, all predated *Milligan*. So Stone confined the troubling precedent of that case "as having particular reference to the facts before it," involving a defendant who had never been a member of any armed forces, and therefore not an "enemy belligerent," which the *Quirin* defendants plainly were. This was less than candid; it did not even rise to the level of a lawyer's distinction without a difference. All but Burger were, like Lambdin Milligan, civilians; and Milligan himself had been a member of a band of Confederate paramilitary irregulars, the "Order of American Knights." Stone knew, but could not concede, that the real point behind this unpersuasive intellectual exercise was to legitimate trial before a military panel that would not be inconvenienced by the constitutional safeguards of the treason clauses of Article II and the procedural guarantees afforded in civil courts by the Bill of Rights.

The naked results-orientation of the *Quirin* opinion was bad enough, but in order to reach the result, Stone was forced to a tactical choice that had dangerous repercussions. The defendants were charged with three substantive offenses besides conspiracy: (1) going behind enemy lines in civilian attire to commit espionage or sabotage; (2) relieving the enemy (Article of War 81); and (3) spying (Article of War 82). The first was a violation of the unwritten international law of war, while the latter two were statutory offenses, Congress having codified the Articles of War.[46] Stone upheld the convictions solely on the first charge, because the latter two would pose constitutional challenges that he wished to avoid. (Both duplicated nonmilitary offenses triable in civil courts, and the Articles of War may have been applicable only to American military personnel tried in courts-martial.)

And therein lay the danger. For by permitting trial of enemy civilians before military courts for violations of an international *lex non scripta*, the *Quirin* decision authorized a broad, potentially illimitable power in military courts, and it did so only at the cost of subordinating fundamental guarantees of civil liberty, such as the Bill of Rights and the stringent constitutional requirements for treason.

To add insult to injury, Stone achieved this result by a faulty statutory construction that even the Court's defenders admitted was insupportable. At the outset of arguments in *Quirin*, it was doubtful that any tribunal, military or civil, could apply the laws of war. Early on, the Marshall Court had held in *United States v. Hudson and Goodwin* (1812) that federal courts do not have jurisdiction over common-law criminal offenses.[47] Common-law crimes are not cognizable in federal courts. But what is the law of war but "a great *lex non scripta*," "a centuries-old body of largely unwritten rules and principles of international law," as Attorney General Biddle correctly identified it during his oral arguments before the Court?[48]

Stone got around the difficulty of *Hudson and Goodwin* by holding that Congress, in Article 15 of the Articles of War, had somehow imported or confirmed the laws of war as a body of law concurrent with the Articles of War to be enforced in all military tribunals.[49] But as commentators on this question have noted,[50] Article 15 did no more than confer jurisdiction on military commissions concurrent with courts-martial; Congress had not intended to create or import a foreign corpus of law into the American legal system.[51]

Chief Justice Stone provided an accurate and fair evaluation of his handiwork: "About all I can say for what I have done is that I think it will present to the Court all tenable and pseudo-tenable bases for decision."[52] In contrast with the Stone Court's sensitive and sensible handling of other wartime civil liberties issues, and in melancholy anticipation of the Japanese relocation cases, *Quirin* established several unenviable benchmarks. It drastically constricted the authority of *Milligan*, which until then had been the beacon of wartime liberties. "Practically then," the victorious Biddle crowed, "the Milligan case is out of the way and should not again plague us."[53] Stone's opinion not only tolerated but encouraged presidential incursions into individual liberties. It subordinated the courts and all of Article III's grant of judicial power to the authority of the military. As a specimen of judicial craft, it was transparently and disingenuously results-oriented, based on logic-chopping distinctions and evasion of real constitutional problems. Six men, though unquestionably guilty of some sort of belligerent activity against the United States in wartime, went to their deaths because a president was avid to see them hanged and a Court was disinclined to frustrate his leadership. In the clash of arms in modern total war, the laws were not silent in this case, but they were impotent to deflect executive will. Edward S. Corwin, the dominant mid-century authority on public law, dismissed the Court's effort in *Quirin* as "little more than a ceremonious detour to a predetermined goal."[54]

Michal Belknap, who has provided the most intensive exploration of the constitutional issues posed by the saboteurs' case, concluded that "the justices enlisted in the national military effort," with the result that civil liberties remained "vulnerable throughout the rest of World War II and in the Cold War." The justices were "unwilling to challenge the warmaking branches of the government" and embraced a "constitutional relativism which dictated that the security of individual rights var[ies] inversely with the extent to which their exercise seemed to threaten the capacity of the nation to wage war," a dangerous calculus. Its total-war mind-set rendered the Court "an unreliable guardian of the Bill of Rights."[55] *Quirin* cast a long shadow. The attitudes of the justices carried over into the Japanese internment cases decided the next year. The precedent permitted the Court to ignore challenges to the jurisdiction of postwar military tribunals trying Japanese and German war criminals. The antilibertarian weight of the Cold War civil liberties cases is traceable to *Quirin*'s deference to wartime attitudes.

CRAMER AND THE LAW OF TREASON

The Court partially redeemed its performance in one of the treason and harboring cases that were spawned by the saboteurs' adventure. In these treason cases, the Court for the first time provided a modern doctrinal content to the constitutionally defined crime of treason and hedged in treason prosecutions with strict evidentiary requirements.

The Framers were so concerned with the abuses of treason encountered in English historical experience that they imposed a specific definition of the crime in the text of the Constitution and, for good measure, added tough evidentiary safeguards. "Treason against the United States," they specified in Article III, "shall consist only in levying War against them, or adhering to their Enemies, giving them Aid and Comfort." They deliberately made treason difficult to prove: "No Person shall be convicted of Treason unless on the Testimony of two Witnesses to the same overt Act, or on Confession in open Court." For good measure, they even constrained the power to punish: "The Congress shall have Power to declare the Punishment of Treason, but no Attainder of Treason shall work Corruption of Blood, or Forfeiture except during the Life of the Person attainted."[56] This passage is unique in three respects: it is the only crime defined in the Constitution; it is the only instance where the Framers devised standards of evidentiary proof; and it is the only textual linkage between crime and punishment.

Despite this unusual specificity, much remained in the treason clauses to be defined. The problems, as usual, traced back to the historical heritage within which the Framers labored. The Treason Act of 25 Edward III defined treason, and a parliamentary enactment following the Glorious Revolution imposed the two-witness rule.[57] But these statutory constraints did not prevent the efflorescence of a doctrine of "constructive treason." The 1351 act itself had included the crime of "compassing" (imagining) the king's death, and later doctrinal development permitted words to serve as an overt act. Under these circumstances, the Crown could punish mere political opposition or resistance to law as treason, and it often did so.

The Framers were determined to rid American law of these ominous potentials, and John Marshall interpreted the treason clauses in that spirit in the celebrated cases of Aaron Burr and *Ex parte Bollman and Swartwout*.[58] In these cases, Marshall preserved the restrictive spirit of the constitutional text and set a precedent for requiring a strict, literal reading of the clauses. (That was why Biddle sought so strenuously to avoid a treason trial for Haupt.) But then, doctrinal development of the law of treason in the United States arrested. Despite innumerable opportunities for doing so, the Lincoln administration did not punish Confederates' levying war against the United States as treasonous. The Wilson administration chose to harass opponents of the Great War by prosecution for the lesser statutory crimes of espionage and sedition. Thus by World War II, the law of treason, beyond the constitutional text, was largely unwritten.

Onto this doctrinal tabula rasa came the German saboteurs. Once landed, they exploited connections with family, friends, and former Bund associates. One of them, Werner Thiel, made contact with an old friend and roommate, a naturalized citizen named Anthony Cramer. Cramer met Thiel twice for drinks (once in the company of Kerling), tried to arrange a tryst between Thiel and his girlfriend, and took $3,670 from Thiel for safekeeping and repayment of an old debt. FBI agents observed the drinking sessions but could not hear what was said. Cramer seems to have been ignorant of the specific purpose of Thiel's mission. After his arrest, Cramer at first lied to protect Thiel, then came clean.[59]

Cramer was tried for treason and convicted in 1942. The only evidence tendered by the prosecution that satisfied the constitutional two-witness rule was of his socializing with Thiel and Kerling. Thus the central constitutional issue quickly came into focus: would *any* behavior seen by two witnesses, no matter how innocent, suffice for the "overt Act" required by the Constitution? (In lawyers' parlance, such an act is said to be "colorless to treason.") Or did the overt act somehow have to manifest on its face that it constituted giving "Aid and Comfort" to the enemies of the United States?[60]

This in turn adverted to a rule in conspiracy prosecutions, whereby any action, innocent in itself, sufficed if it was a step in the overall pattern of conspiracy. And *that*, in turn, brought American jurists directly back to the origins of the treason clauses. For if the relaxed conspiracy rule covered treason prosecutions as well, then the Framers' assiduous care to move treason prosecutions in America away from English constructive treasons would have been in vain. On the other hand, to require that the overt act be in itself sinister would make treason convictions more difficult to obtain. This was the dilemma that Cramer's case brought to the Supreme Court.

The first arguments in Cramer's appeal, presented in March 1944, focused on factual, evidentiary issues. In conference, the justices found themselves deeply divided over the constitutional tests. Chief Justice Stone proved to be the most hawkish proponent of the prosecution-friendly weak test, finding "intent alone" adequate to sustain a treason conviction.[61] Opposing his position were the unlikely trio of Frankfurter, Roberts, and Reed, who supported the strict standard. Frankfurter insisted that the Framers had intended to make it "extremely difficult to prove treason."[62] Jackson attempted a draft opinion limited to the evidentiary questions that avoided the thorny constitutional problems; he admitted that his rationales did not "ring quite true, but they are the best I can think of."[63] That was scarcely a clarion, and several members of the Court, above all Stone, determined to reach the constitutional issues.[64] So the Court ordered reargument,[65] and Solicitor General Fahy took the spontaneous and unprecedented step of commissioning an independent historical review of all treason precedents, as much to inform the Court as to buttress the government's position. Acknowledging the significance of this, Jackson, who wrote the majority opinion in *Cramer v. United States* (1945) after all, noted that "the Solicitor General engaged scholars not otherwise involved in conduct of the case to collect and impartially to summarize statutes, decisions, and texts from Roman, Continental, and Canon law as well as from English, Colonial, and American sources."[66]

The principal researcher in this endeavor was James Willard Hurst, a former law clerk for Justice Brandeis, who was to become the foremost figure in the field of American legal history. At the time, he was a lieutenant in the Navy's Bureau of Personnel, on loan to the Solicitor General for the *Cramer* arguments. The product of Hurst's labors appeared first as a 360–page appendix to the government's brief on reargument, then as the definitive historico-doctrinal study of treason in a three-part series published in the *Harvard Law Review*, and finally in revised and updated form as a monograph in the series "Contributions in American History," edited by Stanley I. Kutler.[67] Hurst endorsed the restrictive interpretation of the Framers' intent and the treason clauses, but acknowledged the dilemma posed by *Cramer*: strict requirements for the overt act would make the independent textual specification of intent superfluous, while strict requirements for intent would do the same to the overt act. Though under no a priori pressure to do so, Hurst supported the government's position that the overt act need not be manifestly treasonous; acts innocent on their face would suffice if interpreted in context.

Debates in conference after reargument disclosed that once the justices decided to go beyond merely evidentiary questions, they ranged along a continuum on the substantive issues. Murphy and Rutledge supported the restrictive approach, while Stone and Douglas were determined that treason prosecutions not be made impossible or even difficult by imposing a strict construction of overt acts. A five-member majority coalesced around Roberts's insight that the Framers meant to link the "procedural" requirements of an overt act and two witnesses to the "substantive" elements of the offense. The substantive component, other than "levying War," required two indispensable elements: intent ("adhering to their Enemies") and act ("giving them Aid and Comfort").

Jackson, writing for the majority, held that the government's evidence failed to prove the essential connection between intent and act.[68] In reaching that result, Jackson devised an interpretation of the treason clauses that was expansively libertarian.

Jackson acknowledged the significance of the occasion: "never before has this Court had occasion to review a conviction" for treason; the result was to be "our initial interpretation of the treason clause." Mindful of that, Jackson moved carefully. He rejected the defense view that the overt act had to be manifestly treasonable; in itself it could be colorless to intent, so long as it demonstrated that the defendant provided some sort of assistance to the enemy. It was here that proof of Cramer's treason failed.

> There is no two-witness proof of what they said nor in what language they conversed. There is no showing that Cramer gave them any information whatever of value to their mission or indeed that he had any to give. No effort at secrecy is

shown, for they met in public places. Cramer furnished them no shelter, nothing that can be called sustenance or supplies, and there is no evidence that he gave them encouragement or counsel, or even paid for their drinks.

The long-term speech-protective value of *Cramer* lay in Jackson's concoction of history. The synthetic history of his *Cramer* opinion typified many of the Stone and Vinson Courts' most influential decisions. Relying heavily on Hurst's work, Jackson nevertheless depreciated its ability to resolve the specific case before them: "historical materials are, therefore, of little help." To eke out the little guidance found in the primary sources, Jackson provided his own construction of their meaning (hence my choice of the term "synthetic"). The result was law-office history driven by policy goals that Jackson sought to impose. It was liberal in a speech-protective sense, severely disabling the power of government to convert political opposition into the ultimate offense. He condemned constructive treasons, calling on the past to affirm the values of the present.

The idea that loyalty will ultimately be given to a government only so long as it deserves loyalty and that opposition to its abuses is not treason has made our government tolerant of opposition based on differences of opinion that in some parts of the world would have kept the hangman busy. But the basic law of treason in this country was framed by men who, as we have seen, were taught by experience and by history to fear abuse of the treason charge almost as much as they feared treason itself.

Jackson emphasized Marshall's dictum in *Bollman*: "the crime of treason should not be extended by construction to doubtful cases." "The treason rule, whether wisely or not, is severely restrictive." The Framers were determined to proscribe the use of treason prosecutions "by established authority to repress peaceful political opposition." Thus they defined the offense strictly and restrictively. They did not intend for disloyal thoughts, hostile sentiments uttered in passion, or even conspiracies to be adequate to convict. "The concern uppermost in the framers' minds [was] that mere mental attitudes or expressions should not be treason." Jackson's opinion reflected Frankfurter's view that the treason clauses originated in "wise old Ben Franklin['s view that] prosecutions for treason were generally virulent" and that "war also is fine pickins for professional informers and generally men of low character."[69]

Cramer reaffirmed the long-standing Marshallian constrictive approach to treason and thus served liberal values. But it had an unanticipated short-term consequence: by denying a determined prosecution the opportunity to suppress opposition and radicalism by treason prosecutions, it rechanneled the impulse to crush political opposition. In a few years, resurgent conservative majorities would invent other means of punishing political heterodoxy. Putting a short leash on treason only stimulated ingenuity to come up with substitutes. Cold War experience was to demonstrate that if treason was unavailable, something like constructive treason would do.

Douglas and the other dissenters in *Cramer* feared that its stringent "sufficiency" test would make future treason convictions impossible. Their concerns were proved unfounded two years later when the Court sustained the conviction of Hans Haupt, father of the saboteur Herbert Haupt, for giving aid and comfort to his son, knowing in general the objects of the mission. Haupt *père* had housed Herbert for six nights, had bought him a car, and had helped him seek re-employment in a factory that made bomb sights, which the younger Haupt hoped to sabotage. Jackson, in effect commenting on his earlier opinion, described the father's actions as having "the unmistakable quality which was found lacking in the *Cramer* case of forwarding the saboteur in his mission."[70] *Cramer* provided a workable construction of the treason clauses that recognized the substance of the offense while surrounding it with securities that prevented it from being used for mere political offenses.

WAR CRIMES AND THE COURT: THE *YAMASHITA* CASE

The Court served the American libertarian tradition well in the treason cases, but it was disinclined to challenge military authority in war crimes trials. In the trials of Japanese commanders accused of permitting or abetting atrocities, the Court reaffirmed and extended *Quirin* on both substantive and procedural issues.

As early as 1942, FDR had warned the Axis powers that those committing atrocities would be tried "in courts of law."[71] Over the opposition of Winston Churchill and some of his own advisors, who favored summary execution of leaders like Hitler, this idea evolved into the charter creating an international military tribunal that tried the Nazi war criminals at Nuremberg. It authorized trials for crimes already recognized by the laws of war, as well as crimes against humanity and crimes against peace.

The situation of Japan was different. There, Americans believed, General Douglas MacArthur, Commander in Chief of U.S. Army Forces Pacific, had authority to set up military commissions to try Japanese war criminals. Charles Fairman's influential *Law of Martial Rule* (reprinted in 1943) supported this procedure, and *Quirin* confirmed it. The Potsdam Declaration (1945) promised that "stern justice shall be meted out to all [Japanese] war criminals."[72] The imperious MacArthur, already growing into his viceroy's role and obsessed with avenging his 1942 defeat in the Philippines, was avid to try and then hang major Japanese war criminals as soon as possible. By September 1945, within a month of the Japanese surrender, he authorized a military commission and provided its procedural rules, including a crucial provision that it might "admit such evidence as in its opinion would be of assistance in proving or disproving the charge, or such as in the commission's opinion would have probative value in the mind of a reasonable man."[73] These and other elements of the procedures merely copied ideas suggested by the War Department's War Crimes Office.

The first defendant to be tried by the military commission created under MacArthur's regulations was Tomoyuki Yamashita, commander of Japanese forces in the Philippines at the time of the Japanese surrender.[74] During the last year of the war, Yamashita's communications and control disintegrated. His troops slaughtered between thirty and forty thousand Filipinos, mostly civilians, during that period. Yamashita neither ordered nor condoned these atrocities; he probably did not even know of them. In any event, he was fully occupied with directing the rapidly disintegrating defense against the onslaught of overwhelming American force. Nevertheless, occupation authorities charged him with failing to control his troops, "permitting them to commit brutal atrocities and other high crimes against people of the United States and of its allies and dependencies, particularly the Philippines."[75] The military commission, composed of five American general officers, found him guilty and, on the fourth anniversary of the Pearl Harbor bombing, sentenced him to be hanged.

Yamashita's conviction was attended by grave problems. The principal charged offense, that he should have known of his troops' conduct and controlled them more effectively, was unknown to the unwritten laws of war. The evidentiary standards promulgated in MacArthur's regulations were intolerably sloppy, even by the standards of wartime military justice, to say nothing of the Bill of Rights and civilian law. The defendant's appointed defense counsel did not have enough time to prepare an adequate defense. The principal charges against the particular defendant (as opposed to the troops under him) went unproven at the hearing. The commission admitted hearsay and faked documentary evidence. It restricted defense counsel's opportunity to cross-examine. MacArthur was indecently eager to hang his enemy, justifying his position by appeals to the military mystique, to "the sacred trust" and "entire cult" of soldiering, "the traditions of fighting men," the "military profession," and ultimately to the enemy's "soldier faith."[76]

The irregularities, to say the least, of Yamashita's trial and conviction came before the Supreme Court by petition for a writ of habeas corpus on his behalf.[77] Despite the precedents afforded by the *Vallandigham* and *Quirin* cases, the justices found themselves confronting a complex of legal issues that combined elements of the Scottsboro Boys cases and the *Insular Cases*. Yamashita's petition was particularly unwelcome to Chief Justice Stone because of his exasperation at the Nuremberg war crimes trials. Writing about his absent colleague, Stone opined that "Jackson is over conducting his high-grade lynching party in Nuernberg [*sic*]. . . . I don't mind what he does to the Nazis, but I hate to see the pretense that he is running a court or proceeding according to common law. That is a little too sanctimonious a fraud to meet my old-fashioned ideas."[78]

Like many other contemporary critics, Stone regarded the war crimes trials as ex post facto victors' justice, and he resented high-minded efforts to draw over them the veil of legality. Thus he thought that if MacArthur wanted to hang his enemies, the Court should not become involved, and certainly not for the purpose of endowing the proceedings with an aura of legitimacy. Meanwhile, MacArthur was indignant that defense counsel had had the presumption to appeal to the Supreme Court; his regulations terminated review of the sentence with himself. He advised his superiors in the War Department that he intended to go ahead with his review anyway. Only the direct countermand of his order by Secretary of War Robert Patterson delayed Yamashita's imminent appointment with the hangman. The Court stayed proceedings as the justices tried to figure out what to do about the unwelcome petition.

The justices agreed to hear argument, and ended up listening to an extraordinary total of six hours of argument over two days on the legality of MacArthur's orders. The ensuing split of the Court on the merits accounts for the strained and unsatisfactory nature of the majority opinion that eventually emerged. Stone, Frankfurter, Douglas, and Burton thought that civil courts lacked jurisdiction over hearings before military commissions.[79] Murphy and Rutledge indicated their determination to dissent, and Rutledge challenged the adequacy of the commission's evidentiary standards. When Stone attempted to refute that, he lost Black, who on that point agreed with the dissenters.[80] Stone backed off, leading Rutledge to charge that "the fact is, and I say it deliberately, that in this respect the [*Yamashita*] opinion is the most aggravated instance of run-around in the history of the Court."[81]

Stone, writing for the majority of six, repeated his *Quirin* performance.[82] He insisted that civil courts retained the power to review the legality of the proceedings before a military commission on a petition for a writ of habeas corpus. But beyond that, he was adamant that the principle of separation of powers mandated that courts refrain from claiming appellate jurisdiction over military trials. "We consider here only the lawful power of the commission to try the petitioner for the offense charged." Military tribunals "are not courts whose rulings and judgments are made subject to review by this Court." This basic position enabled the majority to avoid all the real issues in the case: the novelty of the basic charge, unknown to the laws of war; the flawed evidence; failure to conform to the Articles of War; and the truncated review procedures. "From this viewpoint, it is unnecessary to consider what, in other situations, the Fifth Amendment might require."

Murphy and Rutledge scorned such evasion. Rutledge assigned himself responsibility for challenging the evidentiary standards of the hearing. In a lengthy, eloquent, and moving dissent, Rutledge lamented the Court's failure to come to terms with the utter lack of evidence of the defendant's personal responsibility for the atrocities committed under his watch. In scriptural language, he recalled the majority to the ideal of "justice administered according to law," the "universal law, albeit imperfectly made flesh of our system and so dwelling among us." Measured by that criterion, the *Yamashita* hearing failed miserably. The result violated basic standards of fairness and placed military justice, if not above, then at least "beyond the fundamental law" of the Constitution. The Court abdicated its responsibility for keeping all American institutions, including the military, under the rule of law. The military commission was illegally constituted; defense counsel were denied an adequate opportunity to prepare for the hearing; and MacArthur's evidentiary orders violated the Articles of War and the Geneva Convention. Worst of all, the proceeding violated the spirit and the commands of the Fifth Amendment, with the tacit complicity of the Court.[83] Privately, Rutledge insisted that "the *big* cases are cases in POLITICS an' the LAW takes a back seat. That is, the language of the LAW always remains but its substance goes out the back window."[84]

If Rutledge's conscience was disturbed, Murphy's was ignited. The result was the most vehement and yet idealistic dissent of his career. Reflecting the contemporary movement afoot for creating a United Nations, Murphy noted that if humanity was ever to achieve "an orderly international community based upon a recognition of human dignity," the punishment of atrocities must be "as free as possible from the ugly stigma of revenge and vindictiveness. Justice must be tempered by compassion."[85] Continuing on that positive note, he tried to salvage what he could out of the disappointing majority, noting that at the least it had spurned "the obnoxious doctrine asserted by the Government" that war crimes trials were political questions beyond judicial review. He emphasized Stone's starting point, that habeas corpus would lie to question the legality of any detention by military tribunals.

But beyond that Murphy could only try to retrieve through eloquence what the majority had ignored, "the immutable rights of the individual [that] belong to every person in the world, victor or vanquished, whatever may be his race, color or beliefs." (In private correspondence, Murphy explicitly insisted that the Constitution must follow the flag: "The Bill of Rights must be adhered to wherever the flag flies."[86]) Neither the "popular frenzy of the moment" nor "the mightiest army in the world" could destroy these "universal and indestructible" rights. MacArthur and the military commission created the offense ex post facto, "a practice reminiscent of that pursued in certain less respected nations in recent years." In a passage that brought down on his head the wrath of MacArthur and others in the War Department, he warned darkly that "the fate of some future President of the United States and his chiefs of staff and military advisers may well have been sealed by this decision."[87] "The enemy has lost the battle but has destroyed our ideals," he concluded. The Constitution embodies "all the high hopes and aspirations of the new world" then emerging from the ashes of

World War II. The spirit of revenge and retribution "can do more lasting harm than all of atrocities giving rise to that spirit." "The hearts of all mankind [might be] embittered and filled with hatred, leaving forlorn and impoverished the noble ideal of malice toward none and charity to all."[88]

MacArthur fulminated about the dissents: "No trial could have been fairer." Murphy and Rutledge demanded "arbitrariness of process" because they were squeamish about "the stern rigidity of capital punishment."[89] But another of Murphy's antagonists took an uncharacteristically conciliatory view. "Frank," Justice Frankfurter wrote, "I wholly disagree with your view as to the duty of this Court in *Yamashita* because of my deep conviction as to the limitations upon the *power* of this Court. BUT, . . . I wholly respect the utterance of your conscience taking a contrary view. This applies to Wiley [Rutledge], too. I wish I could say as much all around!"[90]

Yamashita further eroded the force of the *Milligan* precedent.[91] Stone's minimalist approach, forced on him by disagreements among the majority justices, left the major constitutional issues unaddressed and gave his opinion the air of expediency and political accommodation, which in fact it was. It left one narrow constraint on military trials: habeas corpus to determine the legality of the tribunal's authority. (Potentially, that might be a significant check, even if it was not in *Yamashita*.) But beyond that, military justice got carte blanche for trials of enemy personnel. As the *Insular Cases* held a half century earlier, the Constitution and its Bill of Rights did not follow the flag—or the cannons.

MARTIAL LAW IN HAWAII

Cicero's epigram was most strikingly implicated in the regime of military governance that ruled Hawaii between 1941 and 1944. From the day of Pearl Harbor until October 1944, when military rule was terminated by presidential order, the army displaced all civilian government in the Hawaiian islands. Civil and criminal trials were conducted by military provosts courts; the writ of habeas corpus was suspended; army officers assumed all executive, legislative, and administrative functions of the territorial government; and potentially dangerous confrontations between military and civilian power began to erupt as the threat of actual invasion receded.[92]

Even though *Milligan*'s authority had been discounted to some disputed extent by *Quirin*, lawyers assumed that its fundamental principles still structured civil-military relations in wartime: the military could not displace civil judicial authority except when an actual invasion, not merely a feared one, had occurred, and the civil courts were not open and functioning.[93] "Martial law cannot arise from a *threatened* invasion," Justice David Davis had written. "The necessity must be actual and present; the invasion real, such as effectually closes the courts and deposes the civil administration."[94] But the clarity of these principles was clouded after December 7, 1941. For one thing, Congress had provided in the original Hawaiian Organic Act that the territorial governor could impose martial law in a case of "invasion, or imminent danger thereof."[95] More to the point, Hawaii had clearly been invaded by the Japanese air assault, and until the Battle of Midway (June 3–6, 1942) at the earliest, it lay exposed to further air or amphibious attack. Thus there was no question that the governor might proclaim martial law when he did. The problems came from its continuance after the need for complete military control had passed. The consequences of military rule for the entire Hawaiian population were unprecedented in American experience.

Immediately after the bombing of Pearl Harbor, Joseph Poindexter, the territorial governor, issued a proclamation declaring simply that "the public safety requires [*sic*]" and that "I do hereby place the said territory under martial law." It authorized the commanding general and his subordinates "to exercise the powers normally exercised by judicial officers."[96] He suspended the writ of habeas corpus and handed over all governmental functions to the commanding general of the Hawaiian department, Walter Short, who promptly proclaimed himself "Military Governor of Hawaii." The army could impose martial law literally overnight because its legal officers, anticipating some sort of calamity, had already drafted a program for that eventuality. Abeyance of civilian rule was drastic and complete. The army issued regulations covering all aspects of economic and social life in the islands, including such mundane (but important) matters as traffic control. Army officials were particularly concerned about labor conditions because of the islands' crucial role as a staging base for all American trans-Pacific military and naval actions. In 1942, Attorney General Biddle condemned army administration in the islands as "autocratic, wasteful, and unjust."[97]

The army also interned hundreds of Japanese, some of them nearly for the duration of the war—though, to its credit, it resisted pressure from FDR and Navy Secretary Frank Knox for the internment or evacuation of thousands more. Knox, writing to FDR in early 1942, expressed his impatience with concerns over "the matter of interfering with the constitutional rights of American citizens of Japanese descent." American forces on Oahu were "in what is, in effect, enemy country . . . in the presence of a population predominantly with enemy sympathies and affiliations." He insisted that "we get the Japanese out of Oahu and establish them on one of the other islands where they can be made to work for their living and produce much of their own food."[98] FDR saw no constitutional problems if the Japanese were evacuated, as Knox was demanding, because "Hawaii is under martial law."[99]

For their part, the Joint Chiefs of Staff at first recommended that "all Japanese residents of the Hawaiian Islands (either United States citizens or aliens) be transferred to the United States mainland and placed under guard at a concentration camp."[100] In scrapping these ideas and resisting Knox, army officials were not motivated by a tender concern for the civil liberties of racial minorities; they simply feared disruption of the labor supply that loss of the Japanese population would entail. They were also deterred by the logistical problems involved in their proposals. Detention of selected Japanese on the islands provided the most feasible alternative.

Those internees were held on the basis of suspicion and rumor. They were not allowed to defend themselves before judicial or administrative tribunals, nor to confront those who called their loyalty into question. Japanese who were not interned were forbidden from congregating in groups of ten or more; they were prohibited from having flashlights, cameras, portable radios, and even road maps; they were restricted from certain areas; and they had to wear special I.D. badges. (The army did not notice the disconcerting resemblance its regulations bore to antebellum slave controls and to contemporary measures for population control in the Third Reich.) Because Euro-American soldiers claimed that they could not distinguish Koreans from Japanese, the same regulations applied to Koreans, a bitter irony in view of the brutal Japanese occupation of Korea.

The military governor and his executive officer (an army lawyer, Thomas Green) wielded comprehensive controls over all civilian activities in the islands. They censored press and radio broadcasts, took over price-control supervision that would have been the responsibility of the Office of Price Administration, issued regulations for the sale and consumption of alcohol, tried (without success) to suppress gambling and prostitution, and imposed curfews and blackouts. They scrutinized labor relations intensively, controlling wages, hours, and overtime. The "Five Companies," a small group of corporate and business interests that controlled the islands' economy, shipping, and plantations, virtually enserfed their field hands and longshoremen, enforcing seventy-hour weeks by military coercion. The president of the Hawaiian Chamber of Commerce told the territorial attorney general that his organization "was not interested in the courts or the rights of civilians, but was only interested in the obtaining of priorities and the freezing of labor."[101] An official of one of the Five Companies, Walter Dillingham, dismissed civil liberties and citizens' rights as so much "hooey that nobody cared a damn about."[102]

Aside from suspension of the writ of habeas corpus, the most severe incursions into civil liberties routinely occurred in the provost courts that displaced civilian justice. The army permitted civilian territorial and federal courts to resume hearings in early 1942, but their jurisdiction was restricted to noncriminal cases tried without a jury. (The army referred to civilian judges as "agents of the Military Governor."[103]) All felonies were tried before military judges, without juries and usually without counsel. Not surprisingly, 90 percent of them ended in convictions, with harsher sentences than might have been imposed in civil trials. Fourth, Fifth, and Sixth

Amendment protections were unknown in their precincts. Defendants were not allowed to cross-examine witnesses. Provost judges (often nonlawyers) handled much of the direct and cross-examination themselves and discouraged defendants from seeking the assistance of counsel. Judgments could not be appealed to civilian courts. The army resisted restoration of civilian trials because Japanese Americans would sit on juries; army officers considered them unreliable and subject to racial bias. Moreover, the government would later contend, military personnel stationed in the islands who were "unaccustomed to living in such a community" might be disturbed by racially mixed juries.[104] United States Attorney General Francis Biddle concluded that after a year of operation, "the provost courts . . . disregard the safeguards of our judicial tradition and of the Constitution [and] impose punitive and lawless discipline upon the civilian population."[105]

The result of this absolute control of the island population was what a contemporary observer, W. W. Garner, described to Secretary of the Interior Harold Ickes as "a basic element of totalitarian government: unlimited authority without direct responsibility to the people governed." Ickes called for the liberation of "the American 'conquered territory' of Hawaii." One of his subordinates, who was in charge of the Interior Department's office of the territories, discerned a "drift to a complete military dictatorship in the army's attitudes."[106]

Not surprisingly, this stern regime came under increasingly vocal criticism from 1942 on. Territorial civilian officials, judges, and lawyers joined civilian lawyers in the Interior and Justice Departments in denouncing the scope and severity of military rule. The army responded with an absolutist defensive posture, claiming military necessity and demanding unfettered discretion. The War Department backed the generals, and FDR, the only person who could resolve these problems by fiat, remained aloof, preoccupied with other things. This eventually led to a dangerous impasse.

By 1943, the War, Justice, and Interior Departments worked out a political compromise embodied in a "Restoration Agreement," by which the army retained control over all matters directly related to military security, while the territorial and federal courts reassumed jurisdiction over all civil and criminal cases that did not implicate security concerns. But this accord was almost shattered in July when a new and stubborn military commander, General Robert Richardson, defied a habeas order issued by a federal District Court judge, Delbert Metzger, relating to two German American internees. Richardson ordered MPs to rough up the U.S. marshal who served the writ and refused to produce the internees. Judge Metzger then cited the general for contempt and fined him. The general responded by issuing an order prohibiting all civilian courts from receiving habeas petitions and threatened the judge with arrest and trial before a military commission if he did not revoke the habeas order. At this point cooler heads prevailed, forcing the soldier and the jurist to back off from their confrontation. The German Americans were transferred to internment on the mainland, beyond the authority of either man. This conflict became the prelude to the final contest between military power and judicial authority.

The army arrested and tried a stockbroker in Honolulu for embezzlement in August 1942 and a civilian shipfitter for assaulting Marine sentries in February 1944. Both were convicted, then sought a writ of habeas corpus, alleging that their detention was illegal. The District Court issued the writ but was reversed by the Court of Appeals. In *Duncan v. Kahanamoku* (1946), the Court held their trials illegal.[107] Black, writing for the majority, confined his holding to the issue of statutory interpretation, construing the Hawaii Organic Act as not authorizing the army to supplant civilian courts with military tribunals. But in an opinion typical of his approach to constitutional issues, Black relied on his understanding of "the birth, development and growth of our governmental institutions" to demonstrate that military courts were antithetical to the Framers' intentions. Skimming through English and American history, from the Petition of Right (1628) through the Coeur d'Alene strike of 1899, Black found military rule—"government that placed in the hands of one man the power to make, interpret and enforce the laws"—antithetical to American institutions.

In conference, Stone had plumped for a narrower holding. His concurrence suggested that the Court limit itself to the specific facts of the Hawaiian situation, leaving the door open for greater executive and military discretion in some future emergency. Murphy took the opposite tack. He was outraged by the militaristic mentality the army had displayed and the racism implicit in its distaste for civilian authority. He wanted to place the Court's holding squarely on constitutional grounds, and systematically went through the government's brief to demolish every component of the army's position. "Rampant militarism and the glorification of war . . . is not our way of life," he defiantly concluded.

Justice Harold Burton, new to the Court and under the influence of Frankfurter, dissented. He urged the Court to defer to military judgment, which, after all, had been consistently supported by the president and Congress. With Frankfurter, he insisted that that judgment had to be assessed by the conditions of 1942 and 1944, not the peacetime era of 1946. After the bombing of Pearl Harbor, Hawaii "was like a frontier stockade under savage attack." Judicial self-restraint was all the more urgent where the principle of separation of powers was at stake, and judges enjoyed the luxury of second-guessing military and presidential decisions made under the pressure of threatened enemy attack. Burton, who had been an infantryman in the previous war, proudly sent a copy of his opinion to his former comrade-in-arms, Harry Truman (a Captain of Artillery in that conflict), "emphasizing the zones of discretion" the commander in chief had to be allowed.[108] Truman was pleased.

The lessons we might draw from the wartime cases are mixed, as were the results of the cases themselves. *Quirin* cautions us that in a period of national emergency, judges defer to presidential and military authority when they are sufficiently convinced of its necessity. Crisis evokes an unhealthy deference to military judgment and military views of necessity, as was displayed by Frankfurter and Jackson. Later courts have extended this deference to peacetime.[109] A healthy suspicion of the executive branch's tendency to overreach its power goes into abeyance for other judges when they share the general anxiety induced by enemy threat.

Murphy's Argos-like vigilance and Rutledge's skepticism are necessary, but not sufficient, to rouse other judges out of their torpid or panicked acquiescence in presidential or military ambition and opportunism. The judges' normal acuity revives in peacetime, as *Cramer* and *Kahanamoku* suggest. But the Court's sense of its responsibility tends to fade just when it is most needed. The laws are not wholly silent amidst the clash of arms, but they sometimes speak with a muted voice.

NOTES

1. Marcus Tullius Cicero, "*Pro Milone*," in *The Speeches, with an English Translation*, trans. N. H. Watts (New York: G.P. Putnam's Sons, 1931), 11. Cicero's aphorism has furnished a favorite theme to chroniclers of the wartime Court; see, e.g., Mason, *Harlan Fiske Stone*, ch. 39.
2. *Ex parte Merryman*, 17 Fed. Cas. 144 (C.C.D.Md. 1861) (No. 9487).
3. Wall. (68 U.S.) 243 (1864).
4. *The Prize Cases*, 2 Black (67 U.S.) 635 (1863).
5. Kutler, *Judicial Power*.
6. *The Selective Draft Law Cases*, 245 U.S. 366 (1918).
7. *United States v. MacIntosh*, 283 U.S. 605, 622 (1931).
8. Hyman, *More Perfect Union*, 65–67; Paludan, *Covenant with Death*, ch. 2.
9. *Ex parte Milligan*, 4 Wall. (71 U.S.) 2, 121 (1866).
10. Neely, *Fate of Liberty*.
11. Edward S. Corwin would have disagreed with this claim. He characterized America's World War II experience as one of "constitutional relativity," something considerably less than an absolute regard for citizens' liberties. Corwin, *Total War and the Constitution*, 78–132.
12. Comprehensive treatments of the Court's response to wartime issues are surprisingly few. In addition to Corwin, *Total War and the Constitution*, see Murphy, *Constitution in Crisis Times*, 213–247; Mason, *Harlan Fiske Stone*, 647–97; and the symposium-like collection of war-related articles in the first volume of the *Journal of Supreme Court History* for 1996, especially Melvin I. Urofsky's introduction, "The Court at War and War at the Court." I discuss these more benign cases, as well as the Japanese internment cases, in a work in progress on the history of the U.S. Supreme Court, 1941–1953.
13. All eight divulged copious information about themselves during their hearing, which was recorded in a massive trial transcript. Eugene Rachlis relied primarily on that source for the only available secondary account of the episode,

They Came to Kill. George Dasch, one of the eight, told his story in *Eight Spies Against America*. His account varied in significant details from Rachlis'. Dasch portrayed himself as having undertaken the mission to escape from Nazi Germany and help a nation he had come to love.

14. FDR, Memorandum for the Attorney General, June 30, 1942, President's Secretary's File, Departmental Files: Justice, 1940–44, Franklin D. Roosevelt Presidential Library, Hyde Park, New York. I will hereafter cite this archive as "FDR Library," and this file as "PSF."

15. *Ex parte Merryman*, 17 Fed. Cas. 144 (C.C.D.Md. 1861) (No. 9487).

16. Biddle, *In Brief Authority*, 331.

17. For surveys of these legal complications, see Belknap, "Supreme Court Goes to War"; and Danelski, "Saboteurs' Case."

18. Henry L. Stimson, diary entries of June 29, 1942, July 8, 1942, microfilm copy of typed diaries in Yale University Library, in the Manuscripts Division of the Library of Congress, Washington, D.C. I will henceforth cite this archive as "LCMSS." See also Attorney General [Biddle] Memorandum for the President, June 30, 1942, Official File 5036, FDR Library. The Official File (one of three major collections of the president's papers at the FDR Library) will henceforth be cited as "OF," followed by a file number.

19. 1 Wall. (71 U.S.) 2, 127 (order of sentences inverted), 124–125 (1866) (Chase, C. J. and Wayne, Swayne, and Miller, J. J., concurring). Their position was that Congress could authorize military trials of civilians, but had not done so. See Kutler, *Judicial Power*, 89–95; Fairman, *Reconstruction and Reunion*, 182–237; and Lurie, *Arming Military Justice*, 38–42.

20. Biddle, Memorandum for the President, June 30, 1942, OF 5036; Memorandum for the President, October 29, 1942, OF 3603, FDR Library.

21. Executive Order 9185, "Appointing a Military Commission," *Federal Register* 7 (1942): 5103.

22. Articles of War 46, 501/2, codified as 10 U.S.C. §§ 1517, 1522 (1940 ed.).

23. See generally, Randall, *Constitutional Problems under Lincoln*, ch. 6.

24. President, Proclamation 256, "Denying Certain Enemies Access to the Courts of the United States," *Federal Register* 7 (1942): 5101.

25. Lauson Stone, son of the Chief Justice and an army reserve major assigned to assist Royall, later explained the reason for this bifurcated route. In cooperation with Biddle, Royall sought a writ of habeas corpus from Justice Black, designated for the purpose as a circuit judge. From Black's denial, Royall petitioned the full Court. But Justice Roberts expressed doubts about the Supreme Court's jurisdiction, citing *Marbury v. Madison*. Thus Royall decided to supply another route to the high court. Lauson Stone to Alpheus T. Mason, June 27, 1952, quoted in Mason, *Harlan Fiske Stone*, 657.

26. Brief in Support of Petitions for Writ of Habeas Corpus, reprinted in Kurland and Casper, eds., *Landmark Briefs and Arguments*, 39: 317–369. Due to the haste in which the briefs were prepared, the points in the text were not marshaled in so coherent an order. Chief Justice Stone complained to his clerk Bennett Boskey that "both briefs have done their best to create a sort of legal chaos." Stone to Boskey, August 5, 1942, Harlan Fiske Stone Papers, LCMSS.

27. 299 U.S. 304, 320 (1936).

28. U.S. Const., Art. I, § 10.

29. Biddle's argument, reprinted in Kurland and Casper, eds., *Landmark Briefs and Arguments*, 39: 603. Munson, "Arguments in the Saboteur Trial," is a review of the government's arguments by a member of the prosecution team.

30. Morison, *Battle of the Atlantic*, 114–57, 198–201.

31. Roberts quoted in Fine, *Frank Murphy*, 404.

32. *New York Times*, July 29, 1942, 11.

33. *New York Times*, July 28, 1942, 10.

34. Frankfurter had been commissioned a Major in the Army Judge-Advocate General's Corps in 1917, but he was not on active duty in 1942, as Murphy was.

35. The per curiam opinion is printed as part of the opinion in *Ex parte Quirin*, 317 U.S. 1, 18 (1942).

36. Such as Norman Cousins, who dismissed the entire proceedings as an ostentatious "farce." *Saturday Review*, August 8, 1942, cited in Belknap, "Supreme Court Goes to War," 76.

37. E.g., Raymond Moley, "The Supreme Court on the Job," *Newsweek*, August 10, 1942, 64; *New York Times*, August 1, 1942, 10; Bernstein, "Saboteur Trial."

38. Stone, Memorandum for the Court, September 25, 1942, Harlan Fiske Stone Papers, LCMSS.

39. In extensive correspondence with his clerks (Bennett Boskey and James L. Morrison), Stone expressed his substantive doubts and asked them to find precedents supporting his *a priori* conclusions. See Stone's letters of August 5, 9, 14, 20, and September 5, 1942, and the draft memorandum to the Court, September 25, 1942, box 69, Harlan Fiske Stone Papers, LCMSS. Danelski, "Saboteurs' Case," reviews this correspondence in detail.

40. Belknap, "Supreme Court Goes to War," 83.

41. Stone to Boskey, August 14, 1942, Harlan Fiske Stone Papers, LCMSS.

42. Robert H. Jackson, printed, undated memorandum, and typed draft captioned "FOOTNOTES" in Robert H. Jackson Papers, box 124, LCMSS. His experiences at Nuremberg would change that view.

43. "F.F.'s Soliloquy," carbon copy in William O. Douglas Papers, box 77, Ex parte Quirin, LCMSS, reprinted in Belknap, "Frankfurter and the Nazi Saboteurs," 68–71.

44. Stone to Sterling Carr, June 13, 1942, box 9, Harlan Fiske Stone Papers, LCMSS.

45. *Ex parte Quirin*, 317 U.S. 1, 19, 25, 29, 37, 45 (1942).

46. U.S.C. §§ 1553, 1554 (1940 ed.), respectively.

47. *United States v. Hudson and Goodwin*, 7 Cranch (11 U.S.) 32 (1812).

48. U.S. at 13, citing *Ex parte Vallandigham*, 1 Wall. (68 U.S.) 243, 249 (1864).

49. Article 15 provided that: "the provisions of these articles conferring jurisdiction upon courts martial shall not be construed as depriving military commissions, provost courts, or other military tribunals of concurrent jurisdiction in respect of offenders or offenses that by statute or by the law of war may be triable by such military commissions." Article 12 extended personal jurisdiction of courts-martial to "any other person who by the law of war is subject to trial by military tribunals." Logically, it was a circular or bootstraps intellectual move to import the law of war by these provisions.

50. Danelski, "Saboteurs' Case," 73.

51. U.S. Senate Subcommittee of the Committee on Military Affairs, *Hearings on S. 64 a Bill to Establish Military General*, 66th Cong., 1st sess., 1919, 250.

52. Stone to Frankfurter, September 16, 1942, box 68, Harlan Fiske Stone Papers, LCMSS.

53. Attorney General memorandum for the president, October 29, 1942, OF 3603, FDR Library.

54. Corwin, *Total War and the Constitution*, 118.

55. Belknap, "Supreme Court Goes to War," 61, 77, 90, 95.

56. U.S. Const., Art. III, § 3.

57. Edward III, c. 2; 7 & 8 William III, c. 3.

58. *Ex parte Bollman and Swartwout*, 4 Cranch (8 U.S.) 75, 126 (1807) (requiring actual levy of war and not just conspiracy); *United States v. Burr*, 25 Fed. Cas. 55 (C.C.D.Va. 1807) (No. 14,693)(constructive presence insufficient). On the early American law of treason, see Chapin, *American Law of Treason*.

59. See generally, J. Woodford Howard's excellent dissection of the trials and appeal, "*Cramer* Treason Case," and his more extensive "Advocacy in Constitutional Choice."

60. *United States v. Robinson*, 259 F. 685 (S.D.N.Y. 1919) (per Learned Hand, D.J.)

61. William O. Douglas conference notes, March 13, 1944, box 112, William O. Douglas Papers, LCMSS.

62. Frankfurter to Roberts, March 22, 1944, reel 59, Felix Frankfurter Papers, LCMSS.

63. Robert H. Jackson, Memorandum for the Conference, April 24, 1944, box 112, William O. Douglas Papers, LCMSS.

64. Stone memorandum to the Court, March 22, 1944, and Frankfurter to Stone, March 15, 1942, box 71, Harlan Fiske Stone Papers, LCMSS.

65. *Cramer v. United States*, 325 U.S. 8, fn. 9 (1945).

66. 325 U.S. 1, 8 (1945). The research group included the late canonist Stephan Kuttner.

67. Hurst, "Treason in the United States," 226, 395, 806; Hurst, *Law of Treason*, vii, 213.

68. *Cramer v. United States*, 325 U.S. 1, 20, 21, 24, 27–28, 37, 45, 47–48 (1945) (Douglas, Black, Reed, J.J., and Stone, C.J., dissenting in an acerbic opinion by Justice Douglas).

69. Frankfurter to Roberts, March 22, 1944, Felix Frankfurter Papers, microfilm reel 59, LCMSS.

70. *Haupt v. United States*, 330 U.S. 631, 635 (1947); Murphy, J., dissented. Haupt's original conviction had been set aside on procedural and evidentiary grounds: *United States v. Haupt*, 136 F.2d 661 (C.A.7, 1943).

71. "Statement Warning Against Axis Crimes in Occupied Countries," August 21, 1942, in *The Public Papers and Addresses of Franklin D. Roosevelt*, comp. Samuel I. Rosenman (New York, Random House, 1950), 11: 329–30.

72. Potsdam Proclamation, July 26, 1945, in *Treaties and Other International Agreements of the United States of America, 1776–1949*, comp. Charles I. Bevans (Washington, D.C.: U.S. Government Printing Office, 1968–71), 3: 1205.

73. Quoted from the transcript of the Yamashita hearing in Lael, *Yamashita Precedent*, 75.

74. Richard Lael provides the fullest account in *Yamashita Precedent*. Philip R. Piccigallo defends the procedures and results of the Yamashita hearings in *Japanese on Trial*, 49–67. Arnold C. Brackman locates their trials in the larger context of the International Military Tribunal for the Far East in *Other Nuremberg*.

75. Quoted from the transcript of the hearing in Lael, *Yamashita Precedent*, 80.

76. From MacArthur's review of the order for Yamashita's execution, quoted in Lael, *Yamashita Precedent*, 118.

77. Simultaneously, defense counsel sought certiorari to the Philippines Supreme Court, which had declined to review the proceedings of the military commission in *Yamashita v. Styer*, 75 Philippines 563 (Sup. Ct. 1945).

78. Stone to Sterling Carr, December 4, 1945, box 9; Stone to Louis Lusky, November 13, 1945, box 19; Stone to Luther Smith, January 2, 1946, box 27, Harlan Fiske Stone Papers, LCMSS.

79. Rutledge conference notes (n.d.), box 137, Wiley B. Rutledge Papers, LCMSS.

80. Black to Stone, January 28, 1946, box 73, Harlan Fiske Stone Papers, LCMSS.

81. Rutledge to John P. Frank, February 13, 1946, Wiley B. Rutledge Papers, LCMSS.

82. *In re Yamashita*, 327 U.S. 1, 7, 23 (1946). Justice Jackson did not participate because he was in Nuremberg; Murphy and Rutledge dissented.

83. *Ibid.*, 41–42. The embedded biblical reference is to John 1:14.

84. "Richard Roe" (Rutledge) to "Johnny Doe" (John P. Frank) [February 1947], box 21, Wiley B. Rutledge Papers, LCMSS.

85. This passage produced the contemporary quip that he sought to achieve "justice tempered with Murphy." Howard, *Mr. Justice Murphy*, 338.

86. Quoted in Fine, *Frank Murphy*, 459.

87. Joseph Keenan, one of the army counsel in the Yamashita case, indignantly denied Murphy's dire prediction that there would be "a procession of judicial lynchings." Quoted in Fine, *Frank Murphy*, 461. Both Taylor, *Nuremberg and Vietnam*, 182, and Falk, *Global Approach to National Policy*, 154, have suggested that the *Yamashita* principle of command responsibility could have been applied to American military commanders in Vietnam.

88. U.S. at 26, 28, 29, 41.

89. Quoted in Howard, *Mr. Justice Murphy*, 373.

90. Quoted in *ibid.*, 375.

91. The Court followed *Yamashita* in a case decided at the same time involving General Masaharu Homma, who had been Yamashita's predecessor in command of Japanese forces in the Philippines at the time of their conquest and the notorious Bataan death march. *Homma v. Patterson*, 327 U.S. 759 (1946).

92. Harry N. Scheiber and Jane L. Scheiber provide the most thorough study of this subject to date, "Bayonets in Paradise," which is part of their ongoing project on army rule in Hawaii during the war. See also their "Constitutional Liberty in World War II."

93. *Cf.* Frank, "Ex parte Milligan," and Anthony, "Martial Law, Military Government" (*Milligan*'s principles prevailed), with Fairman, "Law of Martial Rule"(supporting the power of the army to proclaim martial law in the islands).

94. *Ex parte Milligan*, 4 Wall. (71 U.S.) 2, 127 (1866) (italics in original).

95. Hawaii Organic Act, ch. 339, § 67, 31 Stat. 141 (1900).

96. Governor Poindexter's proclamation is reprinted in Anthony, *Hawaii under Army Rule*, 127.

97. Attorney General Biddle to FDR, December 17, 1942, PSF, 1942, FDR Library.

98. Knox to FDR, February 23, 1942, PSF, Confidential, Hawaii, FDR Library.

99. FDR to Secretary of the Navy (Knox), February 26, 1942, PSF, Confidential, Hawaii, FDR Library.

100. Quoted in Weglyn, *Years of Infamy*, 175.

101. Quoted in Scheibers, "Bayonets in Paradise," 507.

102. Quoted in Israel, "Military Justice in Hawaii," 243, 251.

103. Quoted in Scheibers, "Bayonets in Paradise," 499.

104. From the government's brief, as paraphrased in the concurring opinion of Murphy, J., in *Duncan v. Kahanamoku*, 327 U.S. 304, 334 (1946).

105. Biddle and Acting Secretary of the Interior Abe Fortas to John J. McCloy, December 19, 1942, quoted in Scheibers, "Bayonets in Paradise," 518.

106. Garner, Ickes, and the subordinate are quoted in Scheibers, "Bayonets in Paradise," 487, 524, 538.

107. 327 U.S. 304, 319, 322, 335–336, 341 (1946). Stone, C.J., and Murphy, J., concurred (on diametrically opposed grounds); Burton and Frankfurter, J. J., dissented; Jackson, J., still in Nuremberg, did not sit.

108. Harold H. Burton to Harry S. Truman, February 25, 1946, box 49, Harold H. Burton Papers, LCMSS.

109. *Goldman v. Weinberger*, 475 U.S. 503 (1986).

CHAPTER 3

Redeeming Whiteness in the Shadow of Internment: The Racial Redemption of Earl Warren

Sumi Cho

Earl Warren is a civil rights and civil liberties icon. During his reign as Chief Justice of the U.S. Supreme Court from 1953–69, the Court set standards of liberal judicial activism on race issues by which future Courts would be judged. Chief Justice Warren presided over momentous decisions that outlawed segregation in public education facilities, Jim Crow laws designed to prevent African Americans from exercising the vote, and found antimiscegenation laws to be unconstitutional. President Eisenhower came to regret his wayward Republican appointment, and "Superchief" Warren's legacy certainly rivals those of Eisenhower and the other presidents of his era. Warren's tenure, perhaps the most significant since John Marshall's, is understood in overtly political terms as a "revolution in race relations."[1]

Despite this iconography, there is another less-detailed aspect of Warren's career that looms large in a critical understanding of the Warren Court's race jurisprudence. This aspect predates his work on the Supreme Court, going back to World War II when Warren was attorney general of California and a gubernatorial candidate in the 1942 elections. During this period, Warren counted himself among California's anti-Asian "native sons and daughters." In fact, Warren was a key actor in the anti-Asian movement that culminated in the 1942 internment of over 120,000 persons of Japanese ancestry, two-thirds of whom were U.S. citizens.[2]

In this chapter, I examine Warren's prominent leadership in advocating for the internment. Warren's political career intersected with the internment of Japanese Californians at three crucial intervals: (1) his response to the bombing of Pearl Harbor as California's attorney general; (2) his successful bid for governor in 1942; and (3) his continued activism against Japanese Californians while governor.[3]

As I have argued elsewhere at greater length, the significance of this self-imposed historical amnesia about Warren's role in the internment is more than biographical. Rather, it illustrates a broader phenomenon in civil rights jurisprudence. Although the Civil Rights era did repudiate the white supremacy that had underpinned the internment, the disparate legal treatment of Asian Pacific Americans ("APAs") and Asian immigrants, the segregation of African Americans under Jim Crow laws, and countless other forms of legally sanctioned racism, it has not kept our legal system from treating the condition of being white as a higher status than of other racial conditions. Thus the reputational value of whiteness has been diminished to the extent that it takes the form of the blatant, biological racism of the Jim Crow era, but it has continued in a new guise.[4] The law has continued to valorize whiteness through a psychosocial and ideological process I call "racial redemption." I have explored the general phenomenon elsewhere; here I show Warren's place in the process of "racial redemption," a phase of his career that has been obscured by the uncomplicated heroization of Warren in many historical accounts.[5]

I do not suggest that Warren intentionally meant to contribute to the redemption of whiteness in the post-Jim Crow era of race relations or any particular racial project (except internment).[6] Rather, I believe that his equivocations regarding his (and society's) racial past became central to the conditions that permitted the later retrenchment of a reformulated version of white supremacy. Nonetheless, one could take this argument a step further and say that Warren himself—directly through his biographers and indirectly through neoconservative and neoliberal mythological invocations of *Brown v. Board of Education*—is now but an effect of the racial project of redemption that is the dominant lens through which the man and the era are understood.

CALIFORNIA'S NATIVE SON

Morton Horwitz observes that of the Warren Court's seven liberal members, "six grew up in extremely poor families." This, he suggests, might explain why the liberal band of "outsiders" had a greater affinity for the underdog and downtrodden. Warren's childhood in Bakersfield, California, may have inclined him to the Progressivism that formed during the first decade of the twentieth century. Drawing strength from the working and middle classes, Progressivism challenged elite economic and political monopolies. Its emphasis on honesty, anticorruption, public versus special interests, and public accountability resonated with Warren's upbringing and early experiences. His Bakersfield childhood, though, did not escape the anti-Asian sentiment of California Progressives. In California, Progressives were as decidedly anti-Asian as they were antimonopoly, equating the Japanese immigrant presence in their state with a form of alien tyranny. One Warren biographer observed that "Orientalist racism and 'reform' were compatible values for California Progressives."[7]

Scholars have documented California's long tradition of anti-Asian legislation, violence and intolerance. Prior to World War II, discrimination against Asian Americans across ethnicities was legal, overt, and widespread. Early immigrants of Asian/Pacific Islander (A/PI) descent were considered nonwhite and socially undesirable. A number of laws were passed to harass, restrict, stigmatize, and eventually exclude each A/PI ethnic group from the United States. Outright exclusion and discriminatory quotas in immigration laws, racial restrictions on naturalization rights and property ownership, antimiscegenation laws, segregated schools, and non-protection from racial violence were some of the most serious legal barriers and injustices Asian Pacific Americans faced through the middle of the twentieth century.[8] This anti-Asian tradition underscored the Progressivism with which Warren would identify during his political career.

Warren found a political mentor and lifelong hero in Hiram Johnson, the Progressives' choice for California governor in 1910 and a leader in the passage of the 1913 Alien Land Law. In his memoirs, Warren associated his political views most closely to those of Johnson's Progressivism, shunning other labels: "I did not care to be categorized as either a liberal or a conservative.... I believed in the progressivism of Hiram Johnson, who had broken the power of predatory interests." Nowhere in his memoirs does Warren attempt to distance himself from, or even discuss, Johnson's or the Progressives' approach to the Japanese in California. Later, as a senator from California, Johnson joined leading anti-Japanese crusader V. S. McClatchy in organizing the "Executive Committee of the Western States"—a lofty name for a steering committee of one senator and one representative each from the eleven western states, designed to guide anti-Japanese legislation through Congress. The prominent California politician and socialist Carey McWilliams noted that Johnson was "very anti-Oriental," and that "Warren greatly respected Johnson, and ... from this source ... Warren sort of had this [anti-Oriental] point of view."[9]

Throughout his years in California politics when he held positions as clerk of the California Assembly Judiciary Committee (1918–19), deputy district attorney of Alameda County (1920–26), district attorney of Alameda County (1926–38), state Republican Party chair (1934–38), attorney general (1938–42), and governor (1942–53), Warren was true to his party's vision of assisting the disadvantaged and the outsider. Like many nativist California Progressives, however, he believed that governmental largesse should be bestowed selectively to promote an ideal vision of California that excluded "undesirable" persons, ideologies, and cultures. With this ideological background and training in mind, I will examine in greater detail three areas of activity from 1942–45: (1) Warren's civil defense planning as California's attorney general; (2) his gubernatorial campaign; and (3) his role as governor.

REDLINING THE YELLOW MENACE

Scholars have identified Warren as the "single most powerful voice for the [internment] decision" and "one of the individuals most responsible for bringing the relocation program into being."[10] Others, however, have disputed this characterization, declaring that "there remains no proof that Warren ever publicly declared himself in favor of mass evacuation prior to mid-February [1942]," and concluding that Warren's "minor role" has been overemphasized due to his later prominence.[11] The following sections synthesize archival materials and other sources to present a more comprehensive record of Warren's involvement with internment efforts.

Two days after the Pearl Harbor attack on December 7, 1941, Secretary of the Navy Frank Knox toured the devastated site and put into circulation unfounded rumors that Japanese Hawaiian saboteurs were responsible for "the most effective fifth-column work that's come out of this war." Although Knox's allegations were never verified, his words carried considerable weight. Newspapers in California sensationalized his comments with headlines that read: "Secretary of Navy Blames Fifth Columnists for the Raid," "Fifth Column Prepared Attack," and "Fifth Column Treachery Told." On January 25, 1942, a committee chaired by Supreme Court Justice Owen J. Roberts released a report on the investigation into the Pearl Harbor attack. Like Knox, the Roberts report insinuated that Japanese Hawaiian spies had aided the Pearl Harbor attack by collecting and transmitting information on island military and naval installations to the Japanese Empire. The Roberts report stirred the anxious imagination of the public. Soon, no tale of treachery was too outrageous for public consumption. Moreover, politicians urging restrictive measures against issei and nisei on the West Coast now had an official report at their disposal.[12]

On January 29, four days following the publication of the Roberts report, Warren met with army officers and considered their concerns: because it was difficult to determine whether residents of Japanese ancestry were alien or citizen and because it was even more difficult to assess their loyalty to the United States, the close proximity of these people to key military facilities posed a distinct security threat. What state laws, the army officers asked Warren, were available to "break up this proximity?" Upon reflection, the attorney general concluded that stricter enforcement of the state's Alien Land Law might provide a partial solution. Under the nativist-inspired Alien Land Law of 1920, property in the control of an alien ineligible for citizenship would be forfeited to the state through escheat actions. Warren also told General John DeWitt, commander of the Western Defense Command, that he favored mass evacuation of the Japanese Californians. On January 30, the day after his conversation with DeWitt, he declared that "the Japanese situation as it exists in California today may well be the Achilles heel of the entire civilian defense effort. Unless something is done, it may bring about a repetition of Pearl Harbor."[13]

To facilitate the escheat actions he had discussed with General DeWitt, Warren convened a statewide conference of over one hundred district attorneys and law enforcement officials in San Francisco on February 2, 1942, to coordinate the campaign against Japanese Californians county-by-county. One federal official in attendance recalled that the attorney general opened the meeting by cautioning against hysteria, "but then proceeded to outline his remarks in such a fashion as to encourage hysterical thinking."[14]

It was agreed that each county official in charge of locating all Japanese-occupied land would forward the information to Warren's office, which would then share it with the army. The attorney general executed this mission with the precision of a military operation, using large-scale maps of each reporting county drawn to uniform scale. He instructed his subordinates that "all property which is owned, controlled or occupied by persons of the Japanese race, whether citizens or not, should be marked on the maps in red." He also asked each county official to designate "important installations" so that proximity of Japanese Californians could be easily compared.[15]

From these maps, Warren concluded that the "distribution of the Japanese population appears to manifest something more than coincidence." He hypothesized that the Japanese Californians were "ideally situated with reference to points of strategic importance, to carry into execution a tremendous program of sabotage on a mass scale should any considerable number of them be inclined to do so." The attorney general presented his maps and conclusions in testimony before the House of Representatives Select Committee Investigating National Defense Migration (Tolan Committee), which convened in San Francisco on February 21, 1942, to address concerns regarding civil defense and Japanese Americans.[16]

There were several problems with the methods and conclusions forwarded by Warren to the Tolan Committee. First, the definitions of strategic "military installations" and "proximity" were so vague and overbroad that it would have been difficult to locate any significant cluster of residents outside an area of strategic military importance. Officials in Warren's office "worked by rule of thumb" and "without any definition" of a "military installation" and "without any defined limitation" of "proximity." In his letter to state officials, Warren defined strategic areas to include "power plants, radio stations, factories and industrial plants, oil and gas wells, power lines, bridges and tunnels, airports and the like," as well as the "city hall, gas plant, hospital, water reservoir, water plant, . . . freight yards, power substations, sewer plant, telephone exchange and war industries." Certainly, as a postwar internment commission concluded, if another immigrant farming group had been mapped in a similar fashion, it would likely have produced "an equally alarming and meaningless pattern."[17]

In addition, the methodology for measuring strategic residencies was inconsistent and prejudicial toward Japanese Californians. The attorney general's desire to drive Japanese Californians off their lands biased the sampling tactics in the project. For example, Warren's sample concentrated only on Japanese Californian rural landholders. Even among rural Japanese Californians, however, many lived in nonfarm areas or on plots operated by non-Japanese that were not included on the maps. Moreover, Warren's study completely ignored the vast majority of Japanese Californians who were non-rural dwellers. As a result, one scholar estimates that the redlining project captured at best only about one-third of the state's Japanese population, thus grossly distorting the empirical case for the alleged conspiracy.[18]

Another bias was the sample's exclusion of "most coastal defenses and war industries" from the list of strategic installations. Few Japanese Californians owned land in these coastal areas. Thus, the exclusion of such low-residency regions from the mapping project upwardly biased the alleged concentration of strategic residencies observed. The one coastal area where Japanese Californians owned a significant amount of land, Santa Barbara County, was included in Warren's report.[19]

Further, Warren's study provided no comparative analysis that would have assessed the data concerning Japanese Californians living near strategic areas in light of data concerning those who did not.[20] Indeed, those deemed to be "in the vicinity" of military installations were simply listed in Warren's Tolan testimony, devoid of any comparative context. Moreover, there was no control group against which the percentage of Japanese Californians living "in the vicinity" of strategic installations could be measured. Thus, taking the Santa Barbara statistics as an example, even if 10 percent of the Japanese Californian population in the county were close to strategic installations, these figures have little significance unless they were compared to other groups, such as citizens and aliens of German or Italian ancestry.[21] The absence of such comparative frameworks from the study strongly indicates that Warren and his team intended to concoct a "scientific" basis for the removal program.

In addition to the methodological defects of the study, Warren's suggestion that Japanese Californians had conspired to live near designated strategic locations ignored the commonsense understanding and history of land use and development. For example, the alarm expressed over Japanese residing near airports obscured the fact that the issei had made their homes in these now-sensitive locations long before airports existed. As a former naval intelligence captain remarked, "[a] lot of Japanese had been living in such areas while the Wright Brothers were still flying kites."[22] Warren also ignored the historical basis for settlement patterns around railroads. In an appendix to his Tolan Committee report, Warren referred to Japanese Californians who resided near railroads, presumably to facilitate sabotage of the railways. It was common knowledge, however, that some issei immigrants from an earlier period, who had worked for the railroads, were paid in grants of cheap, undesirable land along the noisy right-of-way. Similarly, there was nothing conspiratorial about the proximity of Japanese Californians to water conduits, given the irrigation demands of truck farming.[23]

Warren told the Tolan Committee of his suspicion of Japanese Californians who farmed land beneath power lines. " 'Very strange isn't it, gentlemen, that they should be farming here,' " Carey McWilliams recalled Warren testifying. Years later, however, McWilliams thought the ownership of the land by Japanese Californians was "completely innocent," because they were the only ones who could "do anything" with the "little pinches of land" along the rights-of-way taken by power companies. And in fact, law and social practice had long restricted Japanese Californians to marginal tracts in remote areas around abandoned lands, often near industrial areas or dams, reservoirs, electronic transmission stations, or railroad yards. That the issei's success with these unwanted areas became the basis for Warren's racial conspiracy theory was thus a cruel irony.[24]

Warren made particularly good use of the rare instances when Japanese had access to desirable coastal lands, such as in Santa Barbara County. Then district attorney for Santa Barbara County, Percy Heckendorf, had a mundane explanation for the pattern. Issei had originally settled there because it was close to the sea and the temperature was cool, the ideal environment for immigrant farmers to cultivate vegetables and seeds.[25] At the time, however, Warren suggested that the immigrants had settled near the coast to abet an eventual program of sabotage.

In sum, the problems with Warren's mapping project were so numerous that they rendered it little more than propaganda designed to serve the attorney general's goal of dispossessing Japanese Californians. The vague and overbroad definition of key terms and the weaknesses in methodology rendered the findings of the massive research project statistically meaningless. Finally, the misreading of historical, economic and social contexts of landholding and settlement undermined the conclusions of a racial conspiracy theory that glibly found such patterns represented "more than mere coincidence."[26]

Yet none of these shortcomings prevented the project from playing a significant role in the issuance of the internment order and its aftermath. First, the project provided considerable evidence for General DeWitt's recommendation that President Roosevelt intern Japanese Californians. Warren's discussion of the strategic location of Japanese Californians' residences in Santa Maria Valley and Santa Barbara appear almost verbatim in DeWitt's final report. Other borrowed passages formed DeWitt's main justification for Roosevelt's authorization of internment through Executive Order 9066.[27]

Second, the mapping project provided a support for upholding the curfew order in *Hirabayashi v. United States.* In *Hirabayashi,* the Supreme Court observed that Japanese were concentrated in California and Washington—two states significantly responsible for aircraft production and shipbuilding. In his concurring opinion, Justice Douglas emphasized the "real" threat of Japanese invasion of the West Coast by referring to the presence of "many thousands of aliens and citizens of Japanese ancestry in or near to the key points along the coast line." This presence, Douglas noted, had aroused "special concern" among "those charged with the defense of the country."[28]

Third, Warren's mapping project influenced important members of the media. Walter Lippmann, for example, carefully studied one of Warren's maps at a meeting with Warren and Assistant Attorney General Tom Clark and then published a widely read call for internment. "Nobody's constitutional rights include the rights to reside and do business on a battlefield," Lippmann declared in his February 12 column.[29] Other journalists credited Lippmann with access to inside information and repeated his refrain. "The Japanese in California should be under armed guard to the last man and woman right now—and to hell with habeas corpus until the danger is over," Westbrook Pegler brayed. Lippmann's column was passed from Army Chief of Staff George C. Marshall to Secretary of War Henry L. Stimson to Assistant Secretary of War John J. McCloy, and it carried substantial weight with Roosevelt himself.[30]

Fourth, the intensive research and documentation behind the project led to a dramatic proliferation of escheat actions under the Alien Land Law, amounting to "one of the biggest land grabs" in Californian history. Seventy-three of the seventy-six escheat actions brought under the statute between 1912 and 1946 targeted Japanese Californians, and 80 percent of these were brought after the Pearl Harbor attack and during Warren's tenures as attorney general and governor.[31]

According to his second-in-command, Warren used his discretion to enforce the largely symbolic Alien Land Law even beyond the scope suggested by army officials. After escheat proceedings for lands adjacent to military installations were completed, the Attorney General's office expanded the program to general enforcement of the Alien Land Law, "with the resulting escheat of large land areas without regard to whether they were or were not near military or other important installations."[32] Moreover, Warren knew that district attorneys around the state were interested in purchasing lands made valuable by the issei. Under the guise of national security, the attorney general's office aggressively filed an unprecedented twenty escheat actions in 1942 alone.[33]

In sum, by the time Roosevelt signed Executive Order 9066 on February 19, 1942, Warren had organized a methodologically flawed research project to map disloyalty. He also had worked closely with key actors in the military, Congress, local and state politics, and the media, pressing steadily, and often behind the scenes, for drastic action against Japanese Californians. Having established this clear record on "civil defense," Warren set his sights on higher office—the California governorship. In an attempt to distinguish his record from that of the incumbent governor, his campaign would boast of his treatment of Japanese Californians.

THE BID FOR GOVERNOR

After initial demurrals, Warren eventually agreed to run for governor, citing incumbent Governor Culbert Olson's response to Pearl Harbor as his main motivation. Incensed that Governor Olson's civil defense plan included no role for his attorney general, Warren set out to "instruct and organize the public offices of the State in the technique of fifth column, sabotage, and modern warfare" so that the state's civil defense would be prepared "whenever the inevitable occurred."[34] Warren, the Republican challenger, announced his candidacy on April 10, 1942. According to one biographer, his campaign was "corny," "old-fashioned flag waving." Capitalizing on wartime fears and anxieties, his full-page campaign ads proclaimed "This is War!" and "Nero Fiddled and Rome Burned, It must not happen here."[35]

America's war with Japan and the West Coast's war against Japanese Californians provided Warren with the compelling bipartisan appeal that would sweep him into office—no small feat for a Republican candidate in a state with a Democratic majority. Under the lofty theme of "leadership—not politics," the campaign played heavily on the anti-Japanese sentiment that pervaded the state. Warren used the Japanese wartime threat to reach across traditional Republican-Democratic party lines. "I believe that you recognized, as did I, that with the attack on Pearl Harbor, party differences became relatively unimportant," he declared. Just as the platform of the state Republican Party did, Warren's campaign conflated enemy Japanese with Japanese Californians, decrying the Japanese threat and trumpeting Warren's role in interning Japanese Californians.[36]

Warren coupled these broad appeals with specific solicitations of two of the most vitriolic anti-Asian hate groups in the state—the American Legion and the Native Sons (and Daughters) of the Golden West. Warren had close ties to both groups, which comprised the most effective anti-Japanese coalition in California's history, the California Joint Immigration Committee.[37]

Patriotism was the key distinction between the two gubernatorial candidates—a patriotism that was racially loaded and defined by Warren's active part in internment. Warren's campaign contrasted his "constructive leadership" with Governor Olson's "mismanagement" and "bungling" response to Pearl Harbor. Warren's role in initiating the mapping project became a central example of his patriotic leadership, and he boasted of the project's foresight and critical evidence-gathering role in effecting internment. His campaign literature emphasized how in February 1942, while Governor Olson was receiving "delegations of Japs at Sacramento" and intimating that "evacuation was unnecessary," Warren "saw the menace when it was only a shadow on the horizon" and "went to work quietly and did something about it" by "supplying Federal authorities with factual data necessary for the prompt evacuation of the Japanese from California."[38]

Throughout his campaign, Warren played up the fears of the enemy lurking within. He warned that one-third of Japanese Californians were aliens living near military installations and vital war industries and that enemy saboteurs might land on the West Coast at any time, even after internment. Even the "fact that we have as yet experienced no sabotage" was no reassurance; it was "merely evidence that the saboteurs are under discipline and are merely awaiting the zero hour when they should strike." On one occasion, Warren dramatically read from a 1940 book published in Tokyo by a Japanese naval intelligence officer that described how Japanese Angelenos in the San Pedro fishing area could be used to perform acts of sabotage. He neglected to tell his audience that he was reading from a work of fiction.[39]

Perhaps the most effective ploy of the Warren campaign was its portrayal of Governor Olson as a sort of "White Jap" or "Jap lover."[40] According to his campaign literature, while Warren was working hard to round up Japanese Americans, Governor Olson was entertaining Japanese delegations in the state capitol. While Warren was fully prepared "to uphold the right of the military to take action against [West Coast] Japanese," Olson was ridiculed for believing, at least initially, that internment was not necessary. While the incumbent governor's indecisiveness constituted a threat to the West Coast's security interests, the challenger firmly advocated internment of Japanese Californians, and worked to "shut the door" on the concentration camps by submitting amicus curiae briefs in *Hirabayashi* and *Korematsu*. "Earl Warren was fully prepared," one of his campaign pieces stated, "to take a leading part in the legal battle to uphold the right of the military to take such action against the Japanese as might be required by military necessity on the Pacific Coast."[41]

During the campaign, Warren's media strategists, Clem Whitaker and Leone Baxter, seized upon Olson's proposal to alleviate the farm labor shortage by releasing internees to harvest crops under armed guards. In a July 7, 1942, memo to Whitaker, Baxter observed that "Olson wants Japs put to work on farms" by bringing back "'deserving' enemy aliens in farming and fishing industries." She suggested that the American Legion and naturalized American citizens attack Olson's plan along nonpartisan lines and circulated a draft press release to that effect on July 13, 1942. Within days, numerous news stories appeared across the state with such headlines as "Olson Assailed for Jap Plan: Use of Orientals for Farm Labor Called 'Unthinkable' " and "Olson Called War Failure."[42]

Newspapers often quoted verbatim from the campaign's press release, in which outraged naturalized citizens denounced Olson. These stories ended with a blatant endorsement of Warren's candidacy. Warren used the incident to highlight the governor's inability to lead in time of crisis, and he dismissed the notion of using Japanese Californians as farm labor—even under armed guard—as ludicrous:

> The public was not impressed by this [proposal] of the Governor. When the evacuation of the Japanese was first announced, the people of California heartily approved it as a necessary war measure. Nothing has changed their minds since, and the specious argument of the Governor that the Japs could be guarded by troops while harvesting crops was not impressive. They would still be where they might commit sabotage or turn into a fifth column in the event of an enemy raid upon the coast or an attempt at invasion. If all that is needed is to put a guard over them, there would have been no reason for evacuation. A cordon of troops could have been thrown around every Japanese district in the State, but the Japs would still have been in our midst to endanger the safety of our people in the event of enemy action.

After it was reported that some internees were "energetically seeking absentee ballots" for the 1942 elections, editorials implied that Governor Olson was catering to Japanese Californian voters. "Isn't it a fair inference that the Governor was seeking, by an empty gesture, to line up the Jap vote in his favor?" one editorial queried.[43]

Such editorials, carrying sensational titles such as "Olson and the Jap Vote" and calculated to defame Olson's political and racial standing as a "loyal" (white) Californian, were possible because he had been less aggressive than his opponent in capitalizing upon the popular, anti-Japanese Californian sentiment in an election year. These same editorials characterized interned Japanese Californians who were American citizens as an ongoing racial threat in light of their interest in exercising their right to vote. Warren's ability to speak to the fears and paranoia of California's wartime voters in the language of long-standing anti-Asian racism amounted to a winning campaign strategy.

So did his relations with the American Legion and the Native Sons of the Golden West. Warren helped the groups make their case against Japanese Californians, and the organizations enthusiastically supported him for governor. His campaign took full advantage of his insider status with these core supremacist organizations.

Even before the outbreak of hostilities between Japan and the United States, American Legionnaires contemplated internment of Japanese Californians residing on the West Coast. In 1939, for example, the *Saturday Evening Post* quoted the boast of the head of the American Legion's National

Defense Committee to the Japanese American Citizens League that "if we ever have war with Japan and I have anything to say about it, the first thing I'll do will be to intern every one of you." As early as January 5, 1942, the California Legion War Council passed a resolution noting the pattern of Japanese Californian residencies near "strategic locations" and demanding that "all such enemy aliens be placed in concentration camps and that the land and/or property owned . . . by such aliens be placed under government supervision." The Legion later defined enemy aliens and nationals as "Japanese, both aliens and American citizens."[44]

The American Legion national leadership took a formal position on internment on January 19, 1942, unanimously adopting a resolution demanding "immediate action by the Government in evacuating and interning all enemy aliens and nationals in combat zones, such as the Pacific Coast." By early March 1942, after Warren had testified before the Tolan Committee, the California Legion released its survey declaring Japanese Californians to be a "menace to the safety of our country" on the basis of the more than 200,000 aliens and citizens living near railroads, aqueducts, power and oil lines, and defense factories.[45]

At the time, Asians were the only racial group legally prohibited from gaining citizenship under the naturalization statutes' whiteness requirement and Supreme Court precedent excluding Asians from whiteness.[46] The Legion's "one hundred percent Americanism" creed was therefore a facially neutral but racially loaded slogan. Using this same theme, Warren delivered one of his most important campaign addresses at the California Legion's convention in front of 40,000 delegates. Warren identified himself as a proud Legion member and credited the Legion's Americanism Committee for the removal of Japanese Californians from coastal areas. He also supported a pending Legion resolution to keep Japanese aliens out of California "for all time." Departing from his prepared remarks, Warren weighed in on the resolution: "I say to you now that they must not come back to our State—we must keep them away from California so long as the flag of Nippon is flying over the Philippines."[47]

In contrast to Warren's warm reception, Legion members attacked Governor Olson for criticizing the Legion's antisubversive activities. Newspapers reported enthusiastic ovations for Warren at his Legion address side-by-side with a stinging critique of Olson's record by the former American Legion national commander Thomas Riordan. Although the article appeared under Riordan's byline, it was masterminded by Assistant Attorney General W. T. Sweigert, a campaign adviser to Warren.[48]

The American Legion's only true rival in exclusion was the Native Sons of the Golden West (NSGW). Dedicated to the preservation of California as the divinely intended "White Man's Paradise," the NSGW had trumpeted the dangers of the "Asiatic Peril" with the inaugural 1907 issue of its official publication, the *Grizzly Bear*.[49] After Pearl Harbor it congratulated itself on the foresightfulness of its decades of anti-Japanese propaganda. "[H]ad the [Native Sons'] warnings been heeded," the editor of the *Grizzly Bear* boasted, "the treacherous Japs probably would not have attacked Pearl Harbor on December 7, 1941, and this country would not today be at war with Japan."[50]

Warren had joined the NSGW during his successful bid for Alameda County district attorney in 1926. His biographers have explained his decision as a political necessity. Having foresworn contributions and the support of political parties, they have argued, Warren needed to cultivate alternative sources of support from fraternal, civic, and patriotic groups. From 1926 until late middle-age, however, Earl Warren enjoyed an esteemed status within the NSGW.[51]

The Native Sons' wartime agenda mirrored Earl Warren's agenda as attorney general. An editorial appearing in the *Grizzly Bear* in February 1942, for example, argued that the "Japs must be dispossessed of every foot of California land they now hold, and the land must be escheated to the state!" Warren was already working on exactly such a plan through his mapping project. Like Warren, the NSGW advocated not only that aliens and citizens of Japanese ancestry be interned, but also that persons of Japanese ancestry be "permanently routed from these shores."[52]

The organization regularly informed the attorney general of its activities. For example, after its Board of Grand Officers urged the removal of "all Japanese," whether citizen or alien, on February 14, 1942, it sent the resolution and a press release to Assistant Attorney General Warren Olney on March 24, 1942. In May, the Grand Parlor (NSGW headquarters) adopted an even more extreme measure calling for a lawsuit to challenge the birthright citizenship of Japanese American nisei and for a constitutional amendment to exclude persons of Japanese ancestry from U.S. citizenship. This resolution was promptly forwarded to the attorney general's office in early June. Within days, Warren's office responded to the NSGW mailing and replied that he would be "glad" to serve on the "Americanization Committee" of the NSGW.[53]

Unlike Justice Hugo Black, whose membership in the Ku Klux Klan repeatedly surfaced during his years on the bench, Warren's membership in these supremacist organizations has largely escaped serious notice by judicial biographers and historians. Biographers who have addressed Warren's involvement with supremacist groups have tended to sanitize it by eliminating, downplaying, or explaining away his affiliations.[54] But Warren's affiliation with the Native Sons was more than a marriage of political convenience, for the attorney general's campaign files indicate that he knew and approved of the hostile measures forwarded by the NSGW.[55] Warren's anti-Asian activist record while attorney general cannot be explained away, as Hugo Black's membership in the Klan has been, as the only alternative to political suicide. Warren provided leadership, prestige, and legitimacy to two of the most extreme, racist organizations in California history, organizations that engineered the anti-Asian movement and supported a plethora of anti-Asian restrictions and exclusions.

GOVERNOR WARREN GOES TO SACRAMENTO

Warren's hostility toward Japanese Californians did not end with his election as governor. If anything, the passage of time and the security of his office strengthened Warren's animosity toward those interned. In mid-1943, he referred to them as "150,000 potential aiders and abetters of this kind of [sabotage] warfare," all of whom "have been indoctrinated with the imperial designs and have had them coupled with Shintoism—the religion of the race." Internment, the governor argued, "saved our state from terrible disorders and sabotage." He vehemently opposed proposals to return "loyal" Japanese to California, calling it a "body blow" to national security. "If the Japs are released," he reasoned, "no one will be able to tell a saboteur from any other Jap."[56]

While denouncing Japanese Californians with his crude set of stereotypes, Warren simultaneously claimed to maintain a sense of fairness. "This is not a personal view," he explained. "Have you ever heard an Army or Navy man advocate release of these Japs? Have you ever heard any one connected with the FBI indicate such action would be consistent with the national security?" Even while he was declaring his opposition to having "Japs back in California during this war if there is any lawful means of preventing it," he added that "this isn't an appeal to race hatred." Rather, he suggested, "it is an appeal for safety."[57] Even toward the end of the war, Warren could not distinguish between Japanese American citizens and Japanese from Japan. In a 1944 speech before the Newspaper Publishers Association on the "Japanese Problem," Warren suggested that the return of the Japanese Californians would hinge upon the number of casualties suffered by Japan. "When, if ever, these Japanese are to be permitted to return to California is not a question we can decide now. There will have to be many more lives lost far out across the Pacific before the question is germane."[58] This position was particularly ironic in light of the extraordinary high casualty rates suffered by the nisei soldier 442nd regimental combat team recruited from the internment camps that distinguished itself as one of the war's most decorated units.[59] Only when the War Department declared that Japanese Californians would be released from the camps at the end of 1944 did Warren fall into line by pledging his support for the peaceful and safe return of the internees.[60]

THE PROMISE OF REDEMPTION

In the law of property, redemption refers to the freeing of property from mortgage by paying the debt for which the property stood as security.[61]

One form of property recognized by law, as Professor Cheryl Harris has shown, has been a white racial identity or "whiteness." In the landmark segregation case of *Plessy v. Ferguson* (1896), for example, the Court acknowledged that had the plaintiff Plessy been white, he would have had an action for damages against the railway company for his wrongful exclusion from the "white car":

> If he be a white man and assigned to a colored coach, he may have his action for damages against the company for being deprived of his so-called property. Upon the other hand, if he be a colored man and be so assigned, he has been deprived of no property, since he is not lawfully entitled to the reputation of being a white man.[62]

In the *Plessy* era, the property value of whiteness was maintained under a legal system and social order based on the logic of white supremacy.[63] But in a post-civil rights era, open forms of white supremacy have been legally prohibited and socially discredited and, to that extent, the value of property in whiteness has been "mortgaged" and diminished.

Logically, whites have an interest in defending the advantages they enjoyed from their vested, property interest in the racial hierarchies, structures, and cultures of the old regime.[64] At the same time, however, they cannot ignore the post-*Brown* rejection and moral decrepitude of white supremacy. As they have sought to restore the property interest in whiteness to its full pre-*Brown* value, they have also sought ways to reconcile the fundamental tension between their knowledge of the immorality of the old privilege and their desire to enjoy the fruits of that tainted tree. Since *Brown*, the process of racial redemption has permitted them to achieve their twin aims, to denounce supremacy while continuing to enjoy the benefits of its continued operation.

The process has three features: (1) the repudiation of the old forms of white supremacy; (2) the burial of historical memories of racial subordination; and (3) the transformation of white supremacy into more sustainable forms. Repudiation has taken various forms, such as the declaration of racial apologies or racial equality "covenants." For present purposes, the discovery of the Nazi death camps and the popular reception of Gunnar Myrdal's *American Dilemma* were decisive. Both thoroughly discredited the biological racism that sustained old forms of white supremacy and made it impossible for such views to serve as a public rationale for the racial caste system in postwar America.[65]

The burial feature of racial redemption has taken the form of censorship, historical amnesia, selective recall, euphemizing, and revisionist historicizing. The process has obscured individual, institutional, and cultural complicities with the old forms of white supremacy that would otherwise have left "blood on the hands" of those who participated in the repudiated regime, and even damaged the moral currency of those who passively benefited from it. Such burials have manifested themselves as outright denials, glaring omissions, silences, absences, and counterfactual or decontextualized assertions.[66]

The third, and most important, feature of racial redemption has involved the simultaneous transformation and reassertion of white supremacy. The process of racial redemption has retired an outmoded form of white supremacy while introducing a new, more resilient form. What has been billed as revolutionary racial change was a "mere change in the form of investment" in white supremacy.[67] Burial of racial historical context has made it analytically difficult for the public to detect how subordination evolved into a new context. Before *Brown*, white supremacy clearly manifested itself in the system of segregation supported by an ideology of biological determinism. After *Brown*, white supremacy has continued in the new form of formal legal equality abetted by the ideology of color-blind fundamentalism.

Through the stages of repudiation, burial, and transformation, the racial redemption process has effected and depended upon a retrieval of innocent whiteness. This retrieval has decoupled whiteness from the stigma of white supremacy by imagining a kinder, gentler whiteness—one that would never have cloaked itself in white sheets and hoods, one that has not benefited from centuries of a racial caste system, one that has not posited inherent biological differences between people of color and whites, and one that has not tolerated outright violence and malign neglect. For Warren (and, although I do not address these matters here, for the Supreme Court and the nation), the rejection of the principle of separate-but-equal and the practice of segregation in *Brown* and its progeny has decoupled whiteness from white supremacy. Those cases have also had the effect of restoring white innocence and relegitimating the state and its institutions through the embrace of color-blind ideology.[68]

WARREN'S SEARCH FOR REDEMPTION

Earl Warren, I believe, experienced a transformation during World War II when he realized how mistaken he had been—that instead of leading the effort to deny Japanese Americans their rights as citizens, he should have been defending those rights. But what was the nature of Warren's search for redemption? Was it, as his biographers suggest, a sincere attempt to acknowledge fully his past wrongdoing, a search for redemption in something like its religious sense? Or was it an attempt to restore his reputation and the transparency and innocence of his racial identity, a search for redemption in the legal sense developed here?

The first feature of racial redemption requires an admission of racial wrongdoing. Warren's admission came not in the form of a public apology, but in his posthumously published memoirs:

> I have since deeply regretted the removal order and my own testimony advocating it, because it was not in keeping with our American concept of freedom and the

rights of citizens. It demonstrates the cruelty of war when fear, get-tough military psychology, propaganda, and racial antagonism combine with one's responsibility for public security to produce such acts.[69]

Moreover, Warren intended his civil rights cases, including his efforts to produce a unanimous opinion in *Brown*, as a renunciation of his former supremacist views. As his law clerk Tyrone Brown would later write: "In my year on the Court, [Chief Justice Warren] seemed to have embarked on a course to distinguish out of existence the *Hirabayashi* decision in which the Court had validated the Japanese exclusions."[70]

The second feature of racial redemption is an attempt to bury one's racial transgressions. Warren's attempt is best seen in his request to a biographer, John Weaver, not to reprint portions of a wartime letter in which he had balanced constitutional principle against civil defense. In 1943 Warren made his case to Alfred Lundberg:

Either we take the protective measures that we know in our hearts are necessary to insure the safety of our country or we abandon them as being in conflict with some principle of law. We cannot do both in this situation, and our Supreme Court unanimously recognized this fact recently in sustaining the curfew regulations on those of Japanese ancestry. It arrived at its conclusion reluctantly as we all do in such situations. Nevertheless it was firm and unanimous in its conclusion that because of the peculiar situation of those of Japanese extraction, a distinction could, under the Constitution be made.[71]

In 1969 Warren told Weaver that the internment was "controversial" and "emotional" and that publishing the letter would abet "those who would like to stir up the controversy at this tin.e." "[W]hen these people were returned to California after the War," he explained, "I mobilized all the forces in the State to welcome them and even to prosecute successfully those who violated their rights." Perhaps most ironically, the same person who, as California's attorney general, had aggressively initiated escheat actions against issei and nisei, claimed in 1969 that under his supervision the state had "carefully husbanded" the financial matters of those interned, and "as far as [he could] remember," had "repaid [the owners] in full." Further, Warren noted that immediately after the war, and "with [his] approval," the state legislature set aside judgments for violations of the Alien Land Law, many of which Warren had initiated as attorney general. Weaver complied with the Chief Justice's wishes and omitted all references to the letter.[72]

The third feature of racial redemption is the transformation of white supremacy into more sustainable forms. In Warren's case the process was subtle and took the form of his retrospective justification of his actions during the war. As late as 1972, Warren continued to provide a race-neutral explanation for the internment, echoing the rationales he had served up while governor: "[E]verybody who had anything to do with the relocation of the

Japanese, after it was all over, had something of a guilty conscience about it and wanted to show that it wasn't a racial thing as much as it was a defense matter."[73] In fact, the redemption Warren sought entailed neither contrition nor any serious attempt at reparation for his individual wrongdoing. His primary aim was to clear his name by maintaining, as he did during the war, that he acted not out of "race hatred" but for the sake of "safety."[74]

"It was wrong to act so impulsively, without positive evidence of disloyalty," Warren conceded in his memoirs. "Whenever I thought of the innocent little children who were torn from home, school friends, and congenial surroundings, I was conscience-stricken." Yet he also asserted that "we felt we had a good motive in the security of our state."[75]

Three aspects of this passage merit comment. First, Warren did not address the racialized nature of "national security," the extent to which the claims on its behalf were founded on racial hysteria and stereotypes.[76] Second, he did not acknowledge that the constitutional rights of the internees had been violated, probably because he still believed they had not been. As he wrote in 1962, "Where the circumstances are such that the Court must accept uncritically the Government's description of the magnitude of the military need, actions may be permitted that restrict individual liberty in a grievous manner."[77]

Third, Warren's expression of regret was posthumous. Many members of the Japanese American community hoped that Warren would speak out against the internment and retract his wartime attacks on the loyalty of Japanese citizens. A straightforward and sincere apology might have aided the racial healing of issei and nisei victims, many of whom carried the guilt, shame, and injustice of internment to their death. Yet as Professor Eric Yamamoto has observed, Warren failed "to participate in a joint analysis of the conditions of conflict and underlying grievances, to accept appropriate responsibility for injuries inflicted, and to discharge that responsibility through action."[78]

Warren's mostly private expressions of regret have become public only through the historical record. His apology, in other words, was not intended as a public reparation or remedy to those he injured, but as a personal pitch for racial redemption and a formal distancing of himself from his earlier days as a nativist politician. By not apologizing to Japanese Americans directly, Warren perhaps unwittingly indulged (again) his feeling of supremacy over them, thereby maintaining the same hierarchical structural relationship he perpetuated during the war. *He* would set the terms of interaction, including that of apology, and would avoid subjecting himself to criticism or dialogue. Thus, his racial apology for internment, in and of itself, represented a moment in the reconstruction of racial hierarchy and the transformation of white supremacy.

Furthermore, by reprising wartime rationales for internment in his apology, Warren drew on the unrestrained arrogance of transformed whiteness in a manner that does further violence to the interned community.[79] By rationalizing his race-based decision-making in terms of wartime defense and security needs, Warren claimed racial innocence in a way that sacrificed the integrity of the process by which he engaged the injustices of the past. His refusal to acknowledge the legal wrongs inflicted by internment left intact the "military necessity" myth adopted by *Hirabayashi* and *Korematsu*, and rhetorically reimposed the injury of internment. As apologies go, Warren's mea culpa is woefully deficient, but as a component of racial redemption it skillfully restored his own racial integrity and made possible his reassertion of personal supremacy over the victims and events of the past. The apology was an act of repudiation, burial, and transformation, one that has been too often uncritically restaged by Warren's biographers.

CONCLUSION

My objective in this chapter is not to impugn the record of Earl Warren, but rather to understand the complexity of his actions during World War II and later as Chief Justice. In so doing, I have sought to understand the meaning of the silence, downplaying, and apologia surrounding Warren's role in internment practiced by both judicial biographers and internment historians. In one sense, I agree with the many admiring biographers who have suggested that Warren stands as the personification of the American spirit and character. That spirit and character, however, embody a troubling dualism inherent in the simultaneous promise and betrayal of equality at the individual, judicial-institutional, and societal levels, which are assessed here and in previous work through the theory of racial redemption.

Standing at the threshold of the Second Redemption, we might wonder how things would now be if earlier actors such as Warren had proven themselves truly heroic. As we look to past leadership for inspiration for future action, it is unfortunate that we observe Chief Justice Warren being personally unable and judicially ineffective at transgressing what historian George Lipsitz calls the "possessive investment in whiteness."[80] Because Warren settled for a halfway racial politics, he left his legacy available to regressive racial projects that have sought white supremacy's "preservation through transformation."[81] Using racial redemption theory to link Warren's personal past with his Court's racial trajectory allows us to defeat facile understandings of his and other liberal reform efforts that indulge the narrative of "putting race out of business." Warren's story shows that as a project of racial redemption, these reforms were all about an ongoing racialization of the political and the legal. Race got a new storefront perhaps, but it has not gone out of business as a primary axis of social subordination and organization.

NOTES

This work is made possible by a collaborative grant from the Civil Liberties Public Education Fund (CLPEF), of which I am honored to be a part. The staffs at the Bancroft Library at the University of California, Berkeley, the Bancroft Library's Regional Oral History Office, the California State Archives, and the Manuscripts Division of the Library of Congress were most helpful and informative. I am indebted to my research assistants, Pamela Alford, Marlo Johnson, and Marty Moore for their meticulous reading of my manuscripts and their Bluebook expertise. Glennis Jones-Marshall coordinated outstanding faculty support services throughout this project. Finally, I thank my colleagues in Asian American Studies for my interdisciplinary training that informs this work, especially Ronald Takaki for my early training in Asian Pacific American history and Michael Omi for my understanding of sociological theories of race.

1. See Cray, *Chief Justice*, 337; Horwitz, *Warren Court*, 3.
2. See Executive Order No. 9066, 3 C.F.R. 1092 (1942).
3. I intend the term "Japanese Californians" to include both "issei" (first-generation immigrants from Japan) and "nisei" (the offspring of the issei; that is, second-generation immigrants). Both were targeted for internment.
4. Cheryl I. Harris delineates how the law treats "the reputational interest in being regarded as white" as a form of status property in "Whiteness as Property," 1734.
5. Cho, "Redeeming Whiteness."
6. Nor do I argue that "but for" Warren's individual need for redemption from the shame of internment there would have been no Warren Court as we know it. The judiciary's more structurally functional move to redeem itself from overt forms of white supremacist adjudication and society's redemption of whiteness were vital parts of a complex process.
7. Horwitz, *Warren Court*, 13; White, *Earl Warren*, 18–20, 35; Daniels, *Politics of Prejudice*, 49 n. 15; Mowry, *California Progressives*, 154.
8. For excellent historical overviews of discrimination against Asian Pacific Americans, see generally Chan, *Asian Americans*; Takaki, *Strangers from a Different Shore*; Ancheta, *Asian American Experience*; Kim, *Legal History*; McClain, *Search for Equality*; Chan, ed., *Entry Denied*. On the legal treatment of Asian immigrants, see Hing, *Making and Remaking Asian America*; Jensen, *Passage from India*; U.S. Commission on Wartime Relocation and Internment of Civilians, *Personal Justice Denied* (hereafter cited as CWRIC); Kim and Kim, "Asian Immigrants in American Law." On naturalization and land ownership see Chuman, *Bamboo People*, 38–51, 73–89, 117–23; Haney-Lopez, *White by Law*; Ichioka, *Issei*, 226–43; Kettner, *Development of American Citizenship*; Aoki, "No Right to Own?"
9. White, *Earl Warren*, 21; Warren, *Memoirs*, 171; Daniels, *Politics of Prejudice*, 96; Interview of Carey McWilliams, "Earl Warren: Views and Episodes," 29, Earl Warren Oral History Series, Regional Oral History Office, Bancroft Library, University of California, Berkeley, 1981.
10. Chuman, *Bamboo People*, 151; White, *Earl Warren*, 74. White further notes that Warren was able to influence important military and federal policy-makers. From January 1942 on, White writes, he was "a persistent advocate of some form of evacuation, and his skillful marshaling of arguments, some of them spurious

and others based primarily on racial prejudice, significantly contributed to the decision to intern and evacuate the Japanese."

11. tenBroek, Barnhart, and Matson, *Prejudice*, 200; Daniels, *Camps*, 51–52. On the meaning of "issei" and "nisei," see note 3.

12. U.S. CWRIC, 55–57; tenBroek, Barnhart, and Matson, *Prejudice*, 70; Daniels, *Camps*, 49–50.

13. Interview of Warren Olney, III, "Law Enforcement and Judicial Administration in the Earl Warren Era," 228, Earl Warren Oral History Series, Regional Oral History Office, Bancroft Library, University of California, Berkeley, 1981; Cray, *Chief Justice*, 119; Daniels, *Camps*, 51; Severn, *Mr. Chief Justice*, 83–84; Katcher, *Earl Warren*, 142. On the escheat of alien-owned land, see Aoki, "No Right to Own?" 59.

14. Olney interview, 228; Daniels, *Camps*, 62. At the meeting, Warren warned the law enforcement officers that the "Japanese as an entire race of people, men, women, and children alike—especially United States citizens of Japanese ancestry—[are] poised to take disloyal action against the United States at any moment, to move to commit acts of sabotage, espionage, and disloyalty upon some mysterious signal to be issued to them by the Japanese enemy." Chuman, *Bamboo People*, 150–51.

15. Olney interview, 228–29; Earl Warren to Jerome B. Kavanaugh, March 6, 1942, San Bernardino County file, Material on the Pre-evacuation Location of Japanese Americans in California, C-A 172, Bancroft Library, University of California, Berkeley.

16. Earl Warren, Testimony Before the House of Representatives Select Committee Investigating National Defense Migration, March 11, 1942, 5, Warren Papers, University of California, Berkeley; see also National Defense Migration: Hearings Before the House of Representatives Select Committee Investigating National Defense Migration, H.R. Res. 113, 77th Cong., 2d sess., 1942, 10973–11023 (hereafter Tolan Committee Hearings); CWRIC, 98.

17. Grodzins, *Americans Betrayed*, 156; Warren to Kavanaugh, March 6, 1942; CWRIC, 98.

18. Grodzins, *Americans Betrayed*, 156–57.

19. Ibid.

20. The most cited example of purposeful migration of Japanese Californians involved Santa Barbara County, where the 1940 census revealed 2,187 citizens and aliens of Japanese ancestry, and 441 heads of household. Of the 136 land-holdings by Japanese Californians in the county, only 46 were within two miles of strategic installations (excluding highways). Extrapolating an average of 4.7 persons per household, the alleged strategic concentration involved approximately 216 persons, or 10 percent of the Japanese Californian population in the county. In other words, 90 percent of Japanese Californians in Santa Barbara County did not live near strategic installations, yet Santa Barbara was considered the primary example of purposeful suspicious migration. Ibid., 157–58.

21. Ibid., 158–59.

22. Bosworth, *Camps*, 77; Grodzins, *Americans Betrayed*, 156.

23. Tolan Committee Hearings, 10982–87; Bosworth, *Camps*, 76; Grodzins, *Americans Betrayed*, 156.

24. McWilliams interview, 29; Grodzins, *Americans Betrayed*, 159. The irony was not lost on the future Supreme Court Justice Tom Clark, who had advocated internment while at the Department of Justice during World War II:

They would till this land—that is, what's left of it. They would usually have to move rocks and bushes and weeds out. Before long, they would have a pretty good vegetable garden.

Then when the crop was in, people would say, "Well, the rascals have got the best gardens in the world," or "They're located below the dam, or the high tension wire station, or in the switchyard in order to carry out sabotage. That's why they're there." But, as a matter of fact, they had been there for years and had tilled a little plot of ground to make both ends meet.

Interview of Tom Clark, "Japanese-American Relocation Reviewed," vol. 1, "Decision and Exodus," 4, Earl Warren Oral History Series, Regional Oral History Office, Bancroft Library, University of California, Berkeley, 1976.

25. Tolan Committee Hearings, 10111–12; see Interview of Percy Heckendorf, "Japanese-American Relocation Reviewed," vol. 1, "Decision and Exodus," 8, Earl Warren Oral History Series, Regional Oral History Office, Bancroft Library, University of California, Berkeley, 1976.

26. Warren, Testimony, 5.

27. *Final Report: Japanese Evacuation from the West Coast* (Washington: U.S. Department of War, 1943), 9–10; see Grodzins, *Americans Betrayed*, 284–85; CWRIC, 98; Cray, *Chief Justice*, 123. For Warren's meeting with DeWitt, see McWilliams, *Prejudice*, 116; interview of Victor Hansen, "Earl Warren's Campaigns," 4, Earl Warren Oral History Series, Regional Oral History Office, Bancroft Library, University of California, Berkeley, 1977.

28. 320 U.S. 81, 95–96, 105 (1943). For Warren's role in the briefing of this case, see Irons, *Justice at War*, 212–18.

29. Heckendorf interview, 5, i. Lippmann's column of February 12, 1942, is quoted in Bosworth, *Camps*, 60–61.

30. For Pegler's column and the dissemination of Lippmann's, see Daniels, *Camps*, 67–68.

31. Chuman, *Bamboo People*, 201–02; Ringer, *"We the People,"* 865. The quoted language from *Pacific Citizen*, February 2, 1946, appears in Girdner and Loftus, *Great Betrayal*, 429.

32. Olney interview, 229.

33. Tom Scott to Warren, March 26, 1942, Warren Papers, University of California, Berkeley; Chuman, *Bamboo People*, 201.

34. Notes for *Time* Interview, n.d., File 3640:535, Earl Warren Papers, California State Archives.

35. Katcher, *Earl Warren*, 161, 164; Advertisement from unidentified newspaper, n.d., File 3640:482, Warren Papers, California State Archives.

36. Katcher, *Earl Warren*, 157, 161, 162; "Platform of the Republican Party of the State of California," September 17, 1942, File 3640:535, Warren Papers, California State Archives.

37. Inheriting the tradition, membership, and offices of the Japanese Exclusion League, which dissolved in 1924, after plotting the winning strategy for the absolute exclusion of Japanese immigrants through the Immigration Act of 1924, the California Joint Immigration Committee vigorously pursued an exclusionist agenda. Daniels, *Politics of Prejudice*, 108; Grodzins, *Americans Betrayed*, 11.

38. "California Indicts Governor Olson: The Truth about California's Home Defense," n.d., File 3640:457, Warren Papers, California State Archives; "Before and After Pearl Harbor," n.d., ibid.

39. "Warren Tells of Spy Fears," *Los Angeles Times*, July 25, 1942, File 3640:476, ibid.; "Warren Tells of Sabotage Peril Facing Pacific Coast," *Los Angeles Times*, October 17, 1942, File 3640:491, ibid.; Katcher, *Earl Warren*, 148.

40. This was the preferred strategy of the anti-immigrant group, the Native Sons of the Golden West. See tenBroek, Barnhart, and Matson, *Prejudice*, 48.

41. "Before and After Pearl Harbor"; W. T. Sweigert, "Earl Warren and California in Wartime," July 27, 1942, 12, 15, File 3640:5336, Warren Papers, California State Archives.

42. Leone Baxter to Clem Whitaker, July 7, 1942, File 3640:425, Warren Papers, California State Archives; Warren-for-Governor Press Release, July 13, 1942, File 3640:536, ibid.; "Olson Assailed for Jap Plan," *Oakland Tribune*, July 13, 1942, File 3640:445, ibid.; "Olson Called War Failure," *Los Angeles Times*, July 15, 1942, ibid.

43. "Olson Assailed for Jap Plan"; Warren-for-Governor Press Release, ibid.; Earl Warren Campaign Speech, 30–31, n.d., File 3640:5336, ibid.; "Olson and the Jap Vote," *Los Angeles Times*, August 19, 1942, File 3640:536, ibid.

44. Ringer, *"We the People,"* 850; Grodzins, *Americans Betrayed*, 39.

45. Grodzins, *Americans Betrayed*, 39.

46. The Naturalization Law of 1790 required whiteness as a prerequisite for naturalization eligibility. See Act of March 26, 1790, ch. 3, 1 Stat. 103. This racial requirement was amended after the Civil War to include persons of African descent. See Naturalization Act of 1870, ch. 254, §7, 16 Stat. 254. Racial restrictions were not lifted completely until the passage of the McCarran-Walter Act of 1952. See Immigration and Nationality Act of 1952, ch. 477, §311, 66 Stat. 163, 239 (codified at 8 U.S.C. §1422). Although primarily an immigration statute, the Chinese Exclusion Act not only prohibited Chinese from immigrating to the United States, but also barred persons of Chinese descent from naturalization eligibility. See Act of May 6, 1882, ch. 126, §14, 22 Stat. 61 (repealed 1943).

47. See "American Legion Convention Brings 40,000 Vets to L.A.," *San Francisco News*, August 17, 1942, File 3640:481, Warren Papers, California State Archives; Earl Warren, Address at Los Angeles American Legion, August 17, 1942, 2, File 3640:457, ibid.; "Legion Leader Scores Apathy," *Los Angeles Times*, August 18, 1942, 6; "Legion Hears Warren," *Oakland Post Enquirer*, August 17, 1942, F.

48. See "Governor's Race: Ex-Legion Chief Blasts Olson's Record on State War Preparedness," *San Francisco Chronicle*, August 18, 1942, 20, File 3640:481, Warren Papers, California State Archives; "Legion Assails Lag in Defense," *Los Angeles Times*, August 18, 1942, ibid.; "Olson Record Denounced by Legion Aide," *Los Angeles Times*, August 18, 1942, ibid.; W. T. Sweigert to Helen R. MacGregor, July 30, 1942, File 3640:457, ibid.

49. See tenBroek, Barnhart, and Matson, *Prejudice*, 46–47; Grodzins, *Americans Betrayed*, 12, 49; Daniels, *Politics of Prejudice*, 85.

50. Grodzins, *Americans Betrayed*, 48.

51. See Cray, *Chief Justice*, 51; White, *Earl Warren*, 31; Carey McWilliams, "The Education of Earl Warren," *The Nation*, October 12, 1974, 326.

52. Grodzins, *Americans Betrayed*, 48–49.

53. Cover Sheet from Native Sons of the Golden West to Warren Olney, March 24, 1942, File 3640:17885, Warren Papers, California State Archives; tenBroek, Barnhart, and Matson, *Prejudice*, 195; Native Sons of the Golden West, Grand Parlor Resolution, June 1, 1942, File 3640:17885, Warren Papers, California State Archives; Charles W. Johnson to John T. Regan, June 10, 12, 1942, ibid.

54. *Cf.* Frank, "Hugo L. Black," 2326. To support his view that Warren "said nothing to indicate he agreed with the American Legion and NSGW that 'the Yellow Peril' was here and going to take over," Ed Cray cites the following passage from Warren's speech to an American Farmers convention in December 1940:

> It should be remembered that practically all aliens have come to this country because they like our land and our institutions better than those from whence they came. They have attached themselves to the life of this country in a manner that they would hate to change and the vast majority of them will, if given a chance, remain the same good neighbors that they have been in the past regardless of what difficulties our nation may have with the country of their birth. History proves this to be true. . . . We must see to it that no race prejudices develop and that there are no petty persecutions of law-abiding people.

Cray, *Chief Justice*, 115–16. As Morton Grodzins writes, such sentiments may have instilled in Warren "a scrupulous regard for the legal status of resident Japanese," but they did little if anything to diminish his "determination to foster the evacuation by every possible lawful means." Grodzins, *Americans Betrayed*, 124, 127.

55. McWilliams thought Warren was "very active" in the NSGW. McWilliams interview, 29.

56. Earl Warren, Address at the 35th Annual Meeting of Governors Conference, 5–6, June 21, 1943, box 788, Earl Warren Papers, Library of Congress; Cray, *Chief Justice*, 157; Katcher, *Earl Warren*, 148.

57. Warren, Governors Conference Address, 5–6.

58. Earl Warren, Speech before the Newspaper Publishers Association, n.d., box 789, Warren Papers, Library of Congress.

59. The U.S. Commission on Wartime Relocation and Internment of Civilians noted that the 442nd nisei battalion had a casualty rate of 300 percent and recognized it as "one of the war's most decorated combat teams, receiving seven Presidential Distinguished Unit Citations and 18,143 individual decorations—including one Congressional Medal of Honor, 47 Distinguished Service Crosses, 350 Silver Stars, 810 Bronze Stars and more than 3,600 Purple Hearts." CWRIC, 258–59.

60. See Cray, *Chief Justice*, 158–59; Daniels, *Camps*, 158. The War Department stated that it would release Japanese Californians only after the unanimous Supreme Court decision in Ex parte Endo, 323 U.S. 283 (1944), announced on December 18, 1944.

61. In this sense *Black's Law Dictionary*, 6th ed. (St. Paul, Minn.: West, 1991), 884, defines "redeem" as:

> To buy back. To free property or article from mortgage or pledge by paying the debt for which it stood as security. . . . It implies the existence of a debt and means to rid property of that incumbrance.

62. Harris, "Whiteness as Property"; Bell, "Xerces and the Affirmative Action Mystique"; *Plessy v. Ferguson*, 164 U.S. 537, 549 (1896).

63. My working definition of white supremacy is a set of reinforcing and synergistic beliefs and institutional practices and policies consistent with superiority based on white racial identity or inferiorization of nonwhite racial identity, and reflected in societal group power relations. See Cho, "Multiple Consciousness and the Diversity Dilemma," 1036 & n.6.

64. See Crenshaw, "Race, Reform and Retrenchment," 1381.

65. Kluger, *Simple Justice*, 690; Myrdal, *American Dilemma*.

66. Wildman, *Privilege Revealed*.

67. The "mere change in the form of investment" phrase comes from *Lone Wolf v. Hitchcock*, 187 U.S. 553, 568 (1903), in which the federal government claimed that the doctrine of "plenary power" permitted it to abrogate treaties with Native nations unilaterally and without consent. Reva Siegel offers a related term, "preservation-through-transformation," to refer to the changing, yet ongoing nature of subordination through the Equal Protection Clause and antidiscrimination law more generally. Siegel, "'The Rule of Love,'" 2178–87.

68. See Cho, "Redeeming Whiteness," 143–54.

69. Warren, *Memoirs*, 149.

70. Brown, "Clerking for the Chief Justice," 281. Professor Morton Horwitz also identifies Warren's personal experience with internment as one motivation for the Chief Justice's successful efforts to forge a unanimous opinion in *Brown*. Horwitz, *Warren Court*, 24–25.

71. Warren to Alfred J. Lundberg, July 16, 1943, box 6, Warren Papers, Library of Congress.

72. Warren to John D. Weaver, February 3, 1967, Warren Papers, Library of Congress; Weaver to Warren, February 8, 1967, ibid. Far from being "repaid in full," the internees suffered significant financial losses for which they were inadequately compensated. CWRIC, 117–33; Girdner and Loftus, *Great Betrayal*, 428–38; Myer, *Uprooted Americans*, 245–56; and Hatamiya, *Righting a Wrong*, 174.

73. "Conversations with Earl Warren on California Government," June 22, 1972, 260, Earl Warren Oral History Series, Regional Oral History Office, Bancroft Library, University of California, Berkeley, 1981; see also White, *Earl Warren*, 76.

74. Warren, "Address at the 35th Annual Meeting," 6.

75. Warren, *Memoirs*, 149.

76. For this analysis, see generally, Gott, "A Tale of New Precedents," 179–274.

77. Warren did write that situations that place the judiciary in this position must be kept to "an absolute minimum" to preserve judicial review as "a meaningful restraint upon unwarranted encroachments upon freedom in the name of military necessity." Warren, "Bill of Rights and the Military," 193.

78. Hosokawa, *Thirty-Five Years in the Frying Pan*, 271; Weglyn, *Years of Infamy*, 299 n.8; Yamamoto, *Interracial Justice*, 195.

79. For this use of violence in a discursive context, see Cover, "Violence and the Word."

80. Lipsitz, *Possessive Investment in Whiteness*.

81. Siegel, " 'The Rule of Love,' " 2178–87.

Chapter 4

Reconsidering *An American Dilemma*: War, State-building, and the Politics of Black Militancy in the Twentieth Century

Daniel Kryder

> Long-range planning, in my judgement, is of the utmost importance. In such planning, consideration of the color and race problem is of first-line significance. But there is a danger of such long-range planning becoming projects of wide influence in escape from the realities of war. I am not convinced that we can be realists about the war and planners for the future at this critical time.
>
> FDR, March 16, 1942[1]

According to measures of both spontaneous and organized mass action, the four major wars of the twentieth century—World War I, World War II, Korea, and Vietnam—have stimulated black militancy.[2] First, while the incidence of interracial crowd violence has waxed and waned, the three peaks—around 1920, 1943, and the middle to late sixties—occurred during and just after major wars.[3] Second, major wars occasioned the largest, the most successful, and the most radical militant black liberation movements of the twentieth century, respectively: Marcus Garvey's Universal Negro Improvement Association (UNIA); A. Philip Randolph's March on Washington Movement; and the Black Power movement of the 1960s, based on Stokely Carmichael's SNCC and the Black Panthers. To take the UNIA as an example, Garvey, during and on the heels of the Great War, denounced almost the entire black leadership for seeking cultural assimilation and white support.[4] Although opposed to black participation in World War I, Garvey was no pacifist. "The first dying that is to be done by the black man in the future will be done to make himself free."[5] Driven by the same pessimism about the possibility for blacks and whites to live together that animated his proposed return to Africa, he built the largest and broadest mass movement in African American history up to that time.[6] One biographer has called March 1916, the month Garvey arrived in the United States, "precisely the right time" for his appeal.[7] But by 1925 Garvey was in the Atlanta penitentiary and his movement was doomed. Randolph's and Carmichael's efforts similarly illustrate the sense of opportunity and the constraints that characterize wartime social protest.

How has war both promoted the rise of black militancy and limited the prospects for black liberation in the twentieth-century United States? Historians and social scientists studying the causes and effects of war and its impact on political and social change in America have not examined the implicit theory embedded in Gunnar Myrdal's *An American Dilemma* (1944), a work fundamentally influenced by a contemporaneous world war. This chapter will draw out and attempt to explicate Myrdal's theory of war-induced political change. Although he conceptualized several of the broad effects of war very effectively, Myrdal devoted disproportionate attention to white people's ideologies while underestimating the cumulative effect on black militancy of a series of four "wars for democracy." Finally, the essay will offer amendments to Myrdal's view to correct his underestimate of the wartime imperatives that drive state and party actors to attempt to neutralize challenges to wartime social policy, in this case, black liberation movements.

AMERICA AGAIN AT THE CROSSROADS

Finishing his revisions to the manuscript in 1942 and 1943, the Swedish social economist Myrdal could not have avoided documenting the contemporary debates about race.[8] The young Swede was chosen partly for his relative insulation from and, it was therefore hoped, his objectivity about the race question in the United States, but he collaborated with a stellar array of American social scientists, including Ralph Bunche, J. G. St. Clair Drake, E. Franklin Frazier, Arthur Raper, Edward Shils, and Louis Wirth. The result was roughly 1,500 pages of unparalleled comprehensiveness. Optimism about human nature and confidence in the practical application of the new social science led Myrdal to expect that efforts to bring racial policy into line with core American values would launch a virtuous process of "cumulative causation," in which gains in one sphere of social or political relations would spur progress in other areas.[9]

Many have noted that Myrdal was too sanguine and underestimated the chameleon-like adaptability of racially biased attitudes to changes in law, the political system, and the economy. Even today, wholly American if archaic racial beliefs remain embedded within an overarching democratic national creed, and the legacy of racial disadvantage continues to shape the experience of all Americans in schools and labor markets. Since 1940 the black quest for political power, employment, and educational opportunity has met with as many obstacles as triumphs, including overt racism, white paternalism, and endless ideological debates and organizational rivalries over the justification, goals, and mechanisms of reform. Myrdal overlooked the possibility that resistant strains of racial prejudice might survive the collapse of a formal system of racial caste. Those criticisms of Myrdal are commonplace enough, but little attention has been paid to the book's treatment of the effects of war on racial ideology and behavior. As one intellectual historian put it, Pearl Harbor allowed Myrdal to "frame his discussion of American race relations in terms of a global war for democracy."[10]

The title of Myrdal's final chapter, "America Again at the Crossroads," refers to the choices posed by war. "Now America is again in a life-and-death struggle for liberty and equality," he wrote. American blacks were wondering what the conflict would mean for them. They watched closely because war had historically served a progressive, liberating function. The final chapter begins:

> The three great wars of this country have been fought for the ideals of liberty and equality to which the nation was pledged. As a consequence of all of them, the American Negro made great strides toward freedom and opportunity. The Revolutionary War started a development which ultimately ended slavery in all Northern states, made new import of slaves illegal and nearly accomplished abolition even in the South—though there the tide soon turned in a reaction toward fortification of the plantation system and of Negro slavery. The Civil War gave the Negro Emancipation and Reconstruction in the South—though it was soon followed by Restoration of white supremacy. The First World War provided the Negro his first real opportunity as a worker in Northern industry, started the Great Migration out of the South, and began the "New Negro" movement—though the end of the War saw numerous race riots and the beginning of a serious decline in employment opportunities. After the advances on all three occasions there were reactions, but not as much ground was lost as had been won. Even taking the subsequent reactions into account, each of the three great wars in the history of America helped the Negro take a permanent step forward.[11]

Following their release from slavery during the Civil War, most African Americans believed in the transformative potential of war and the concurrent centralization of political and coercive power in the executive branch. In a sentiment repeatedly expressed by black leaders throughout this century, an officer of a "Negro" Masonic organization in Texas early in World War I announced that the conflict would lead to "our second emancipation."[12] Myrdal's argument regarding the effects of war on racial politics is unsystematic, but of all the historical events reviewed in *American Dilemma*, war clearly served as the most powerful mechanism by which what he termed the "American Creed" and the "American Dilemma" came to be understood by the black and white masses.[13] The book's historical analysis of the first half of the twentieth century contains an implicit theory of war's effect on social and ideological change.

World War I

Following the Civil War, a short-lived and ineffectual period of Radical Reconstruction and the eventual abandonment of freedmen by the Republican Party disappointed hopes that conventional politics and formal institutions would offer equality to black Americans. That hope gave way to the belief that black advancement would be best served by individual moral and economic development. Tact, blue-collar skills, and hard work would elevate the individual and the race, according to Booker T. Washington and his associates. Among more militant blacks, the Great War dealt this philosophy a mortal blow. This new black militancy was caused, according to Myrdal, by changes in Southern agriculture, mass migration to northern cities, and the ideological implications of the war itself. The draft of whites, the end of immigration, and the war boom prompted Northern firms to accept blacks; most of these new jobs lasted until the end of the twenties. Myrdal considered the Great Migration a powerful ameliorative force, since urbanization and physical mobility contradicted "the traditionally peaceful and innocent accommodation of rural southern Negroes." Blacks entered the Army optimistically, ready to prove themselves through bravery and devotion to the nation, and although the War Department segregated black soldiers in training and assignments, the effect of the relocation of servicemen was substantial. Roughly 400,000 blacks were drafted, and while many worked in service roles, about 200,000 traveled to France. The nation to which they returned was frighteningly hostile; ten of the seventy blacks lynched in 1919 were soldiers. Still more were killed and injured in the twenty-five race riots during the same year.[14]

Myrdal was primarily interested in the impact of such trends on popular thought. Most whites, he maintained, joined in a revival of democratic ideology. They discussed the "American way of life" and acknowledged a lack of democracy in domestic politics. "The First World War stirred up people's minds and prepared them for change." This foment combined to raise the hopes of blacks and to draw attention to the "anomalous position" of African Americans in a so-called democracy. The lynching of a soldier was sometimes accompanied by complaints that blacks had "gotten 'wrong ideas' about their social status" while serving abroad. The wartime experience, Myrdal claimed, served as a "most severe shock" to American blacks, with lasting effects on their understanding of their subordinate role in the American polity.[15]

Social Trends between the Wars

Myrdal found that the decades prior to World War II had witnessed a decline in racial prejudices nationally and an increase in racial separation in the South. The result was an isolated and bitter black subculture. In the North, Myrdal believed that blacks enjoyed full legal equality, even if they still experienced discrimination in many private relations. The North, if led by courageous leaders, was nearly prepared, he thought, for a "fundamental redefinition" of the status of America's blacks. The Solid South was, in Myrdal's opinion, under pressure from a rising legal culture within the region and from attacks—on the poll tax, for example—from without. The occupational status of black Americans was deteriorating, however, and stagnation and exclusion restrained black workers both in Southern agriculture and urban workforces. Because discrimination was declining in other spheres and because national politics promised to remain liberal and progressive, Myrdal believed that the economic situation for blacks would have improved even without a second world war.[16]

In support, Myrdal pointed to "the most important of all social trends in the field of interracial relations," the slow decline since emancipation of "the popular theory behind race prejudice." He found that theories of racial caste were no longer defended confidently; his researchers had to "hunt them into the open." When drawn out, "they looked shabby and ashamed of themselves." Since the white man was losing confidence in the theory that had structured his racial worldview but had not yet altered his behavior to reflect this ambivalence, "he is in a dilemma." He would resolve the dilemma, Myrdal predicted, by eliminating caste theories and embracing the American Creed, a process already well-advanced by the time of Pearl Harbor.[17]

World War II

Myrdal found that World War II had organizational, socioeconomic, and ideological effects. It increased the political leverage of black leaders and organizations over the state, prompted rapid demographic and occupational change, and clearly revealed the American Dilemma. The new political leverage was both socioeconomic and ideological in origin. "He has seen his strategic position strengthened not only because of the desperate scarcity of labor," Myrdal wrote of the black man, "but also because of a revitalization of the democratic Creed. . . . He cannot allow his grievances to be postponed until after the War, for he knows that the War is his chance."[18]

In addition, the war favored race organizations by requiring a further "concentration of responsibility" through the regulation of labor relations by national unions and by federal law and administration.[19] For the most part, Myrdal simply reported the fact that black leaders recognized what is now called an improved political opportunity structure. This wartime leverage, I would argue, arose from a combination of three factors. The first was rapidly increasing membership in organizations, made possible by the higher incomes blacks enjoyed as a result of tight labor markets. The increased dues, in turn, enabled organizations to mount more effective recruiting campaigns. The second factor was African Americans' realization that the implicit or explicit threat of work stoppages was a source of power in a full-production, war economy. The third factor was the severity and duration of the war itself. By the summer of 1943, *The Crisis* called the "long war" argument "the question currently debated wherever colored Americans gather and talk."[20] "The graver the outside danger to the safety of this country, the more abundant the gains will likely be," as Horace Cayton put it early in the mobilization.[21] Ironically, the American state itself was primarily responsible for strengthening blacks' hand here, as it repeatedly stressed the gravity and persistence of the threat the conflict posed to American security.

Myrdal and his associates may well have expected that the socioeconomic effects of the war would resemble those of the last one. Mobilization would alter the social bases of the black masses by stimulating migration, moving the unemployed into work, and diversifying the occupational status of blacks. In fact, the facts of mobilization, as Myrdal reported them in August 1942, looked grim. No significant black migration had begun, and the demand for new labor was primarily confined to skilled occupations thoroughly dominated by whites.[22] Relatively little defense spending was allocated to the South; a large, Depression-fed reserve pool of white labor clamored for most defense jobs, and, in the North, white resistance to black employment was well-organized and protected by business's and government's recognition of racially exclusive unions. Finally, although the Fair Employment Practices Committee was, in Myrdal's estimation, "the most definite break in the tradition of federal unconcernedness" toward bias in employment, in the summer of 1942 it was "moribund" and only "something of a promise for the future."[23]

Myrdal's discussion of the armed forces was equally discouraging. The majority of Army training facilities during World War II were located in the South, increasing both black and white resentment toward the military's race policy. Relatively few blacks served in the Army and in the National Guard, and they did so most often in labor battalions. The Navy only employed blacks as messmen or menial laborers.[24] In addition, the war interrupted a process of increasing interracial cooperation and fellowship in the South of the 1930s and replaced it with a sense of impending crisis. Many observers foresaw race riots in the immediate future, and Myrdal himself predicted a reaction against any wartime gains.[25]

How could this dire analysis lead to any optimism at all? Myrdal sensed that as the war continued, trends would rapidly improve. Black Americans were better educated and, with a more robust press and stronger organizations and leaders, much better prepared to press their claims than ever before. The Depression and the war had broken the tradition of noninterference by government in employment, and Myrdal believed this would favor the prospects of blacks, apparently because he believed liberal forces to be ascendant at the federal level. In promoting the further unionization of the workforce and the regulation and planning of the economy, the war would break down economic discrimination, particularly in the North. Demobilization, and the threat of mass unemployment it entailed, would require large-scale federal intervention. No presidential administration would allow unemployment to fall disproportionately on blacks. Instead, federal agencies would present fair-employment policies as essential to national economic development in order to secure public support. Other forms of bias would then decline "according to the law of cumulative causation" (a favorite concept of Myrdal's). Even if a reaction set in after the war, history suggested, in Myrdal's opinion, that black Americans were "not likely to be driven back as far as they would have been had their previous gains been smaller."[26]

Such organizational and political-economic developments were less important in Myrdal's reckoning than an ideological one. In keeping with his theory that the "Negro problem has its existence in the American's mind," so that significant developments in race relations stemmed from "changes in people's beliefs and valuations," Myrdal was interested in "social trends" only insofar as they caused or influenced the ideology of Americans, particularly whites. Myrdal believed that World War II was an ideological war inasmuch as the Allies were trying to resuscitate democracy in continents dominated by totalitarian regimes that endorsed principles of racial superiority. Blacks were calling for the nation's equal dedication to democracy at home. "They can, with new reason, point to the inconsistency between American ideals and practices." Under these conditions, their cause possessed "supreme logical strength." Northern whites were beginning to feel the force of the "belief-behavior" contradiction, and thus the war was accelerating the defeat of the nation's illegal and unconstitutional caste theory. Whites simply no longer had the "moral stamina to make the Negro's subjugation legal and approved by society" in the face of the overriding moral power of the American Creed.[27] The war's relation to the cause of democracy was forcing a "deeper split" in the "moral personality" of the white southerner than in that of the white northerner. The South's increasing isolation and the nationwide spread of the political-economic problem of race combined to undermine the unstable interregional race compromise of 1877.

Myrdal also believed that the United States needed to prove that it could integrate blacks into the polity as it assumed a leadership role in world affairs. With whites forming a progressively smaller proportion of the world's population and nonwhite nations developing economically and politically, the nation had a responsibility to prove the practicality of its ideals. The world needed to believe in the youthful, moralistic optimism of America, and by extension in the feasibility of "peace, progress, and order." If America could live up to its convictions, its domestic welfare and its international prestige and power would be enhanced. Most declarations of rights derived from American manifestos such as Wilson's Fourteen Points and FDR's Four Freedoms, and many observers expected the creation of an international legal apparatus to hear appeals from oppressed minority groups. American power and stability would depend on the support and goodwill of other nations.[28]

In addition to these "compelling forces," America's "innermost desire" for democracy at home remained strong, for once again the primary trend in its history was the gradual realization of the American Creed. As black Americans became more assimilated and better educated, their continued exclusion from various spheres of society had made them increasingly impatient. At the same time, whites were gradually shedding their supremacist caste theory, and the unstable North-South interregnum on race appeared to be at an end. "The international upheavals connected with the two World Wars and the world depression brought these developments to a crisis." Myrdal believed the world situation to be "deeply unbalanced" and ripe for a "world revolution" that would alter race relations significantly. The Swede counseled action, for peace would bring new and complicated social and economic problems. The times demanded the use of social engineering based on social scientific theories of causal relations, because many spheres of life formerly considered matters of "individual adjustment" would be governed by "political decision and public regulation."[29]

A schematic representation of Myrdal's implicit theory (see Figure 1) will underscore the centrality of the white belief-behavior contradiction to his explanation of political change. Subsequent historical experience prompts a question: why did the collision of egalitarian ideals and racist practices in the United States between 1941 and 1945 not fulfill Myrdal's expectations and produce significant and lasting changes in the law, practice, and the ideology of racial equality?[30]

WAR AND MILITANCY: THE BELIEF-BEHAVIOR CONTRADICTION IS NO CONTRADICTION

As Myrdal suggested, the American war mobilizations of the first half of this century and the ideological contradictions they entailed stimulated black advocacy and race conflict in the United States But the most striking aspect of the history of all four of the major wars the United States fought in the twentieth century was the cumulative effect of the sequence of promise and disappointment that attended each. With each iteration, the fraudulence of the American Creed became clearer for black Americans. As a result, resistance intensified over time and fueled the militancy with which blacks expressed their grievances. Black leaders, no less than their military counterparts, resolved not to "fight the last war." By the mid-sixties, black radicals were openly advocating armed insurrection—notwithstanding the irony that black Americans moved from under- to overrepresentation in the armed forces.[31]

Figure 1
An American Dilemma: Myrdal's Model of the Effects of War upon Racial Attitudes and Black Liberation

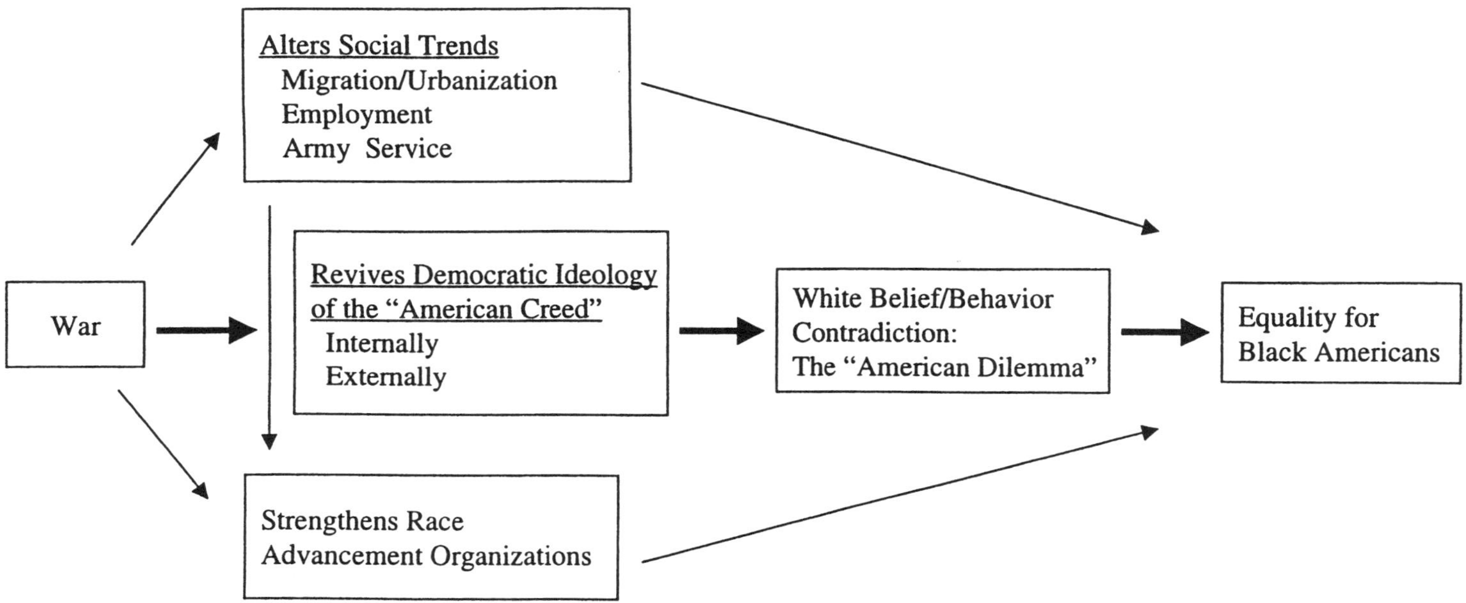

That black militancy accumulated can be seen in a brief review of four successive mobilizations. World War I, of course, had its violent crowd actions, but most of these were white-on-black affairs. Armed resistance by blacks was primarily defensive. Black Americans either subscribed to Garvey's return-to-Africa project or concurred with W.E.B. DuBois's well-known appeal to "close ranks" for the duration of the war.[32] Yet the conflict brought not greater civil rights and fairer treatment but a rash of lynchings and violent invasions of black neighborhoods.

By the start of World War II, the failure of a passive strategy was all too clear. When the nation entered the war, Myrdal explained,

> Negroes were not optimistic as to what its significance for them would be. They knew the democratic war aims were not meant for them . . . but there was more reason and more opportunity for protest. The democratic ideology stimulated by the war . . . outweighed the emphasis upon "wartime unity and harmony," and gave the Negro protest an ear among the whites, at least in the North. These same things made the Negro want to protest more.[33]

The lessons of the recent past were sobering and drove the elderly DuBois to renounce bitterly the advice he had once given. The first war "proved a disillusioning experience for the Negro," wrote Horace Cayton.[34] "The people are wiser than they were at the time of the first world war," wrote Pearl Buck.[35] In addressing the opening session of the annual conference of the NAACP in Houston in July 1941, Herbert Agar, editor of the Louisville *Courier-Journal*, warned listeners of the lessons of history. "The promises made to the Negro after the first world war by politicians and leaders were not kept," he declared. "It was all a lot of eyewash but they think of the Negro when the crisis comes." Similarly, Kenneth Clark noted that the morale of the black soldier had grown more "reality-bound" since World War I, when appeals to patriotism were effective. To "use those methods now . . . would be a blundering mistake."[36]

From World War II onward, black organizations pursued reform much more forcefully. In July 1941, for example, a militant March on Washington Movement threatened to flood the capital with impatient African Americans just as the Nazis invaded the Soviet Union, and the city struggled with a well-publicized and racially charged "crime wave." Militancy persisted into the Cold War. With war in Korea looming in 1948, for example, A. Philip Randolph openly advocated resistance to the draft before the Senate Armed Services Committee. He prepared for a campaign of noncompliance until Truman's Executive Order 9981, directing "equality of treatment and opportunity" for all races in the armed services, made the matter moot.[37]

Finally, the intensification of the Vietnam war in the 1960s corresponded with the turn in the civil rights movement toward a radical, black power agenda. Although the precise connections remain somewhat unclear, they involved the widely held belief among black Americans that the increased deployment of African Americans was a sign of entrenched racial bias and the implausibility of the claim, successfully made in earlier conflicts, that Americans were aiding the resistance of tyranny abroad.

The militancy of the sixties was therefore an accumulated militancy, having gained strength from the experiences of past generations. As each war successively failed to fulfill its promise, it focused attention on the belief-behavior contradiction implied by the American Creed.

IF MILITANCY, WHY NO LIBERATION? STATE INSTITUTIONS AND THE DEMOCRATIC PARTY DURING WARTIME

Two wartime political imperatives pursued by presidents—social order and reelection—combine to account for the lack of policies of racial liberation in wartime. Myrdal did not consider the presidency to be an independent political force in these cycles of reform, war, and reaction, but in every case, the central state in the person of the executive sought to neutralize emergent militant movements.

In each of the four major twentieth-century wars, Democratic presidents faced two imperatives. The first was the need to expand military capacity dramatically, both by mobilizing industry and by drafting and training soldiers. This was a surprisingly anarchic process and, as such, required the cooperation and allegiance of key organized social groups, including industrial workers, employers, and civil rights groups. The state could bargain for the groups' allegiance or, if not forthcoming, repress their resistance. The second was the need to keep the Democratic Party permanently in office ("party permanence"). In each case except Lyndon Johnson's in the Vietnam war, this meant, in practice, that the administration's strategists had to attempt the difficult task of mollifying the segregationist southern wing while constructing a new clientele relationship with black workers and voters. Social unrest threatened to disturb both efficient war-making and party permanence.

The Central State and Black Militancy: The Pursuit of Social Order and Efficient War-making

Although wars generated increasingly militant "antiestablishment movements," they failed to propel the cause of black liberation because they were checked by the development of the federal government's capacity to control their protests. If the civil rights protests of the fifties originated in institutions deeply buried in the black community and thus insulated from white control, racial struggle in wartime has occurred in the context of a temporary but significant extension of federal economic and police power. Consider the dangers of mobilizing the discontented. The number of black inductees into the military in World War II surpassed by more than

50 percent the number of blacks who joined unions. And American military units participated in serious racial disorders during this war on at least twenty occasions.[38]

The American state controlled the friction and violence of the growing unrest with both old tools and new policies.[39] The military's predominant concern with force and discipline and its instinctive turn toward policing and repression to control unrest in its ranks constrained rather than facilitated the efforts of activists seeking egalitarian reform. Civilian officials at first relied upon such familiar regime "tools" as symbolic appointments, including highly visible black officers and "black cabinet" officials. Small steps toward reform followed, such as the announcement—if not the enforcement—of the desegregation of post facilities and transportation in 1943 and 1944. Over time, state officials devoted new resources and developed new techniques for the pacification of the races, including intelligence, recreation, indoctrination, and the incremental relaxation of segregation. Innovation was particularly substantial in the field of surveillance. Although the state began World War II, for example, with a rather crude and reactive coercion-intensive system—collaborating with local civilian police forces to gain physical control of black soldiers and workers—it finished the conflict with a more complex repertoire of measures to reduce unrest and thereby stanch the forces of reform.

The administration of war by the central state has typically required it to favor black citizens more than it did in peacetime. Though slight in practice, this solicitude came at the expense of states and localities. The relatively thorough regulation of the economy and workforce unintentionally created an antagonistic relationship to authorities in the states, particularly as federal administrators routinely interfered with local laws governing segregation and labor control. They stormed into previously isolated communities with extraordinary coercive powers and occasionally built entirely new cities, such as Oak Ridge, Tennessee. In the process, longstanding but fragile racial norms were often violated—by military police, for example, patrolling cities and towns on weekends or by fair employment investigators as they reviewed the hiring practices of local factories. Whether and when to enforce federal law or local custom was a difficult question, answered pragmatically but inconsistently. Release from this wide-ranging regulation by the central state must be considered one of the likely causes of violent postwar racial reactions.

As state officials bargained more openly and directly with peak organizations, the mobilization for and prosecution of the war drove the state to routinize and consolidate its relationships to social groups through quasi-corporatist arrangements. Wars generally lead to changes in the relationship between a central state's system of "obligations" and social groups' claims from "rights," and World War II was no exception.[40] So long as the central state offered black manpower a combination of concessions and controls, leading "race advancement" groups turned their attentions toward it. That state of affairs usually ended, abruptly, with the peace.

The Democratic Party and Black Militancy: The Pursuit of Political Permanence

The second reason why wartime militancy failed to propel the cause of black liberation was the need of Democratic presidents to preserve the party's governing coalition in the face of friction generated by new, centralized controls of soldiers and workers. The four major American wars of the twentieth century were fought by Democrats who, after having apparently exhausted the country's appetite for reform, redirected the polity toward war: Woodrow Wilson (who presided over the New Freedom and the Great War), Franklin Roosevelt (the New Deal and World War II), Harry Truman (the Fair Deal and the Korean war), and Lyndon Johnson (the Great Society and the Vietnam war). In each case the cycle of entry, war prosecution, and exit was governed by a reform Democrat who was sensitive to the party's schizophrenic attitude toward race and labor regulation.

Wilson set the pattern, winning the 1912 election on a New Freedom platform that all but ignored foreign concerns. He helped bring the Progressive movement to fruition in his first term—with the Clayton Anti-Trust Act, federal aid to education and agriculture, the Federal Reserve Act, and the creation of the Federal Trade Commission. But the outbreak of World War I in 1914 gradually redirected his energy to international issues, culminating in the American entry into the conflict in April 1917, the waging of war in the trenches, and Wilson's ill-fated efforts to restructure international politics at the Paris Peace Conference and through his prized League of Nations.

This apparent cycle of domestic reform and international war also obtained in the case of Franklin Roosevelt. No president achieved more domestic reform, as he attempted to restore the nation's confidence and revitalize its economy with two full terms of regulatory, relief, and recovery initiatives. He pointed the Congress toward the passage of the Wagner Act, the Social Security Act, and a progressive taxation plan. Voters responded to his leadership in 1936 with a massive reelection victory. The second term, however, saw the defeat of his divisive plan to pack the Supreme Court and his attempt to purge conservative Democrats in the 1938 primaries. His claim to have mastered the Depression were undermined by the recession of the same year. With the arming of England against Nazi expansionism, and the purposeful isolation of Japan, and the beginning of the Pacific War in late 1941, "Dr. Win the War," as he put it, replaced "Dr. New Deal."

Throughout the thirties Roosevelt successfully contained intra-party conflict over issues that normally would have split northeastern reformers from their conservative southern colleagues, the most sensitive being race and labor.[41] The inner contradictions of the New Deal coalition were best revealed in Congress, where the principal partners were a southern white plantation elite and organized labor. By 1940, however, blacks comprised an emergent faction of the party in the urban North, and they pressed the administration to replace symbolic gestures and egalitarian rhetoric with an effective program of federal civil rights. To Congressmen from the Deep South, the expansion of central state authority posed a potentially serious threat to Dixie's highly exploitive, racially biased staple crop economy. The mutual accommodation of the two controlling partners in Congress (and their representatives elsewhere in the national government) was in jeopardy.

The full mobilization of human and material resources forced onto the political agenda questions of race that were very difficult for the Democratic Party to resolve. Some were wholly new, stemming from the peculiar logistics of war; others, long familiar to the party, gained new ideological strength in the Allies' war against fascism. In rapid succession, for example, the World War II Congress considered bills to create a system of absentee voting for armed forces members, prohibit the poll tax in state voter registration systems, prohibit discrimination in the operation of the selective service system, and make permanent the Fair Employment Practices Committee and the U.S. Employment Service. World War II thus transformed the New Deal Congressional debates on race. Limited in 1935 to the somewhat anachronistic problem of lynching, they addressed an array of reforms directed at complex and contemporary forms of inequity.

When Harry Truman became president in 1945 he was determined to fulfill the promises of his predecessor, and after his stunning reelection in 1948, he pursued his own Fair Deal. After battling a bipartisan conservative coalition in Congress, the outbreak of war in Korea in 1950 eliminated whatever chance he had for domestic success. The American people grew tired of the stalemate in Korea and eagerly elected a Republican who promised to end the conflict. Truman left office aware that he had lost the people's confidence.

Lyndon Johnson arrived at the presidency in a very similar fashion. He was determined to carry forward John F. Kennedy's stalled program of domestic reform, and he quickly won passage of major legislation in the area of civil rights and social insurance. Moreover, under the banner of the Great Society, he launched an all-out war against poverty that won him the full support of liberals in the 1964 campaign. No sooner had he won the election, however, than he began the slow escalation of the war in Vietnam, leading to the sustained bombardment of the North, the sending of a half-million ground troops to the South, and a bitter national debate that drove him from the White House. Major wars caused these difficulties for the Democratic Party in that they facilitated civil rights claims at the same time that they promoted new labor controls, for mobilizations lent themselves to the greater regimentation of the working classes.

The United States never fought a twentieth-century war except as a postscript to major reforms and the concurrent reorganization of the capacity of the central state. Repeatedly, presidents have discarded a prewar social agenda and used or developed tools to manage the racial friction that the movement of the races produced. Although sectional economies and political necessity have strictly limited the possible responses of an otherwise strengthened state, temporary and decentralized administrative initiatives have successfully defused race crises and insulated the federal executive from potentially threatening divisions within the Democratic Party coalition. When an election neared, the problem of political survival became an overriding concern, and the president's staff responded with relatively minor, public, and symbolic concessions to secure the black vote. These political considerations, however, remained secondary to the supreme goals of war-making and the accommodation of social unrest. Lacking established, formal bureaus or other mechanisms, the American state "coped" as best as it could by monitoring areas of racial tension, and by responding to the potential crisis on a day-by-day basis.

Although students of political development often remind us that wars and states advance in symbiosis, the scholarship on American political history has paid relatively little theoretical and historical attention to the linkages between war-driven national political-economic forces and patterns of state formation and collective action.[42] Myrdal is a very good start, despite his overestimating the importance of wartime ideology in instilling an invigorated American Creed in the minds of the American masses. He was also mistaken in his belief that black liberation would follow primarily from changes in whites' attitudes rather than the sustained activity of a social movement. But his model of the ways that wars change socioeconomic, cognitive, and organizational patterns is fundamentally sound, if incomplete and unbalanced. The critique and revision offered here attempts to develop, redirect, and augment his causal story in three ways. (See Figure 2.) First, this research has suggested that scholars reframe Myrdal's analysis to focus on the prime mover of twentieth-century race reform: organized "race advancement" activity on the part of blacks. Second, the chapter suggests that scholars adopt a diachronic perspective to understand the accumulated resentment which characterized the collective experience of black citizens in wartime. Successive generations developed increasingly militant responses to a central state unwilling to pursue the American Creed during or after wars for democracy. And, finally, this chapter has augmented Myrdal's model with a consideration of the independent effects of the war-making central state and the Democratic Party in neutralizing wartime militancy. While Myrdal expected social practices to adapt to and reflect ideals made salient by democratic wars, he overlooked the American president, who, in the 1940s at least, was a realist wary of "planning for the future."

Figure 2
War and Social Change in the Twentieth-Century United States: State and Party Imperatives in the African American Case

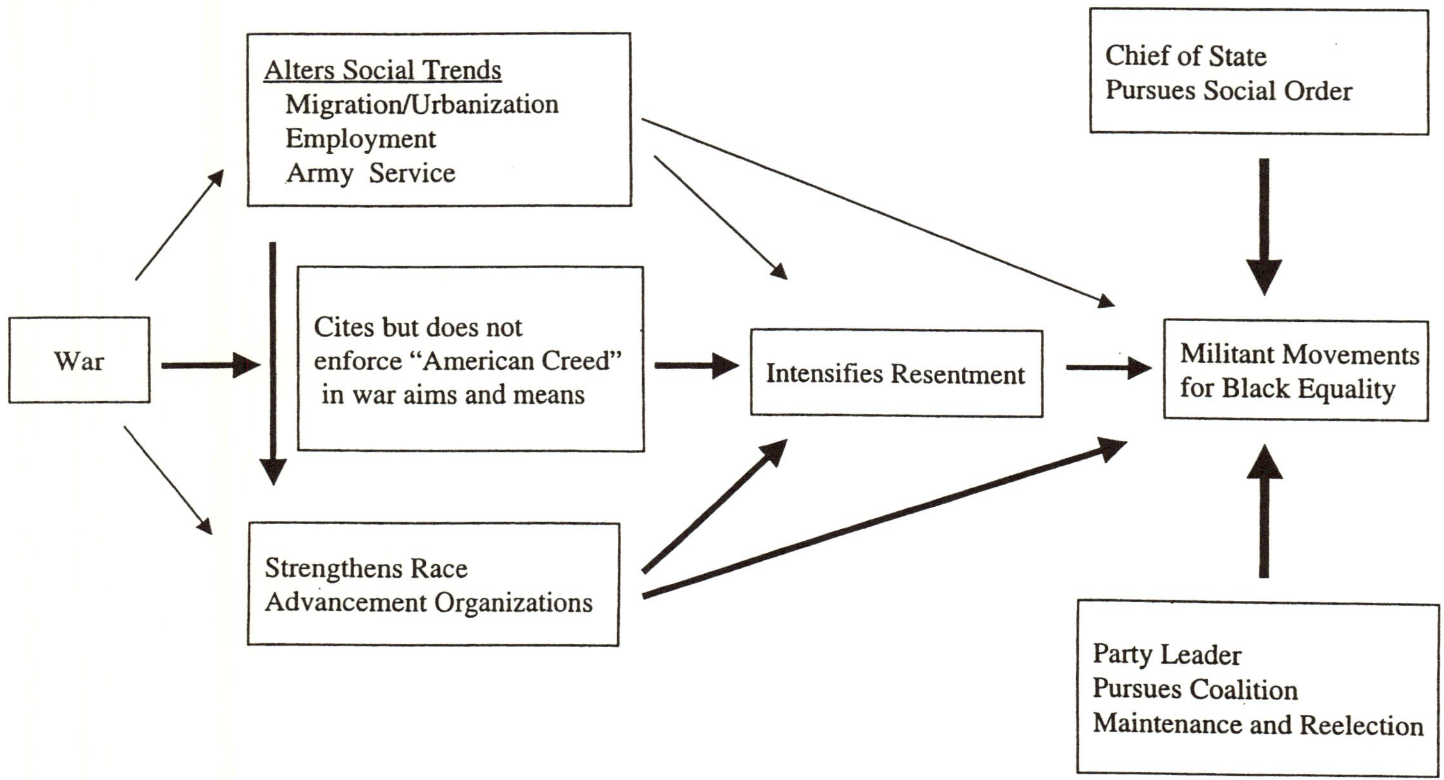

NOTES

1. FDR to Edwin Embree, March 16, 1942, OF 93 (Colored Matters), FDR Library.

2. For the purposes of this essay, an organization is considered militant if it seeks to (1) limit membership to social group members, i.e., all-black organizations; (2) repudiate "acceptable" organization leaders associated with the progressive wings of the major parties; (3) refuse to eschew confrontational or violent tactics; and (4) advocate separatist claims. The spontaneous crowd violence likewise involved black populations combating the symbols or the institutions of white privilege, either through defensive or offensive tactics.

3. Grimshaw, *Racial Violence*; Janowitz, "Patterns of Collective Racial Violence"; Brooks, "Domestic Violence"; Sitkoff, "Racial Militancy."

4. America's black leadership, he said, "had no program, but were mere opportunists who were living off their so-called leadership while the poor people were groping in the dark." Levine, "Marcus Garvey," 116–17.

5. Levine, "Marcus Garvey," 117.

6. By the end of 1919, he claimed two million members for the UNIA, but this statement is, at best, a rough estimate.

7. After a visit to Europe, Garvey returned in 1918. Garvey's "pageantry" or aristocratic courtliness appears to be an analogue to the martial political culture of World War I. The UNIA's first international convention was held in Harlem in 1920, and spectators lined the streets for miles to watch Garvey in his military uniform, followed by contingents of the "African Legion" clad in blue military garb, Black Cross nurses, and uniformed marching bands. Guests at court dinners were seated according to rank, and honors conferred on persons took the form of medals and titles such as the Star of African Redemption. Levine, "Marcus Garvey," 112, 121.

8. Myrdal, *American Dilemma*, x–xvii.

9. In an important break with contemporary scholarship on the relationship between race and socioeconomic status, Myrdal systematically applied a culture-of-poverty rationale commonly used to explain demographic patterns among European immigrants, thus rejecting the notion that economic differences between "white" and "black" families and workers reflected genetic differences. Myrdal's adoption of this framework both promoted and reflected a modification of liberal attitudes to include the notion that African Americans were assimilable into American political culture. Cherry, "Culture-of-Poverty Thesis and African-Americans." See also Southern, *Gunnar Myrdal and Black-White Relations*; Jackson, *Gunnar Myrdal and America's Conscience*; Pressman, "American Dilemma: Fifty Years Later."

10. As Myrdal said, "It became my war work. And I think this meant much for what the book came to be." Jackson, *Gunnar Myrdal and America's Conscience*, 163. See also ibid., chs. 4–6.

11. Myrdal, *American Dilemma*, 997.

12. Quoted in Levine, "Marcus Garvey," 112.

13. The idea that racial segregation contradicted core American ideals was prominent in race discourse and the rhetoric and ideology of race advancement organizations when the book was written. Its proponents reacted to the obvious incongruity between Allied war aims and domestic policies. As an official in the

March on Washington Movement put it in 1941, "Everyone was talking about democracy, even in the dark South, but their actions belied their words. We listened attentively to the cruel words, for all said, "All men are created equal and that in this country all men have equality of opportunity." John Eardlie to FDR, August 16, 1942, OF 4245–G, OPM, COFEP, War Manpower Board, FDRL. One black editorialist wrote before Pearl Harbor that "The defenders of decency in democracy—and their mothers and fathers—have a right to a faith in its existence here before they fight for it far away." *Raleigh News & Observer*, April 7, 1941. In early 1942, the *Pittsburgh Courier* sponsored the popular Double V Campaign to signify victory "over enemies from without . . . [and] over our enemies from within." The letter to the editor that launched the campaign is quoted in Washburn, *Question of Sedition*; Finkle, *Forum for Protest*; and Wesley, "The Negro Has Always Wanted the Four Freedoms," 90. See also the essays by Roy Wilkins, A. Philip Randolph, Willard Townsend, and Mary McLeod Bethune in Logan, ed., *What the Negro Wants*.

14. Levine, "Marcus Garvey," 112; Myrdal, *American Dilemma*, 200, 295, 745. While army training and travel may have had some ameliorating effects, the predominance of Southern attitudes in the War Department largely defeated this trend. According to the *Pittsburgh Courier*, the Great War mobilization transformed a great many indifferent white soldiers into racists by sending Northerners into the South—converting them to local sentiments and practices—and racist Southerners to the North "to spread their infamous of race prejudice wherever they go." "Southern Americanism," *Pittsburgh Courier*, November 23, 1940. A similar effect of army influence was seen in the second war. "The army has done more to develop racial consciousness by segregating black and white soldiers in communities where such is not the practice, then has the Bund or the Ku Klux Klan." "New Edifice Situated in Arlington, Va.," *Chicago Defender*, October 18, 1941. See also Adams, "Southerners Invade the North While Northerners 'Stay Put,' " *(New York) Amsterdam News*, March 25, 1944.

15. Myrdal, *American Dilemma*, 193, 563, 745. James Weldon Johnson wrote of the cynicism and "spirit of defiance born of desperation" that marked the end of World War I. He claimed that postwar radicalism differed from the prewar variant in its "fierce race consciousness." Johnson, *Black Manhattan*, 246. Under Johnson the membership of the NAACP increased tenfold—by 90,000—between 1916 and 1920. Levy, "James Weldon Johnson," 89.

16. Myrdal, *American Dilemma*, 998–99, 1001–02, 1003–04, 1010.

17. Myrdal, *American Dilemma*, 1003–04.

18. Ibid., 409. "The Negro leaders know full well that they have immense possibilities of putting pressure upon the American nation during this War for democracy." Myrdal, *American Dilemma*, 852.

19. Myrdal, *American Dilemma*, 1010.

20. Benjamin Quarles, "Will a Long War Aid the Negro?" *The Crisis* (September 1943): 268; George S. Schuyler, "A Long War Will Aid the Negro," *The Crisis* (November 1943). "The 'hope' here, as we see it, is a war threat so terrible that they will be glad to have engineers and combat pilots regardless of complexion." "Plane Factory Qualifications Don't Mean a Thing When You Are Colored," *Philadelphia Plain Dealer*, September 6, 1940.

21. Horace Cayton, "Negro Morale," *Opportunity* (December 1941): 375.

22. See Weaver, *Negro Labor*.

23. Myrdal, *American Dilemma*, 409–10, 416.
24. Ibid., 419–20. In October 1940 the War Department announced that blacks would be inducted into the Army at rates matching their proportion in the general population, and that they would be represented in all branches, although the policy had not been executed as Myrdal completed his book.
25. Ibid., 1014.
26. Ibid., 423, 426, 1005–06, 1011, 1014. Ironically, if a true peace curtailed the production of armaments at this stage, the losses to black workers might have been minimized, since a number of factors had thus far limited nonwhite gains largely to civilian production. Ibid., 424.
27. Ibid., 426, 998, 1004, 1008–09.
28. Ibid., 1019–20, 1021–1022.
29. Ibid., 1021–23.
30. Historians have generally not ascribed great importance to wars in explaining the eventual achievement of statutory racial equality in the twentieth-century United States. Recent work has suggested that innovative mass advertising techniques, self-interest, and a concern for one's comrades-in-arms, no less than ideology, led Americans to support the war. See in particular Fussell, *Wartime*, 129–43. Critical reexaminations of wartime ideology and practice include Dower, *War without Mercy*; Polenberg, "The Good War?"; Blum, "Unity and Stability"; Adams, *Best War Ever*; King, *Separate and Unequal*; and Gerstle, "Race and the Myth of the Liberal Consensus."
31. The peacetime strength of black troops in the regular Army had been fixed by Congress in 1866 at two infantry and two cavalry regiments, making nonwhites less well represented in the Army than in the general population until the 1940s.
32. "That which the German power represents spells death to the aspirations of Negroes and all the races for equality, freedom, and democracy. Let us, while the war lasts, forget our special grievances and close ranks shoulder to shoulder with our white fellow-citizens and the allied nations that are fighting for democracy." W.E.B. DuBois, "Close the Ranks," *The Crisis* (July 1918): 111.
33. Myrdal, *American Dilemma*, 755.
34. Horace Cayton, "Negro Morale," *Opportunity* (December 1941): 371.
35. "Then they were soft after years of peace and prosperity. But now they have had lean years and bitter times and hardness has grown into their souls. If we want unity, at this time of national defense, let it not be thought that our people can be cajoled into that unity by promises or sentimentalized into it by emotionalism or threatened into it by force. They can be unified only by their own free belief in their cause." Pearl S. Buck, "Too Much Unity is a Danger," *Opportunity* (April 1941): 110–11.
36. "Stress Seven Acts Against Democracy," *Chicago Bee*, July 6, 1941; Clark quoted in memorandum, Robert C. Weaver to Jonathan Daniels, September 4, 1943, p. 2., OF 4245–G, OPM, COFEP, WMC.
37. Quarles, "A. Philip Randolph," 159.
38. McAdam, *Political Process*; Vatter, *U.S. Economy*, 127; "Review of the Month," *Monthly Summary of Events and Trends in Race Relations* 2 (1944); Sandler, "Homefront Battlefront."
39. For most "state-centered" Americanists, these army policies would appear to be anomalous cases, for the institutional development literature tends to favor

case studies of the genesis and evolution of peacetime "progressive" national bureaucracies administering social welfare or regulatory programs. This growing literature has not yet fully explored the significance of temporary administrative reforms which aim at goals other than permanent bureaucratic expansion. Instead, studies of American political development have focused disproportionately on two periods of rapid state expansion and consolidation: the rationalizing and regulatory Progressive Era, or the recovery-, relief-, and reform-minded New Deal. Skowronek, *Building a New American State*; Skocpol and Finegold, "Explaining New Deal Labor Policy," 1297–1304; Goldfield, Reply, 1304–15. Weir, Orloff, and Skocpol, *Politics of Social Policy*, includes several articles which directly address the cumulative effects of the New Deal and World War II.

40. A substantial historical literature uses organized labor and women workers to explore the relationship between individuals, groups, and institutions within a wartime industrial policy. See Seidman, *American Labor*; Lichtenstein, *Labor's War at Home*; Meier and Rudwick, *Black Detroit*. On women, see Anderson, *Wartime Women*; Campbell, *Women at War*; Rupp, *Mobilizing Women for War*; Honey, *Creating Rosie the Riveter*; Milkman, *Gender at Work*.

41. V. O. Key made the strongest version of the argument linking southern Democrats to the obstruction of civil rights reform: "on the race question, and on the race question alone, does a genuine southern solidarity exist." Key, *Southern Politics*, 359. See also Bensel, *Sectionalism and Political Development*; Katznelson, Geiger, and Kryder, "Limiting Liberalism."

42. Of the many synthetic treatments of American society during World War II, the best are Polenberg, *War and Society*, and Blum, *V Was for Victory*. For an efficient overview of economic developments during the war, see Vatter, *U.S. Economy*.

CHAPTER 5

Vivien Kellems and the Folkways of Taxation

Carolyn C. Jones

> I mistakenly believed that we were justified in suspending our constitutional rights and liberties in time of great emergency. . . . [Taxes] are fastened down upon us in an emergency and there they remain forever.
>
> Vivien Kellems[1]

In the conduct of total war, a sense of citizen obligation and willingness to sacrifice were essential. While popular images abound of public-spirited unconditional sacrifice by Americans on the home front, some historians have perceived a more conflicted and complex "politics of sacrifice." The Roosevelt administration, they argue, found itself contending with various groups to define the community interest and the meaning of sacrifice in time of war.[2]

Taxation provided one vehicle for wartime sacrifice on the home front. Americans claimed to be willing to pay higher taxes.[3] Financial sacrifice was required to pay for World War II, as federal budget expenditures were twelve times greater in 1945 than they were in 1940.[4] Congress and the Roosevelt administration fundamentally altered the federal tax system during the war by making the individual federal income tax a mass tax.

The tax regime created in World War II has remained the foundation of the federal tax system. Its unprecedented revenue capacities helped finance the Cold War.[5] As it became apparent that the new tax system would outlast the war, an emerging conservative movement used constitutional law and political philosophy to attack the income tax and its withholding mechanism. Mass income taxation overlaid state property laws in ways that produced different taxes for similarly situated married couples during the war. In making mass taxation permanent, Congress addressed inequalities among married couples while creating relatively greater burdens for single taxpayers.

For many observers, Vivien Kellems was, in the words of a *New Yorker* profile, "the most persistent, articulate and controversial opponent of the income tax, both state and federal, that the nation has ever known."[6] A woman who used autobiography as a weapon against the wartime tax system and its continuation, Kellems was a female employer in a managerial world dominated by men and an outspoken libertarian regarded warily even by many conservatives.

Kellems launched her first battle against the federal income tax in January 1944. In a nationally reported speech she declared, "I call upon all business, both big and small, to follow my example and put aside post-war reserves out of their taxes."[7] A second battle involved a tax-collecting innovation introduced during the war, wage and salary withholding. In 1948 Kellems asserted that being required to withhold taxes from her employees' paychecks without compensation from the government violated the Thirteenth Amendment against involuntary servitude.[8] Her aim, as she acknowledged in her 1952 book *Toil, Taxes and Trouble*, was to abolish a fundamental component of the postwar income tax regime, one that made the system less reliant on voluntary compliance.

A third episode of resistance was Kellems's reaction to the adoption of the joint return for married couples in 1948. The mass federal income tax with its high progressive rates highlighted inequities between couples in community property and common-law states and between those who employed tax avoidance techniques and those who did not. Kellems saw the joint return as providing an income-splitting tax reduction not available to single taxpayers. In 1969 Kellems again refused to pay federal income taxes because of the system's discriminatory treatment of single people.[9] She launched a vigorous campaign to change the law through the courts and through pressure on Congress.

As wartime sacrifice extended into the postwar period, as a postwar conservative critique of taxation developed and grew, and as single taxpayers (often women) perceived the inequality of their tax treatment, Vivien Kellems's antitax campaigns dramatized themes of wartime sacrifice, conservatism, and feminism. Her wartime refusal to pay taxes provides a snapshot of the politics of sacrifice in the context of taxation. Her protest against withholding illustrates a developing postwar critique of the federal government's revenue powers. Finally, Kellems's resistance to higher taxation for single taxpayers was one phase of her long advocacy of feminism, in which she utilized arguments that turned upon both differences and similarities between men and women.

INTRODUCING VIVIEN KELLEMS

Kellems was born June 7, 1896, in Des Moines, Iowa, the third of seven children and the only daughter of David and Louisa Kellems. At the time of Vivien's birth, her father was a minister in the Disciples of Christ, Campbellite sect. The family moved to Eugene, Oregon, when Vivien was two years old. Her father and, later, her mother, taught homiletics, exegesis, and other subjects at the Eugene Bible University.[10]

Vivien attended public school in Oregon and graduated in 1918 with a B.A. in economics from the University of Oregon. She became a booker of programs for a western and, later, a southern Chautauqua circuit. During this time she became engaged to a naval doctor who was killed when his ship was torpedoed in September 1918. During this period she was also said to have married briefly and divorced. Kellems, when questioned about this, replied, "We don't talk about this matter. . . . Officially, I am a spinster."[11]

She returned to the University of Oregon and earned a master's degree in economics in 1919. In 1920 she entered a Ph.D. program in economics at Columbia University, where she is said to have studied taxation with E.R.A. Seligman. She left before earning the degree to become a theatrical publicist and later a lecturer, plugging a variety of theatrical productions. Her recommendations depended on subsidies from producers.[12]

Kellems's industrial career was launched in 1928 when her brother obtained a patent for his improved version of a cable grip. She sold the "Kellems Products" grips to several electrical companies in New York. Based on toy finger traps—those little woven tubes into which one's fingers can be easily inserted but then are held tight when one attempts to remove them—the grips were used in "pulling wiring" for such prominent projects as the Chrysler Building, the underground electrical systems in Shanghai and Barcelona, and the Boulder Dam.[13]

Described as "petite, young and dynamic," Kellems was celebrated as a leading woman in industry by the New York Soroptomists and the National Association of Manufacturers (NAM). In 1941 *Nation's Business* reported that "her success in a man's field" had not "decreased her femininity, as witness her selection by the Fashion Academy as one of the 13 best-dressed women in public life." Such notoriety was no accident. From 1939 to 1944, Kellems employed a personal publicity representative.[14]

With the country's entrance into World War II, Kellems grips were used by the Army and in naval shipyards, and Kellems herself became a defense contractor.[15] Her wartime role was not limited to businesswoman. In 1942 Kellems began a series of unsuccessful bids for political office, losing the Republican nomination for her Connecticut congressional district to Clare Boothe Luce.[16] (During the contest, unkind words were exchanged. "Everybody talks of Clare Boothe's sex appeal," Kellems said. "I would be very mad if anyone said I was using sex appeal." Luce responded, "What's the matter with that wild-eyed little woman, anyway?"[17]) Kellems's lack of electoral success continued as she campaigned for the U.S. Senate in 1950, 1956, and 1962 and for governor of Connecticut in 1954.[18]

Kellems was probably the most visible opponent of federal income taxes during World War II and into the early 1950s. During the war Treasury Secretary Henry Morgenthau, Jr., singled her out as uniquely opposed to tax compliance during the war.[19] Her protest against withholding in the 1940s received widespread media attention. She returned to the spotlight in the 1970s, testifying with actress Gloria Swanson and others before the House Ways and Means Committee and heightening her story of unfairness by forming an association for single women who might have married men killed during the war.[20]

For such efforts she won the attention of prominent historians. Clinton Rossiter called her the "Diana" of the ultraconservative camp; Willard Hurst treated this "very determined, stubborn woman industrialist" as the epitome of single-issue civil disobedience in his lectures on American legal history in 1978. Her memory lingers among libertarians and other conservatives, such as Murray Rothbard, who described her campaign against withholding in *For a New Liberty: The Libertarian Manifesto*.[21]

THE POLITICS OF SACRIFICE AND POSTWAR RESERVES

As Randolph Paul, General Counsel of the Treasury put it in a 1942 speech, entitled "Federal Taxation in Total War":

> Change—with its long arm, its disturbing touch, its decree of events not yet manifest—has come to all the "folkways" of taxation. Tax issues are now stated in novel ways; concepts dominant have exchanged places with concepts recessive; new relationships and shifts of base are born of every economic event. Everything we do is brimful of consequences. We are writing a significant chapter in tax history.[22]

During the World War II years, to pay for the war, the income tax was converted from a class tax to a mass tax. From 1918 through the 1930s, a very small percentage of Americans was covered by taxable returns. The portion of the total population covered on taxable returns reached an all-time high of 11.4 percent in 1920, but it fell to an average of 3.7 percent during the 1930s. By the end of World War II, however, 90 percent of the labor force filed income tax returns and 60 percent of workers paid income taxes.[23]

The transformations that World War II wrought in the federal tax system were promoted in a massive government public relations effort. Taxpayers were portrayed as willing and sometimes enthusiastic contributors to the war effort. In radio spots and programs, in movies, and in a Treasury-commissioned song by Irving Berlin, the government sought to promote an image of tax payment as public-spirited participation in the war.[24] Berlin's

1941 song "I Paid My Income Tax Today" expressed the government's notion of a patriotic spirit:

I said to my Uncle Sam
"Old Man Taxes here I am"
And he—was glad to see me
Lower brackets that's my speed
Mr. Small Fry yes indeed
But gee—I'm proud as can be.

I paid my income tax today
I'm only one of millions more
Whose income was never taxed before
A tax I'm very glad to pay
I'm squared up with the U.S.A.
You see those bombers in the sky
Rockefeller helped to build them, so did I
I paid my income tax today.[25]

The reality of taxpaying and the degree of sacrifice it would entail were often more complicated than such messages conveyed. For example, the Roosevelt administration failed to convince Congress of the need for higher levels of taxation during the last years of the war. Roosevelt vetoed what became the Revenue Act of 1943, calling the bill "relief not for the needy but for the greedy." Yet Congress overrode his veto.[26]

Tension clearly existed in wartime notions of appropriate levels of taxation, not only among policy-makers in Washington, but also among the public at large. As Treasury Secretary Morgenthau observed in a meeting with his aides, "After all, this is the one place I suppose, where the United States Government hits more people face to face than any other front. It is a question of domestic morale." Sometimes Morgenthau feared the public's reactions. When changes in the law in 1943 resulted in a form that took an assistant treasury secretary and two others two-and-one-half hours to complete, Morgenthau feared disaster, especially because he believed that the public was already in "a state of irritation. . . . They have open wounds; they are sore; they are mad."[27]

Vivien Kellems's very public refusal to pay her taxes during World War II throws light upon the government effort to convert the federal income tax into a mass tax. The government made extensive use of the media in selling the income tax to millions of new taxpayers. Kellems, too, was versed in public relations. The attention paid Kellems suggests both her media savvy and the government's sense of a certain vulnerability, its fear of incipient volatility in the public's attitude toward taxation.

In a speech before the Kansas City, Missouri, Women's Chamber of Commerce on January 18, 1944, Vivien Kellems announced that she would not pay the December 15, 1943, installment of her income tax. Calling the tax a violation of the Fourth Amendment's protection against unreasonable seizure and of the Fifth Amendment's due process provisions, Kellems urged businesses "both big and small to follow my example and put aside postwar reserves out of their taxes."[28]

Morgenthau issued a press release the next day. While not referring to Kellems by name, the press certainly made the connection to her defiant speech. Morgenthau stated:

> Most Americans are proud to pay their taxes to help win the war. The Treasury, which deals with millions and millions of taxpayers, has constant evidence of this patriotic spirit. . . .
>
> Anyone or everyone has a right to advocate changes in the law by due legislative process. However, to advise citizens to refuse to pay taxes—particularly in time of war—smacks of disloyalty. Such an attitude is especially unworthy of persons profiting from war contracts.[29]

Morgenthau's depiction of Kellems as a person "profiting from war contracts" pointed to a darker image of defense contractors. As in World War I, Congress enacted additional taxes on excess profits, in part to prevent industrialists from profiting from the sacrifices of others. Randolph Paul, in a 1942 speech before the National Lawyers Guild, argued that "[e]xcess profits taxes also have important implication for morale. Like individual income taxes, they are vital in promoting the feeling that comparable sacrifices—at least financially—are being imposed on all alike—civilians as well as soldiers."[30] In calling for sacrifices from labor and industry, the government wanted to show that all citizens contributed to the war effort. A war contractor's refusal to pay either income or excess profits taxes was, from the government's perspective, an egregious offense.[31]

The next day Kellems fired back. She agreed that patriotic American citizens ("of which I am one, Mr. Morgenthau's insulting slur to the contrary") were "eager to pay taxes to win the war." Kellems went on: "But those same millions . . . are not willing to pay taxes so that billions of dollars may be squandered on plain and fancy boondoggling not remotely connected with the war." Kellems offered to testify "before the proper Congressional committee."

> I still think it is a patriotic act for business to set aside a postwar reserve; in other words to put money in the bank so that it may continue to have jobs for its employees when this war is over. When I get enough money that is what I propose to do, Mr. Morgenthau, and if that be treason, make the most of it.[32]

Shortly after this exchange, Drew Pearson's radio show featured correspondence between Kellems and Count Friedrich von Zedlitz, a German national living in South America who was said to be a Nazi propaganda agent and was on the State Department's blacklist as an agent of

Metallgesellschaft. In her letters, Kellems called Zedlitz "my darling boy" and told him, "I love you dearly." Comments in government reports suggested that Kellems and Zedlitz were engaged. Soon after the Morgenthau-Kellems skirmish, Elmer Irey, the revenue agent credited with putting Al Capone in prison, instructed Treasury agents to review the State Department's files on Kellems and Zedlitz. Irey passed the information thus obtained to Morgenthau's deputy.[33]

At a January 27, 1944, meeting of Randolph Paul, Secretary Morgenthau, his secretary Mrs. Klotz, and a Mr. Smith (in all likelihood, Fred Smith, the Treasury Department's public relations advisor), Kellems became the topic of conversation:

Mr. Paul: Drew Pearson handed me a story this morning. He drove me down. It was a complete story about Kellems taken from the Censorship.

Mr. Smith: I think she is just nuts.

Mrs. Klotz: They caught her. They have the letters.

H. M. Jr.: This woman that goes and talks with her somewhere says she has a perfectly gorgeous ring with a South American stone that she wears. Somebody was out with her. She had on this new fur coat. She was asked about why she put her money into that. She said, "I am not going to put it into bonds."

Mrs. Klotz: They have the goods on her about her engagement.

H. M. Jr.: To this Argentinian? It is wonderful.

Mr. Paul: Public enemy number one.[34]

In April, Democratic Congressman John Coffee of Washington urged the Department of Justice to investigate Kellems, whom he accused of treasonable and seditious conduct, in part because of the Zedlitz correspondence, which he read on the floor of the House. According to Coffee:

Miss Kellems poses as a patriotic citizen and yet has consistently played the Nazi game. She is today giving aid and comfort to the enemy and is a tool of the Goebbels propaganda machine.

This woman, who is in constant contact with our hated Nazi enemies, this woman, the lover of a fifth-column Hitler spy in Argentina, admits . . . that right now in Connecticut she is engaged in work for the armed forces of a highly restricted and confidential nature.[35]

For the remainder of 1944, Republican Senator Clyde Reed of Kansas, ranking member of the Post Office and Post Roads Committee, launched inquiries into the leak of Kellems's letters to the press and to Representative Coffee. Senator Reed admitted Kellems "may have been silly in some of this correspondence . . . fond, foolish women frequently are, but that is no reason to violate her constitutional rights." Pearson claimed he got the letters "in Shangri-La" and characterized Kellems as naive. Morgenthau continued to receive reports as Kellems paid off her 1943 income tax liability. The subcommittee hearings were inconclusive.[36]

Before the year was out, Kellems had filed a libel suit against the California Congress of Industrial Organization (CIO) Council and the *Labor Herald*, the Council's newspaper, for stating that she had "engaged in treasonable operations" in her correspondence with Zedlitz and her Kansas City speech. The newspaper made the charge as part of its attack on her brother Randolph ("a rabid reactionary," in the opinion of the CIO Council's lawyer), who ran for Congress in the fall of 1944.[37] At a deposition on March 5, 1946, the CIO lawyer asked Morgenthau what effect he believed "those statements and actions of Miss Kellems" had had on the war effort. The by-then former Treasury Secretary answered, "Well, I felt her statements might be extremely harmful." Of Kellems's Kansas City speech, he said, "[A]s far as I know, I think Miss Kellems's attitude on the payment of taxes—as far as I can remember she was the only person of all the taxpayers . . . that felt that way."[38]

Kellems's libel suit was dismissed in 1946 by U.S. District Judge Louis Goodman. The opinion soon came to the issue of free speech in a time of total war. Goodman drew a connection between speech rights and the responsibility of citizens:

> The evidence discloses plaintiff to be a highly placed woman industrialist enjoying during the war profitable government contracts of a highly confidential nature. She took to the public platform to proclaim her grievances against the government and officers of the government. Moreover she undertook in so doing to mold and shape public opinion, all undeniably proper and lawful activities. But when, in time of grave national peril, she directly urged and invited citizens to refrain from paying taxes payable pursuant to duly enacted statutes and necessary in the prosecution of the war, in my opinion, it was within the area of fair comment to characterize her activities as "treasonable." Those who in public utterances seek to formulate and direct public opinion, have an accompanying responsibility. Particularly this is so at a time when millions of our young men and women were offering life and limb in national defense.

Goodman's opinion then became more personal:

> The court observed the plaintiff's demeanor and attitude upon the witness stand. I found her to be evasive, argumentative, arrogant and indeed brazen in her reiteration of her claimed right to do and say as she pleased, without regard to the possible dire consequence to her country and her fellow citizens. True, these considerations are not legally controlling in the resolution of the issue here presented. But at least they go to the weight of the evidence and serve to throw light upon the spirit and intent backgrounding the utterances and activities referred to in the alleged defamatory publications.[39]

The same insistence on asserting her own notion of the goals for which Americans could be asked to sacrifice was evident throughout Kellems's first episode of tax resistance. The Treasury's public relations campaign closely tied the payment of taxes to victory over Germany and Japan. In the Disney animated film, *The New Spirit* (1942), for example, Donald Duck drives from Hollywood to Washington in his enthusiasm to pay taxes. Stacks of tax revenues are transmuted into guns, planes, and ships. At the film's end, as an American flag is formed by clouds around a setting sun, the narrator intones, "Taxes will keep democracy on the march." Similarly, in the pamphlet *Battle Stations for All* (1943), the Office of War Information sought to rebut allegations that higher taxes were advancing New Deal programs. A box set off from the rest of the page, headlined "Non-War Expenditures Reduced," asserted that "ninety-six cents of every dollar spent by the Government will be for war costs and interest on the public debt and only four cents for so-called 'non-war' purposes."[40]

Kellems responded to such arguments in two ways. First, she claimed that tax revenues were going not to the conduct of total war but to what she called "boondoggling." She told a women's luncheon club in Philadelphia that "our forefathers did not intend that a little group of Communists in the White House should pick our pockets and throw everything we've got into the bottomless pit of relief and support the whole world." In other words, tax sacrifices were not for winning the war and defending "American" values but for promoting the Communism of government personnel and programs.[41]

Second, Kellems argued that wartime objectives ought to include provision for an economically prosperous postwar environment, one in which businesspeople would have more control over economic decision-making than the Roosevelt administration envisioned. As Alan Brinkley has written, "nothing inspired more fear during the war years than the specter of a peacetime economic collapse and a return to the high levels of unemployment that had been the most troubling and intractable problems of the 1930s." Some in the Roosevelt administration proposed using fiscal policies, including progressive taxation, to stimulate postwar economic growth.[42] Kellems advocated a different approach.

In a September 1943 speech to the Chicago Rotary Club, Kellems urged the passage of legislation to allow businesses to "put aside seed money" tax free. "If we plunge into a depression after this war, the rest of the world will follow us right down into the Slough of Despond." She then set forth her "simple," four-point program:

1. Repeal the Capital Gains Tax.
2. Permit Business to Build Up Tax-free Postwar Reserves.
3. Repeal the Idiotic Capital Stock Tax.
4. Allow private citizens to deduct the income tax for the previous year in figuring their net income for the current year.

"If this simple program is followed," Kellems claimed, "you will see a post-war boom in this country beyond our fondest dreams."[43]

In early 1942, the Treasury Department had recommended a tax with a postwar rebate to provide revenue for the conduct of the war and funds to smooth reconversion to a peacetime economy. Secretary Morgenthau suggested that any corporate taxes in excess of 80 percent be refunded after the war for the purchase of equipment or the employment of more workers. In 1943 Morgenthau again proposed forced corporate lending to the government with funds to be returned after the war for reconverting corporations. In her Kansas City speech, Kellems advocated that business put money "in the bank." That approach would, however, have deprived the government of revenues in wartime, a significant distinction. After Morgenthau's rebuke, Kellems urged that the "reserves . . . should be put into war bonds," a more patriotic reservoir.

As for her own situation, Kellems repeated that she did not have the money to pay her taxes because she had sunk her profits into new materials and equipment. "They can't get blood out of a turnip." Kellems's brother and business partner, David, rather more circumspectly said that "those having the necessary money available should pay their taxes promptly."[44]

Kellems's argument about postwar reserves also implicated fears about collectivism and government planning that emerged in the 1930s and extended into the war years. Donaldson Brown of General Motors was concerned that the "public has not come to distinguish between the necessity of centralized planning and regimentation in time of war, and the exercise of corresponding functions on the part of the government in time of peace."[45] If the government collected taxes for postwar reconversion, it would have a greater voice in the terms and conditions of the postwar economy than if those same revenues were retained by the business community.

Apprehensions about central planning contributed to the surprising success of Friedrich A. Hayek's *Road to Serfdom* upon its American publication in September 1944. Condensed in the *Reader's Digest* and distributed by business groups, the book argued that planning, beyond the minimum needed to maintain competition, led to dictatorship. The 1944 edition had little explicit discussion of taxation, but its general argument would have implications for a conservative like Kellems. As Hayek explained in 1976:

> At the time I wrote, socialism meant unambiguously the nationalization of the means of production and the central economic planning which this made possible and necessary. . . . [S]ocialism has come to mean chiefly the extensive redistribution of incomes through taxation and the institutions of the welfare state. In the latter kind of socialism, the effects I discuss in this book are brought about more slowly, indirectly and imperfectly. I believe that the ultimate outcome tends to be very much the same although the process by which it is brought about is not quite the same as that described in this book.[46]

Although no evidence suggests that Hayek was a particular influence on Kellems, her wartime tax resistance was motivated by a similar fear of postwar planning and a consequent loss of liberty. The government responded not by refuting her on policy grounds; rather, it undermined her authority by placing her outside the community of sacrifice. By identifying her as a war profiteer and as a woman entangled in an affair with a Nazi, the government succeeded in undermining Kellems's credibility. While she portrayed herself as a businessperson, Morgenthau rushed to a less attractive characterization—that of a disloyal defense contractor.

WITHHOLDING TAX

At the beginning of the war, income tax was paid in quarterly installments in the year after liability for it was incurred. It was not collected currently at the source. As Randolph Paul explained, this practice was "poorly adapted to the budgets and flow of income of 44 million taxpayers." The Current Tax Payment Act of 1943 required that employers withhold taxes on wage and salary income and put the income tax on a current basis.[47]

In early 1948, Kellems launched what was probably her best-known antitax campaign. In a speech before the Los Angeles Rotary Club on February 13, she announced that she would no longer withhold federal income taxes from her employees' paychecks as required by law. On February 20, Kellems stopped withholding income taxes. Kellems's workers received a calculation of the amount of tax owed and purchased money orders to use in paying their taxes quarterly.[48]

For nearly two years thereafter, Kellems tried to goad Treasury Secretary John W. Snyder into indicting her.[49] The Treasury issued a statement in May 1948 that "[we] are proceeding to exercise all the resources at our command." That month the government attached her property for $1,685 in taxes due, penalties, and interest. Kellems then deducted that amount from her 1948 income tax with the defiant and, in her case, possibly ill-advised announcement to the Treasury: "If you wish that money you can sue me or you can again send your gestapo agent and grab it from the bank."[50]

In August 1949, the federal government seized $6,133 from Kellems for her noncompliance. Kellems sued the United States for these seizures in November 1949. Her claim was split. She and her brother David (a seldom mentioned plaintiff) were given a jury trial on their claim for $6,133 against John J. Fitzpatrick, the Internal Revenue Collector for Connecticut. The Kellemses' claim for $1,678.40, levied during the incumbency of Fitzpatrick's predecessor, was tried to Carroll C. Hincks, a U.S. district court judge.[51]

On a pretrial motion, Judge Hincks ruled that the Withholding Tax Act was constitutional. The jury trial, which turned on the willfulness of Kellems's refusal to withhold, ended with a verdict for Kellems and her brother, which Hincks refused to set aside.[52] With regard to the earlier levy for $1,685, however, the judge found against the Kellemses. Neither

Kellems nor the government were happy with the result, and although Vivien threatened to appeal, she never did.[53]

Kellems's protest illuminated a conservative constitutional critique of the federal income tax, its expansion during World War II, and the greater effectiveness it obtained as a result of withholding. As Alan Brinkley has noted, the American Right, in all of its diversity, has not received "anything like the amount of attention from historians that its role in twentieth-century politics and culture suggests it should." American conservatism was no monolith. One strand, an individualistic, antistatist classical liberalism, came to be called "libertarianism" after the appropriation of the term "liberal" by Rooseveltian reformers. Another, more normative strand was especially concerned for "moral traditions, universal values, and inherited social hierarchies." A third tended toward "a cultural and religious fundamentalism."[54] These tensions parallel a difficult philosophical conflict within contemporary conservatism, which George Will has identified as "the cultural contradiction of conservatism." "Conservatism depends on eliciting from citizens a public-spirited self-denial. But that is not easily elicited in a commercial republic of the sort conservatism celebrates, where individualism enjoys maximum scope for private pursuits."[55]

During the 1930s, advocacy for lower income taxes for the relatively wealthy few who paid them was not unusual. Some conservatives, particularly those in the business community, saw income taxation and the Sixteenth Amendment as central causes of an erosion of American society.[56] During the war, however, many conservatives suspended or dampened their public attacks on the Roosevelt administration and the income tax. The war period has been described by both scholars and conservatives as a low point of libertarian thought in the United States. As George H. Nash has written: "In 1945, no articulate, coordinated, self-consciously conservative intellectual force existed in the United States. There were, at most, scattered voices of protest, profoundly pessimistic about the future of their country."[57]

What distinguished Kellems from most of her fellow "ultraconservatives" was the broad-ranging, constitutional basis of her arguments.[58] Perhaps the libertarian closest to her views was Frank Chodorov. After working as a teacher, advertiser, clothing factory manager, and director of the Henry George School of Social Science, Chodorov established a conservative monthly, *Analysis*, and later edited *The Freeman*. He is best remembered for his essay "Taxation is Robbery" and for two books, *One is a Crowd* (1952) and *The Income Tax: Root of All Evil* (1954).[59]

Chodorov and Kellems continued and elaborated the arguments of the conservatives of the 1930s. Both viewed the enactment of the Sixteenth Amendment, permitting the imposition of the modern income tax, as a rupture of the original constitutional scheme. They saw the federal government's ability to levy an income tax as a threat to private property and, therefore, to freedom. Chodorov wrote in 1952:

The nature of sovereignty, however, is beyond doubt; it is the degree of coercion that the government exerts on the people; and this degree of coercion is in turn dependent on the amount of the nation's wealth the government has at its disposal. . . . Conversely, the immunity of the people is in proportion to the amount of their wealth they can keep out of the government's hands. It follows, then, that the Sixteenth Amendment, which gives the government a prior claim on all the production of the country, puts the government in the way of acquiring as much power as it is possible for a government to exercise; that is, under our revised Constitution it is possible for the government to attain absolutism.[60]

Kellems put the point in similarly strong terms: "In other words when we passed the Sixteenth Amendment we surrendered our RIGHT TO OWN SOMETHING. We took the first, big, requisite step into Communism." Marx and Engels, she noted, had advocated "progressive" income taxation as a way "to destroy the capitalistic system." Tax withholding was the "handmaiden of the graduated income tax," and it stemmed "from the same fountainhead—communist Russia." Kellems considered the original constitutional restrictions on federal taxation as vital. "There is only one freedom on the planet Earth," she declared, "freedom from unjust taxation or, as practiced by England in colonial times and by the gangster Truman Administration today, confiscation."[61]

Although Chodorov and Kellems tended to emphasize the Sixteenth Amendment's threat to individuals, they and other conservatives also feared its effect on the states. In his foreword to Chodorov's *Income Tax*, Utah governor J. Bracken Lee wrote that by putting its "hands into the pockets and pay envelopes of the people," the federal government "drew their allegiance away from their local governments," over which they had some control. With its new economic power, the federal government could "bribe" citizens and state governments "into submission to its will." The result, he concluded, was that "the whole spirit of the Union and its Constitution has been liquidated."[62]

Chodorov and Kellems agreed with Lee and similarly argued for the repeal of the Sixteenth Amendment or the income tax itself. As Chodorov declared (in bold type):

In name, it was a tax reform. In point of fact, it was a revolution.

For the Sixteenth Amendment corroded the American concept of natural rights; ultimately reduced the American citizen to the status of subject, so much so that he is not aware of it; enhanced Executive power to the point of reducing Congress to innocuity; and enabled the central government to bribe the states, once independent units, into subservience. No kingship in the history of the world ever exercised more power than our Presidency, or had more of the people's wealth at its disposal. We have retained the forms and phrases of a republic, but in reality we are living under an oligarchy, not of courtesans, but of bureaucrats.[63]

For her part, Kellems asserted that this dire situation was made worse with the enactment of withholding during the war. In *Toil, Taxes and Trouble*, Kellems wrote as if she had been a compliant taxpayer during the war:

It is an outrageous invasion of the Constitutional rights of the American people, but in common with other frantic citizens, I mistakenly believed that we were justified in suspending our constitutional rights and liberties in time of great emergency. . . . I also had boys, near and dear to me, fighting in our armed forces all over the world and would gladly have done anything and everything to shorten the war by as much as one day. At least this method would enable us to get money back from overpaid war workers with which to prosecute the war and bring our boys home.

Please note that I said "mistakenly." I have changed my mind. I don't believe that we should *ever* suspend our constitutional rights, no matter how great the crisis because I have become convinced that there is no national disaster or emergency, including a world-wide war, that cannot be handled *better* within the framework of our Constitution.[64]

Kellems saw that the government had used the war as an opportunity to alter the tax regime, a point that historians have subsequently made, if not in precisely the same words.[65] As Kellems put it:

The history of the last nineteen years consists of a series of "emergencies" which have been used to chip away at our Constitution, until the men who framed that immortal document would stand aghast at the wreckage which the New Dealers have made of it. This is particularly true of taxes. They are fastened down upon us in an emergency and there they remain forever.[66]

Kellems argued that requiring the withholding of federal income taxes from employees' paychecks constituted involuntary servitude for the employer. She turned to the courts to strike at the withholding tax and, with it, the federal income tax. "The test case is as American as a hot dog," she would later declare.[67] Yet she launched her litigation just after a turning point in American constitutional history had made her challenge quite unlikely to succeed. As Bruce Ackerman has written:

Since the epic struggle between Franklin Roosevelt and the Old Court, the judiciary has consistently upheld democratic efforts to take control of the economy in pursuit of social justice. Under the constitutional regime inaugurated by the New Deal, there are no significant limits on the national government's taxing, spending, and regulatory powers where the economy is concerned—other than the requirement that government compensate owners if their property is taken for public purposes.[68]

Not surprisingly, Kellems could find few supporters for her constitutional arguments, even among staunch conservatives.[69] A fellow "ultraconservative" like Chodorov might concur. Citing her experience, he wrote of tax withholding:

It is a form of conscription. Disregarding the right of privacy, which is an essential of liberty, the government's agents may, under the law, invade the employer's office, demand his accounts, and punish him for any infraction which they believe he has committed; they can impound his property and inflict a penalty for not having collected taxes for the government.[70]

But other conservatives would not go so far, to Kellems's evident frustration. Before the war the National Association of Manufacturers named her a leading woman in industry, but it refused to join her anti-withholding campaign. (Its treasurer and business manager explained that the alternative "would be even higher taxes on business and on higher individual incomes than is now the case.") Kellems fumed, "What hope is there when an organization such as the National Association of Manufacturers not only approves the withholding tax but refuses to let the matter be presented to its membership?"[71]

On at least one occasion, a prominent conservative took steps to avoid her. In April 1952, Robert M. Harriss wrote to Herbert Hoover of his plans to come to New York. "I would like to have the pleasure of seeing you, and if agreeable bringing Miss Vivien Kellems of Conn. with me." A note to his secretary, written on the letter, records Hoover's reply. "If he calls up," Hoover wrote, "tell him I would be glad to see him alone."[72]

Several conservatives were aware of Kellems's activities and, to a certain extent, approved of them but were not close collaborators. One might have expected her to have strategized with her fellow Connecticut resident Rose Wilder Lane, the daughter of Laura Ingalls Wilder and the source, recent scholarship suggests, of some of the conservative sentiments expressed in her mother's *Little House on the Prairie* books. (Lane's views may well be captured in a passage in *The Long Winter* (1940) describing a visit to the Ingalls family of a sympathetic character in flight from his tax obligations.) Lane herself avoided taxation by reducing her income below taxable levels, relying upon herself for her goods and services as much as possible, and refusing to become part of the Social Security system.[73]

Yet when, in the mid-1950s, Lane discussed Kellems with Jasper Crane, a Du Pont executive and a member of the conservative Mount Pelerin Society, she could claim no close relations with the industrialist. Crane had asked, "Do you know whether Vivian [*sic*] Kellems is still refusing to withhold taxes from her employees?" Lane replied, "I met her only once. . . . She is not a thinker at all; she is executive *acting*, vigorous, fearless, honest, a fine person." In September 1956, Lane wrote that she intended to vote for Kellems in a coming election. "I agree with you, of course, that these movements 'won't get very far' (at least not soon)." She "is, and represents, nothing that I *stand* for; in my opinion she expresses only an emotion which I feel, not a principle or a policy."[74]

THE JOINT RETURN

The joint return was a statutory solution to a problem that became obvious during the war. Before 1948 the modern federal income tax was assessed essentially on an individual basis. The progressive rate structure of the income tax meant that a couple would pay the least tax if their income was divided equally between them. With the implementation of a mass income tax and, in particular, the use of marginal rates exceeding 90 percent, taxpayers had great incentives to find ways to split their incomes.[75] One popular and visible technique was the holding of property in joint tenancy, which increased markedly in the 1940s. Another was the adoption of "community property" regimes, which five states and the territory of Hawaii instituted after 1939. A third was the creation of family partnerships, which accounted for much of the almost doubling of partnership returns between 1940 and 1945, notwithstanding the skepticism with which the Bureau of Internal Revenue viewed those submitted by husbands and wives.[76]

In 1948 the joint return was adopted to remedy the "inequality" caused by tax treatment of community property and by the Bureau's hostility to family partnerships. By combining a husband and wife's incomes, dividing the total in half and doubling the tax on half, the joint return provided tax reduction for most married couples. If a husband, for example, were the sole wage earner, the return resulted in exposure to lower marginal rates.

The joint return stopped the "stampede" to community property and curtailed the rush to family partnerships. "Wives need not continue to master the details of the retail drug business, electrical equipment business, or construction business," the tax professor and former Treasury official Stanley Surrey declared, "but may turn from their partnership 'duties' to the pursuit of homemaking."[77] Henceforth income-splitting for tax purposes depended on marital status and not some legal right in a spouse to income or property.

This is where Vivien Kellems came in. In 1952 Kellems had noted that the tax reduction made possible by the joint return was not available to single taxpayers, but she did not make this disparity the basis for a refusal to pay her federal income tax until 1969.[78] In the early 1970s she campaigned to change the law in the courts and in Congress, where she testified with Gloria Swanson and others before the House Ways and Means Committee. Kellems heightened her story of unfairness by forming the "War Widows of America," a group for single women who might have married men killed during the war. She was still resisting at her death on January 25, 1975. Her estate ultimately paid her tax arrearage.[79]

While either single men or single women could be relatively disadvantaged by the joint return, Kellems stressed its unfairness to single women. She stated her criticism in terms of her long-standing views on gender. In one of the articles that first brought her to the attention of the public, Kellems complained that "[e]ven in the United States where they have more advantages than any other place on the globe, women are still denied equal rights." She continued, "I agree that a woman's place is in the home. I have a nice home and I love it. But is there any reason why a woman isn't a woman because she is in business? Business men have homes and love them, don't they?" In 1951 it was said that one of her fundamental tenets was "that the female sex is forever being done out of its rightful deserts by underhanded male machinations." Such views made her a supporter of the Equal Rights Amendment in the 1940s and a critic of so-called protective legislation for working women.[80]

Although Kellems also protested a Connecticut ban on night work by women after the war, her most notorious opposition to protective legislation involved her use of female "homeworkers" to produce smaller grips for wartime use by the Signal Corps.[81] At first Kellems spoke of grip weaving as men's work. The *Saturday Evening Post* reported in April 1942:

> Every now and then she steps in and weaves a grip herself, just to keep her hand in. But weaving grips takes muscle and, ironically, for a feminist who believes that more women should be doing men's work, Miss Kellems employs men only. There are twenty-five all told, and she pays them on a piecework basis.[82]

By June 1943, however, Kellems had begun to tap into the supply of mothers who worked at home. In that month a feature article in *Better Homes and Gardens*, "Yankee Kitchens Go On the Production Line," reported on her plans to hire a thousand women to meet her new contracts, with a preference for those who worked in the home. The editors wrote approvingly:

> *Better Homes and Gardens* believes that no mother of children under 14 should be asked to work outside her home until all other sources of labor have been exhausted. . . . *However, there is a way, which Better Homes and Gardens endorses and applauds, for a woman to get into direct war production without leaving home*. . . . Here is the plan in action.[83]

The article presented the testimony of several women who wove grips by hand at their kitchen tables for four cents per finished grip. Some had sick husbands; all had children at home. Weaving grips was no longer a masculine activity; rather, the woman grip weaver "puts into it the same individual care that she would into sewing a dress for one of her children or making a pie."[84] The article portrayed homework as less noisy and distracting than factory work and less likely to result in juvenile delinquency—a growing problem in "industrial centers where women leave home a full working day and their children roam the streets." ("If a woman is in a factory," the article claimed, "she can't get home till supper time and her children run wild.")[85]

The National Consumers' League protested that Kellems's use of homeworkers violated the 1936 Walsh-Healey Public Contracts Act and may have run afoul of regulations under the Fair Labor Standards Act of 1938.[86] In Connecticut, however, the state commissioner of labor allowed violations of the homework law, and Kellems herself claimed to have had the permission of the governor (although this was disputed).[87]

Kellems responded to her critics with appeals to patriotism and to traditional notions of motherhood. "Isn't it thrilling that a mother rivets the wings of an airplane on which her son may fly to victory," she asked, "but isn't it tragic that while mothers are riveting airplanes our juvenile delinquency has assumed alarming proportions?" "Ardent feminist that I am, I have always maintained that a woman's first job is in her home." Moreover, homework would ease the reconversion process. "[T]he woman has never left her home therefore she does not have to return to it. She has never taken some man's job who naturally wants it back when he returns from the war."[88] As a member of Connecticut's consumer's league, an anti-homework group, marveled, "It is amazing how 'patriotism' is interpreted in cases like this."[89]

Kellems defended homework in terms of the equal freedom of men and women to enter into contracts of their own choosing and the need to recognize of women's distinctive social role. To opponents of the Equal Rights Amendment, she was living proof that the ERA's supporters were "wealthy women and professional women, probably financed by the National Association of Manufacturers, who cared not a whit for the well-being of working women who desperately needed the protection of social legislation to allow them to compete in the labor market."[90] Yet Kellems's reference to the maternal obligations of female workers showed that she did not balk at arguing that public policy should respect natural differences between men and women.

One natural difference Kellems often invoked was women's superior skills or moral attributes. These, she claimed, made them the special guardians of American constitutional values.[91] In 1942 the *Saturday Evening Post* said that Kellems ("the most energetic feminist since Lucy Stone") was "always carping at masculine ways of getting things done."[92] Men were too willing to bargain away their rights. As she scolded the Economic Club of Detroit in 1948:

> How much longer are we going to take it? Is there no more good, old-fashioned American courage, or have we become a nation of spineless jellyfish? . . . We have fought and won a global war to free the whole world and have succeeded only in bringing chaos and misery to that world and making tax slaves of ourselves.
>
> So let's repeal the income tax. You think it can't be done? If we left it to you men, it couldn't. But I'll tell you what's going to happen. We women are going to repeal it. We got you out of that prohibition mess, didn't we? Well, we'll dig you out of this

one. But I want to remind you that we didn't vote for either one—they were exclusively your ideas. . . .

Because we women are just about fed up with all this nonsense, so-called socialized medicine, federal aid to education and all the rest of this paternalistic claptrap, designed to make us incompetent dependents upon the Government. All we want is for the Government to give back to the American people the money which is rightfully theirs, the money for which they work and which they earn, and we'll pay our own doctor's bills, we'll educate our children, and we'll once more become self-respecting, self-reliant citizens.[93]

Yet even in claiming that women held their moral convictions more strongly than did men, Kellems spoke of the *content* of those convictions in terms that did not distinguish between men and women. Both aspired to be "self-respecting, self-reliant citizens." A similar appeal to universal standards dominated her attack on the tax system's differential treatment of single and married persons.

The Tax Reform Act of 1969 limited the "singles penalty" to no more than 120 percent of what a married taxpayer filing jointly would have paid on the same income. Before the 1969 act, a single taxpayer could have paid as much as 42 percent more federal income tax on the same income when compared to a married taxpayer. Kellems, among others, felt that the 1969 reform did not go far enough, and she continued to press the issue in the early 1970s.[94]

Kellems argued that because single women outnumbered single men, the tax law's treatment of singles discriminated against women. The treatment was, further, an unreasonable and unconstitutional one. Testifying before the House Ways and Means Committee in 1973, Kellems argued that "the single people of this country have continued to pay at World War II rates until 1964." By forming War Widows of America, Kellems underlined the demographic disparity between men and women, and, as she saw it, the injustice of lowered tax rates for married couples.[95]

Until the 1960s relatively few Americans would have felt the force of her argument from their own experiences. The joint return was adopted in 1948, coincident with a postwar boom in marriage and family size. Over 96 percent of the women and about 94 percent of the men who came of age during World War II married, and they did so at earlier ages than previously.[96]

Starting in 1960, however, marriage and birthrates declined, and the divorce rate rose, at first gradually and then markedly by the end of the decade. As single adults became more numerous, Kellems gained a constituency for her views. She even appealed to the new sexual mores with a novel constitutional argument. "Justice William J. Brennan declared that under the right to privacy concerning birth control, it is a violation if you deny birth control information to single people," Kellems observed. "Now it would seem to me in view of that decision . . . certainly single people cannot be taxed for a situation which they cannot help."[97]

Constitutional arguments dominated her testimony before the House Ways and Means Committee in 1972 and 1973, but Kellems had not lost the old impulse to civil disobedience. Since 1969, she had refused to pay a portion of her taxes that she claimed corresponded to the amount above that which she would have paid as a married woman.[98] She urged other single women to do the same and provided them with a chart showing the tax penalty for being single.[99] She also appealed to one of the oldest and most celebrated acts of civil disobedience in American history. She urged her correspondents to write their Congressmen and to *"ENCLOSE A USED, DRIED TEA BAG OR SOME COFFEE GROUNDS IN YOUR LETTER."* ("Do not use new tea," she counseled. "There is no reason why we should make the tea companies rich—they haven't contributed one penny to our campaign. A local restaurant will save their tea bags for you.")[100]

One way or another, as Michael Graetz has written, "Ms. Swanson and Ms. Kellems were an effective team protesting the unfairness of income taxes on single persons." In 1969 Congress lowered the rate of tax on single taxpayers, although not without creating the marriage penalty, which continues to plague the federal income tax to this day.[101]

CONCLUSION AND EPILOGUE

World War II changed the folkways of taxation. By making the income tax a mass tax, the architects of wartime finance set in place a regime that has lasted for decades. Kellems's story shows that these changed "folkways" were not uncontested. She spent her career fighting each of the major structural features adopted during the war or its immediate aftermath.

The most obvious aspect of her tax resistance was its lack of success. In part, Kellems failed because her attacks were too narrowly based in her own experiences to persuade others of her case against the new tax regime. Tax resistance by a wealthy war contractor could not withstand the constant, comparative scrutiny of the politics of sacrifice—and probably would not have even if the war contractor in question had not been romantically linked to a German count. "In many ways, I suppose you might say that the letters business ruined my life," Kellems admitted to a journalist in 1951. Although she bravely protested that "the sacrifice will not be important if I am successful in my purpose of turning the Communists out of powerful places in my country and persuading Congress to pass some sensible tax laws," her contemporaries remained unimpressed. "She's got a kind of superwoman complex," a neighbor told the journalist. "Didn't want to pay her taxes during the war, you know. Stands out against the law of the land now and was mixed up with some blacklisted German a few years ago, too. . . . I tell you, she's a dangerous woman."[102]

Even so, Kellems might have had a greater impact had she joined the networks of conservative intellectuals developing around her. Surely the potential for collaboration existed in her critique of the New Deal, which was broadly consistent with the anti-planning themes of Hayek's *Road to Serfdom*. Yet she maintained an isolated posture and was kept at a distance even by her fellow industrialists in the NAM.

But if Kellems's career illustrates the failure of opposition to the tax regime established during World War II, it also reveals weaknesses in that regime that have continued to trouble policy-makers. Her constitutional arguments against withholding may not have garnered broad support, but her subsidiary point about costs of compliance continues to be raised by reformers and scholars.[103] And she lived to see some of her arguments for equal treatment of single and married taxpayers successfully taken up by proponents of a change in the tax law.

About a year before her death, Kellems described herself in a letter to Barbara Walters at NBC-TV. "I am 77 years old and known chiefly as that crackpot old woman who knows nothing but taxes although the Wall Street Journal recently promoted me from crackpot to respectability."[104] Kellems may have persuaded few people with her autobiographical references, but her career of tax resistance effectively raised conundrums that plague taxpayers and politicians to this day. As notions of public sacrifice have altered and the external threat of war has receded, dissatisfaction with our income tax system has grown.[105] When the folkways of taxation change again, "crackpots" like Vivien Kellems might well win recognition for their protests, if not quite respectability.

NOTES

1. Kellems, *Toil, Taxes*, 63–64.

2. See Leff, "Politics of Sacrifice," 1296, 1301; Blum, *V Was for Victory*; Brinkley, *Washington Goes to War*. Historian Mark Leff has traced the politics of sacrifice in two case studies: Roosevelt's unsuccessful executive order capping wartime salaries and the successful coordination of wartime propaganda by the War Advertising Council. The salary cap was seen by some as contrary to American values. Leff described the negative response: "Labeling it a product of communistic philosophy and class hatred, attackers called it an un-American assault on free enterprise that threatened the production necessary for an effective war effort." Leff, "Politics of Sacrifice," 1299. The advertisers were able to appear patriotic through public service messages that maintained brand loyalty and visibility. The goodwill generated through wartime advertising would result in postwar sales. This happy coincidence of self-interest and sacrifice provided a means of avoiding a fundamental clash of values.

3. Leff, "Politics of Sacrifice," 1296–97. For example, in March 1944, Gallup's American Institute of Public Opinion notified Morgenthau "confidentially in advance" of a recent poll indicating that 90 percent of respondents felt the amount of taxes they had to pay was "justified and fair." William A. Lydgate to Secretary Morgenthau, March 10, 1944, Henry Morgenthau, Jr., Diaries, 710:22, Franklin D. Roosevelt Library, Hyde Park, N.Y. (hereafter Morgenthau Diaries). A few days later Fred Smith submitted a proposed senatorial speech celebrating the polling

results to Morgenthau. Fred Smith to Secretary Morgenthau, March 18, 1944, Morgenthau Diaries, 711:237; Speech for Senator Draft #2, March 18, 1944, Morgenthau Diaries, 711:238–44. Smith also indicated that when George Gallup returned from out of town, "we will try to get a statement out of him to send overseas, pointing out that polls show the American public to be more than willing to make any sacrifice for the war." Fred Smith to Secretary Morgenthau, March 18, 1944, Morgenthau Diaries, 711:235.

4. U.S. Bureau of the Census, *Historical Statistics*, 1123–24.

5. Brownlee, *Federal Taxation in America*, 1996.

6. Andy Logan, "Profiles: Grips and Taxes II," *New Yorker* 26 (February 10, 1951): 39.

7. "Will Not Pay Tax, Miss Kellems Says," *New York Times*, January 19, 1944, p. 38, col. 2.

8. *Kellems v. United States*, 97 F. Supp. 681, 683 (1951).

9. Bernhard Knollenberg to Henry Morgenthau, Jr., December 9, 1941, with attached article, Morgenthau Diaries, 472:296–303; Kellems, *Toil, Taxes*, 78–79; *New York Times*, April 15, 1969; *New York Times*, March 17, 1971.

10. "Vivien Kellems, Foe of Tax System, Dies," *New York Times*, January 26, 1975, p. 49, col. 1; Logan, "Grips and Taxes II," 43.

11. Logan, "Grips and Taxes II," 43. Actress Gloria Swanson referred to this brief marriage in her tribute to Kellems. Gloria Swanson, "Unforgettable Vivien Kellems," *Reader's Digest* 107 (July 1975): 144. Kellems described meeting Swanson during the March 5, 1950, broadcast of "Today with Mrs. Roosevelt."

> I was speaking on taxes and Gloria was talking about taxes on actresses and she advocated that as actresses grew older they should be permitted depreciation or a depreciation allowance as actresses. Their income and chances of employment are less as they grow older. In Gloria's case, it doesn't apply. You can take one look at her. She is playing a 40-year-old woman on Broadway, but Gloria had a valid point.

House Committee on Ways and Means, *Tax Treatment of Single Persons and Married Persons Where Both Spouses are Working*, 92d Cong., 2d sess., 1972.

12. Logan, "Grips and Taxes II," 43, 44; Kellems, *Toil, Taxes*, 12. In an introduction to Kellems's book, Rupert Hughes wrote:

> In Columbia, Miss Kellems specialized in taxation, of all subjects for a girl! Her special teacher was Dr. Edwin R. A. Seligman, a world-authority on public finance. She studied also labor problems under Professor Seager, and Marxian socialism under Professor Simkovitch, but she found strange fascination in the dreadful field of taxation.

Gloria Swanson claimed that Kellems returned to school at the age of seventy-one to pursue a doctorate in economics at the University of Edinburgh. "The subject of her thesis: the 16th (Income Tax) Amendment to the U.S. Constitution and its impact on our society." Swanson, "Unforgettable Vivien Kellems," 144, 148, 150.

The intellectual origins of Kellems's views on taxation remain unclear. Kellems herself slighted her interest in formal economics in an interview with the *Los Angeles Times* in 1969. "[S]he made her way through her BA and MA in Columbia in economics 'for no reason at all except I was crazy about the teacher.' " Maggie Savoy, "Single Woman has Proposal for Overtaxed," *Los Angeles Times*, December 14, 1969, p. F16.

13. Joseph M. Weresch, "A Girl with a Grip of Steel," *Nation's Business* 29 (August 1941): 44–56; Logan, "Grips and Taxes II," 47.

14. "On the Cover—Vivien Kellems," *Independent Woman*, March 19, 1940; "Wirepuller," *American Magazine* 130 (August 1940): 79; Weresch, "Girl with a Grip," 56; Andy Logan, "Grips and Taxes I," *New Yorker* 26 (3 February 1951): 42. Soroptimist International was a service organization of executive women in business and the professions. Rupp and Taylor, *Survival in the Doldrums*, 48.

15. Logan, "Grips and Taxes II," 47.

16. "Vivien Kellems, Foe of Tax System, Dies," *New York Times*, January 26, 1975, p. 49, col. 1. Jeffries, *Testing the Roosevelt Coalition*, 119–20.

17. "The Women," *Newsweek* 20 (August 31, 1942): 31.

18. "Vivien Kellems, Foe." Kellems was a candidate for the U.S. Senate in 1950 on the "Independence Party" ticket. The same ticket included the socialist mayor of Bridgeport as the gubernatorial candidate. The ticket failed to qualify for a place on the ballot. "Accepts the Nomination," *New York Times*, August 4, 1950, p. 18; "Miss Kellems Out of Race," *New York Times*, September 27, 1950, p. 35, col. 2.

19. "Deposition of Henry Morgenthau taken by and on behalf of the defendants," March 5, 1946, *Kellems v. Labor Herald*, Box 795, Henry Morgenthau, Jr., Papers, Franklin D. Roosevelt Library, Hyde Park, N.Y.

20. House Committee on Ways and Means, *Tax Treatment of Single Persons*, 4; House Committee on Ways and Means, *General Tax Reform*, 93d Cong., 1st sess., 1973; Graetz, *Decline (and Fall?) of the Income Tax*, 32.

21. Rossiter, *Conservatism in America*, 171; Hurst, *Modern American Legal History*, cassette 13, side 2; Rothbard, *For a New Liberty*, 85–86.

22. Address by Randolph Paul before Cornell University Law School, December 11, 1942, 20, Income Tax—Treasury, Treasury—WPB, General Records of Assistant Directors James Rogers and William Lewis, Records of the Office of War Information, RG 208, National Archives, College Park, Md.

23. Brownlee, "Tax Regimes," 93.

24. Jones, "Class Tax to Mass Tax," 685.

25. Irving Berlin, "I Paid My Income Tax Today," December 26, 1941, Morgenthau Diaries, 480:83.

26. Blum, ed., *From the Morgenthau Diaries*, 76. See Randolph Paul's recollections of his years in the Treasury Department, *Taxation in the United States*. Alan Brinkley has written:

> The erosion of congressional support for liberal measures did not, of course, occur in a vacuum. It reflected a broad growing popular impatience with the New Deal—and with the taxes, deficits, and expansion of bureaucracy that many voters associated with it. . . . Virtually nowhere on the political landscape were there vigorous grassroots movements of the sort so common in the mid-1930s, movements such as those led by (among many others) Upton Sinclair, Floyd Olson, Milo Reno, Robert La Follette and Huey Long, movements attacking concentrated wealth and corporate power and demanding increased social protections for ordinary people. The most energetic forces of popular dissidence during the war were, instead, various groups on the right expressing their hostility toward both communists and liberals and often with one another.

Brinkley, *End of Reform*, 142–43.

27. Taxes Meeting, March 10, 1943, Morgenthau Diaries, 615:145–46; Taxes Meeting, July 29, 1943, ibid., 652:193.

28. "Will Not Pay Tax, Miss Kellems Says," *New York Times*, January 19, 1944, p. 38, col. 2.

29. Treasury Department, Memo for Press, January 19, 1944, Press Releases, 40:595, Morgenthau Papers; "Rebuked for Call Not to Pay Taxes," *New York Times*, January 20, 1944, p. 21, col. 2.

30. Address by Randolph Paul before the National Lawyers Guild, September 26, 1942, 5, Income Tax—Treasury, Treasury—WPB, General Records of Assistant Directors James Rogers and William Lewis, RG 208.

31. Leff, "Politics of Sacrifice," 1299–1306. Newspaper accounts do not reveal whether Kellems took a stand on the excess profits (as opposed to the income) tax.

32. "Miss Kellems Defies Government to Act," *New York Times*, January 21, 1944, p. 13, col. 4.

33. "Miss Kellems Asks for Data on Letters," *New York Times*, April 5, 1944, p. 12, col. 5; Vivien Kellems to Sr. F. C. Zedlitz, April 14, 1942, Correspondence and Papers: 1933–45, Confidential Reports about People: 1944–45, Morgenthau Papers; "Kellems Letters Refused Senators," *New York Times*, June 11, 1944, p. 20, col. 4; Fred C. Pond to Mr. Irey, January 27, 1944, 3–4, Correspondence and Papers: 1933–45, Confidential Reports about People: 1944–45, Morgenthau Papers; Elmer Irey to Mr. Sullivan from Elmer Irey, January 27, 1944, ibid.

34. Meeting re Press Conference, 10:30 a.m., January 27, 1944, Morgenthau Diaries, 697:8. For Fred Smith's position, see Fred Smith to Secretary Morgenthau, May 3, 1943, ibid., 631:90.

35. Kathleen McLaughlin, "Urges U.S. Study of Vivien Kellems," *New York Times*, April 1, 1944, p. 16, col. 5.

36. The director of censorship refused to turn the Kellems-Zedlitz reports over to the Senate subcommittee until it subpoenaed him, citing an opinion of the Attorney General. "Reed to Ask Study of Kellems Case," *New York Times*, April 8, 1944, p. 15, col. 4; "Kellems Asks for Data" *New York Times*, April 5, 1944, p. 12, col. 5; Group Meeting, 9:30 a.m., May 1, 1944, Morgenthau Diaries, 726:14; Group Meeting, 3:15 p.m., July 24, 1944, ibid., 757:191; "Senators Get Copies of Kellems Letters," *New York Times*, June 13, 1944, p. 17, col. 3; "Kellems Letters Refused Senators," *New York Times*, June 11, 1944, p. 20, col. 4.

37. Herbert Resner to Henry Morgenthau, February 24, 1946, Box 795, Morgenthau Papers.

38. "Deposition of Henry Morgenthau taken by and on behalf of the defendants," March 5, 1946, *Kellems v. Labor Herald*, Box 795, Henry Morgenthau, Jr., Papers, Franklin D. Roosevelt Library, Hyde Park, N.Y.

39. *Kellems v. California Congress of Industrial Organization Council*, 68 F. Supp. 277, 278, 279 (N. Dist. Ca. 1946).

40. *The New Spirit* (Disney, 1942), in U.S. Government Film Collection, FAA 188, Motion Picture Collection, Library of Congress, Washington, D.C.; Office of War Information, *Battle Stations for All* (February 1943), 37, in Pamphlets, 1942–43, RG 208.

41. Kellems's references to Communism were more pronounced in her account of her refusal to withhold taxes from her employees' paychecks in 1948. See Kellems, *Toil, Taxes*, 56, 61–62.

42. Brinkley, *Liberalism and Its Discontents*, 55; see ibid., 55–59.

43. Vivien Kellems, "The Underground," Chicago Rotary Club, September 28, 1943, Box 45, Westbrook Pegler Papers, Herbert Hoover Presidential Library.

44. Blum, *From the Morgenthau Diaries*, 36, 68; "Rebuked for Call Not to Pay Taxes," *New York Times*, January 20, 1944, p. 21, col. 2; "Miss Kellems Defies Government to Act," *New York Times*, January 21, 1944, p. 13, col. 4. An interview conducted in 1951 suggests that Vivien's opposition may have been less principled than she protested at the time. "Of course, she says, she had intended to pay her taxes all along—just didn't happen to have the money at the moment, which could happen to anybody, and when she found that she had enough cash on hand after all, why, she simply paid up. 'What's so surprising about that?,' she says." Logan, "Grips and Taxes I," 44.

45. Fones-Wolf, *Selling Free Enterprise*, 26. These concerns are also discussed in Tedlow, *Keeping the Corporate Image*, 118–29, 140–41.

46. Rosenof, "Freedom, Planning and Totalitarianism," 150; Hayek, *Road to Serfdom*, xxiii.

47. Paul, *Taxation in the United States*, 328–32; Current Tax Payment Act of 1943, Pub. L. No. 78–68, 57 Stat. 126, 145–49 (1943). The quoted language is from Paul, *Taxation in the United States*, 333–34.

48. "Tax Law is Defied by Miss Kellems," *New York Times*, February 14, 1948, p. 28, col. 5; "Miss Kellems Objects," *Newsweek* 31 (February 22, 1948): 22; "Woman Employer Ends Withholding of Taxes," *New York Times*, February 21, 1948, p. 28, col. 3; "Kellems's Workers Pay," *New York Times*, June 16, 1948, p. 31, col. 7.

49. "Indictment Asked By Miss Kellems," *New York Times*, May 2, 1948, p. 36, col. 1; "Miss Anti-Withholder," *Newsweek* 31 (May 10, 1948): 27; "Miss Kellems Insists," *New York Times*, December 17, 1948, p. 36, col. 2; "Miss Kellems Dares Snyder to Indict Her," *New York Times*, April 13, 1949, p. 44, col. 7. "I have been trying to get indicted," Kellems is reported to have said, "but Mr. Snyder, as you have noticed, has refused to do so. I don't want to call him a coward, but he seems to be a timid person."

50. "Treasury Will Force Miss Kellems to Pay," *New York Times*, May 6, 1948, p. 44, col. 7; "Kellems Holdings Are Tied Up By the U.S.," *New York Times*, May 15, 1948, p. 19, col. 4; "Miss Kellems Clips Tax," *New York Times*, January 17, 1949, p. 21, col. 4.

51. "Another Kellems Lien," *New York Times*, August 4, 1949, p. 25, col. 5; "Kellems Fund Seized," *New York Times*, August 9, 1949, p. 27, col. 4; "Miss Kellems Sues U.S. for Fine on Tax," *New York Times*, November 22, 1949, p. 20, col. 6; "Miss Kellems Wins U.S. Court Suit Over Defiance on Withholding Tax," *New York Times*, January 25, 1951, p. 1, col. 6.

52. "Miss Kellems Loses Round," *New York Times*, October 29, 1950, p. 49, col. 4; "Miss Kellems's Suit Has a Day in Court," *New York Times*, January 24, 1951, p. 20, col. 4; "Miss Kellems Wins U.S. Court Suit," *New York Times*, January 25, 1951, p. 1, col. 6.

53. "U.S. Wins a Kellems Case," *New York Times*, April 26, 1951, p. 31, col. 2; "U.S. Asks Reversal of Kellems Verdict," *New York Times*, January 26, 1951, p. 4, col. 4; "Criticizes Kellems Jury," *New York Times*, February 4, 1951, p. 31, col. 2; "Kellems Verdict Hit," *New York Times*, March 31, 1951, p. 6, col. 3; "Kellems Appeal Deadline Passes," *New York Times*, July 16, 1951, p. 38, col. 4.

54. Brinkley, "Problem of American Conservatism," 409; Rossiter, *Conservatism in America*, 11; Brinkley, *Liberalism and Its Discontents*, 282–91; Nash, *Conservative Intellectual Movement*. Other scholars have identified the strands differently.

Jerome Himmelstein identified "three elements of conservatism—economic libertarianism, social traditionalism and militant anticommunism." Himmelstein, *To the Right*, 14. For purposes of this chapter, I will use the term "conservative" to refer collectively to these various strands and more specific terms when referring to particular currents of conservative thought, such as libertarianism.

55. Will, "Cultural Contradictions of Conservatism," 55.

56. Ratified in 1913, the Sixteenth Amendment provides that the federal government may collect income taxes without regard to apportionment among the states according to population. This amendment was a response to the Supreme Court's finding that the 1894 income tax was unconstitutional as an unapportioned direct tax in *Pollock v. Farmers' Loan and Trust*, 157 U.S. 429 (1895).

In 1934 a group of conservative businessmen centered around the Du Ponts started to organize what ultimately became the American Liberty League. Among their complaints was that the New Deal was using the Sixteenth Amendment as "an instrument to redistribute wealth to communize the nation, and to confiscate the property of one man and dole it out to others." Some hoped to repeal the Amendment. In addition, Roscoe Pound, the former dean of the Harvard Law School, formed the Committee of Americans to lobby for lower taxes. Burk, *Corporate State and the Broker State*, 138–39, 182, 272.

57. Fones-Wolf, *Selling Free Enterprise*, 27; Nash, *Conservative Intellectual Movement*, xv, 10–11.

58. Cf. Rossiter, *Conservatism in America*, 170.

59. See Nash, *Conservative Intellectual Movement*, 12–15, 23–25.

60. Chodorov, *One is a Crowd*, 153–54.

61. Kellems, *Toil, Taxes*, 34, 56, 61–62.

62. J. Bracken Lee, foreword to Chodorov, *Income Tax*, vii. Lee was not the first to perceive a trend toward national as opposed to state citizenship. For example, Rogers Smith has observed that oath laws passed during the Civil War "compelled citizens to affirm supreme loyalty to the national Constitution as opposed to the states." Smith, *Civic Ideals*, 274–75.

63. Chodorov, *Income Tax*, 46–47. For calls for repeal, see Kellems, *Toil, Taxes*, 27; Chodorov, *Income Tax*, 91, 129–133; Lee, foreword, vii. For Kellems's awareness of the case against the Sixteenth Amendment on federalism grounds, see her summary of the ratification debates in Virginia in *Toil, Taxes*, 55.

64. Kellems, *Toil, Taxes*, 63. Kellems's reference to "overpaid war workers" would seem to be an example of the politics of "comparative sacrifice."

65. Brownlee, "Reflections," 20–22.

66. Kellems, *Toil, Taxes*, 64. On this point Kellems went beyond even Chodorov. "There is no way of conducting war other than by confiscating all that is needed to save the nation from destruction or enslavement," Chodorov wrote. "If [the Sixteenth Amendment] were repealed, and Congress declared that a state of war exists, it could enact an income tax law for the duration; after all, during war the government can suspend the Constitution." Chodorov, *Income Tax*, 133.

67. Kellems, *Toil, Taxes*, 70.

68. Ackerman, "Taxation and the Constitution," 4–5.

69. That said, in 1951 housewives in Marshall, Texas, echoed her claim that paying taxes was a form of involuntary servitude in explaining to Treasury Secretary John W. Snyder why they refused to pay Social Security taxes for their domes-

tic servants. "Texas Housewives Rebel At Paying Tax for Maids," *New York Times*, April 30, 1951, p. 40, col. 4.

70. Chodorov, *Income Tax*, 61–62.

71. Kellems, *Toil, Taxes*, 82–83.

72. Robert M. Harriss to Herbert Hoover, Post Presidential Individual Correspondence, 1952–1963, Box 79, Herbert Hoover Papers, Herbert Hoover Presidential Library, West Branch, Ia.

73. Wilder, *Long Winter*, 110–14; Holtz, *Ghost in the Little House*. Tax lawyers call such self-reliant acts "imputed income."

74. Crane to Lane, May 24, 1955, in MacBride, ed., *Lady and the Tycoon*, 117; Lane to Crane, June 1, 1955, ibid., 177; Lane to Crane, September 4, 1956, ibid., 153.

75. Bernhard Knollenberg to Henry Morgenthau, Jr., December 9, 1941, with attached article, Morgenthau Diaries, 472:296–303; Bittker, "Taxation and the Family," 1400; Chirelstein, *Federal Income Taxation*, 157; Vickrey, *Agenda for Progressive Taxation*, 276; Witte, *Development of the Federal Income Tax*, 117–18.

76. Hines, "Real Property Joint Tenancies," 582; Jones, "Split Income," 266–93; Commissioner of Internal Revenue to Bourke B. Hickenlooper, May 20, 1947, 1–2, in "Legislative File, Sponsored, Taxation, 1947, HR1, Partnerships," Bourke B. Hickenlooper Papers, Herbert Hoover Presidential Library, West Branch, Ia.

77. Jones, "Split Income," 273, 294–95; Surrey, "Federal Taxation of the Family," 1097–111.

78. Kellems, *Toil, Taxes*, 78–79; "Vivien Kellems Resumes Protest over Tax Rates," *New York Times*, April 15, 1969, p. 42, col. 1; "Miss Kellems Again Balks," *New York Times*, March 17, 1971, p. 35, col. 2. Her refusal in 1969 related to her federal income tax liability for 1968.

79. House Committee on Ways and Means, *Tax Treatment of Single Persons*, 4; House Committee on Ways and Means, *General Tax Reform*, 781–837; Graetz, *The Decline (and Fall?) of the Income Tax*, 32; Richard Hatch, *New York Times*, April 9, 1978.

80. Weresch, "Girl with a Grip," 57; Logan, "Grips and Taxes I," 40; "Equal Rights Promised in House," *New York Times*, January 6, 1944, p. 20, col. 1. See Rupp and Taylor, *Survival in the Doldrums*, 59.

81. "Miss Kellems Tests State's Labor Law," *New York Times*, April 9, 1947; "Vivien Kellems Sees Labor Solution in 'Home Work'," *Hartford Times*, June 2, 1943, p. 6.

82. Kobler, "Five-Foot-Two, She Lifts the World," *Saturday Evening Post* 214 (April 18, 1942): 67–69.

83. Webb Waldron, "Yankee Kitchens Go on the Production Line," *Better Homes and Gardens* 21 (June 1943): 17.

84. Ibid., 65. Such domestic imagery was not unusual at the time. Rosie the Riveters, working in factories producing military hardware, were said to be transferring household skills to a new sphere.

85. Ibid., 65–66. On juvenile delinquency and the employment of mothers, see Hartmann, *Home Front*, 82, 213.

86. Boris, *Home to Work*, 271, 273–79, 293–94.

87. Ibid., 293; "Vivien Kellems Sees Labor Solution in 'Home Work'," *Hartford Times*, June 3, 1943, p. 6.

88. "Vivien Kellems Sees Labor Solution in 'Home Work'." Earlier Kellems had somewhat inconsistently declared that "it is an excellent thing for industry to

pour all of these women into our factories." "Speaker Praises Women in Factory," *New York Times*, May 26, 1943, p. 12, col. 8.

89. Quoted in Boris, *Home to Work*, 294.

90. Rupp and Taylor, *Survival in the Doldrums*, 59.

91. This is by no means a point that originated with Kellems. Such arguments, for example, provided a basis for the suffrage movement. "Evangelical Protestantism in the nineteenth century supported the notion that women were morally superior to men and thus encouraged women to value themselves and their own contribution to social life." Cott, *Modern Feminism*, 17.

92. Kobler, "She Lifts the World," 28–29.

93. Ibid., 27–28. The historical accuracy of Kellems's statement is certainly open to question, as is the accuracy of her representation of other women's views.

94. Sylvia Porter, "Single Taxpayers Aided By COST Organization," *Hartford Times*, August 2, 1971; Remarks of Senator Abraham Ribicoff, *Congressional Record*, 92d Cong., 1st sess., February 18, 1982, 3037–38.

95. Audio tape, Vivien Kellems on Taxation, January 18, 1972 (Alexandria, Va.: Audio-Forum, 1972), Babbidge Library, University of Connecticut; House Committee on Ways and Means, *Tax Treatment of Single Persons*, 4; Graetz, *Decline (and Fall?) of the Income Tax*, 32.

96. May, *Homeward Bound*, 20

97. House Committee on Ways and Means, *Tax Treatment of Single Persons*, 6.

98. *Kellems v. Commissioner*, 474 F.2d 1399 (2d Cir. 1973); *Kellems v. Commissioner*, 58 T.C. 556 (1972); *Skau v. Kellems*, 26 AFTR 2d 5921 (U.S. Dist. Ct., Conn. 1970). The 1972 case involved Kellems's unsuccessful claim for a refund for her 1965 income taxes on the ground that she had been discriminated against as a single person.

99. Kellems, "Single Taxpayer," n.d., Box 22, Lucille Cardin Crain Papers, Box 22, University of Oregon Archives, Eugene, Ore.

100. Kellems, "Dear Resentful Taxpayer," May 1971, ibid.

101. Graetz, *Decline (and Fall?) of the Income Tax*, 32; McCaffery, *Taxing Women*, 62–67.

102. Logan, "Grips and Taxes I," 37, 47.

103. Slemrod, "Which is the Simplest Tax System," 360.

104. Vivien Kellems to Barbara Walters, January 28, 1974, Box 2, Polly K. Ruhtenberg Papers, University of Oregon Archives, Eugene, Ore.

105. Brownlee, "Tax Regimes," 104; Graetz, *Decline (and Fall?) of the Income Tax*, 3–5.

CHAPTER 6

The Ideal and the Actual in the State: Willard Hurst at the Board of Economic Warfare

Daniel R. Ernst

The United States' entry into World War II caught the American legal profession at an unsettled moment in its encounter with the administrative state. Until the first decades of the twentieth century, courts had been the natural environment of American lawyers, the venue in which they had acted upon what Tocqueville called "certain habits of order, a taste for formalities, and a kind of instinctive regard for the regular connection of ideas." Yet as early as 1916, even the sober and conservative Elihu Root, a lion of the Wall Street bar, predicted that the delegation of legislative power to executive officials would become a permanent part of the American legal order, notwithstanding its great potential for "oppression and wrong." Later events proved Root right. By one estimate, 70 percent of the practice of major law firms in 1934 was before agencies that did not exist a generation earlier. Even the judiciary was transformed as it added the oversight and articulation of regulatory regimes founded on statutes to its traditional function of resolving private disputes under the common law.[1]

By Pearl Harbor a growing consensus within the legal profession held that the governance of modern societies and economies required more extensive gathering of information, more specialized and expert decision-making, and a broader array of remedies than courts could hope to provide on their own. Whether the federal bureaucracies of the early twentieth century were actually up to the job was another matter. New Dealers, including the protégés of the Harvard law professor Felix Frankfurter, defended the new administrative bodies as efficient and tractable instruments for the promotion of the public good. In fact, the national administrative state had been constructed on a divided polity, whose fault lines pitted localism against national interests, Congress against a burgeoning executive, and nonpartisan expertise against the demands of party officials and organized interests. The realization that they had pinned their hopes on "a hapless administrative giant, a state that could spawn bureaucratic goods and services but that defied authoritative control and direction" was slow in coming and may itself have been a product of the New Dealers' experiences during World War II.[2]

The American war effort required an unprecedented expansion of domestic procurement, allocation, and command-and-control regulation, which was staffed, in significant part, by lawyers. In the preceding decades, lawyers had often appeared before administrative bodies of one sort or another; now the war provided thousands of them with their first experience of federal bureaucracies from the inside. For some, such as a young attorney in the Office of Price Administration named Richard M. Nixon, it was an unhappy experience filled with petty careerism and shortsighted in-fighting.[3] As Reuel Schiller's essay in this volume suggests, a call for heightened judicial review of administrative decision-making was one result. But other lawyers felt that their service in civilian or military bureaucracies materially contributed to the war effort. They returned home with a new appreciation for what the administrative process could contribute to American governance.

One instructive case is that of James Willard Hurst. After the war Hurst would become the dean of American legal historians by showing that the field extended beyond courts and common-law doctrines to include the social history of law. But in December 1941 Hurst was a young and recently married law professor who had only just begun his historical investigations. For several years his principal concern had been developing a course entitled "Law in Society," which tried to give students a broader view of the legal system than the court-centered "case method" that dominated American legal education. After Pearl Harbor, Hurst looked for ways to join the war effort and found it in a new agency headed by Vice President Henry Wallace, the Board of Economic Warfare (BEW).

Hurst served at the BEW for almost a year, commencing in February 1942. As a member of the general counsel's staff, he played the leading role in developing and implementing the policy that was most responsible for the agency's reputation as a New Deal bastion in wartime Washington. The "labor clauses" he developed for the BEW, which wrote minimum labor standards into contracts with the foreign suppliers of raw material, embodied his conviction, evident in the "Law in Society" course, that the general welfare of all members of modern societies could be obtained only through the active intervention of administrators into market relations. Hurst stuck by his labor clauses even though he knew that they addressed a concern that lay beyond the stated mission of the BEW, that they probably ran counter to the wishes of a majority of the Congress elected in the fall of 1942, and that his principal claim for their contribution to the war effort lacked a convincing empirical basis.

As it happened, Hurst's efforts came to nothing when the BEW was abolished in July 1943 after a spectacular quarrel between Wallace and his opponents in Congress and the executive branch. Hurst claimed to have "learned a great deal about bureaucracy" while at the BEW, but he never identified just what he learned, so that the lessons must be inferred from his postwar lectures and writings. These show that Hurst's ideals for the administrative state survived the war intact, but they also displayed a new and idealistic belief that lawyers could provide government with the far-sighted, broad-ranging regard for social interests that businessmen and professional politicians typically lacked. Hurst was well aware that in practice the administrative state and the legal profession often fell far short of his ideals, but he chose to see this not as grounds for revising his views but for urging them upon his students and readers as persuasively as he could. When his critics remained unconvinced, Hurst ultimately responded by attributing the persisting gap between the ideal and the actual in the state to the ineradicable imperfections of human nature.

ADMINISTRATION IDEALIZED

When Felix Frankfurter learned of Hurst's appointment to the BEW, he congratulated the executive director, Milo Perkins, on his good fortune. "I know of no one of his years who excels him in character, disinterestedness, and insight into the relationship between law and economic processes," the Supreme Court justice wrote. At the Harvard Law School of the 1930s Hurst had impressed Frankfurter as a standout in class and an editor of the *Harvard Law Review*. Hurst stayed on after graduation as Frankfurter's research assistant during the 1935–36 academic year and then became Justice Louis Brandeis's law clerk during the momentous October 1936 term of the U.S. Supreme Court.[4] Frankfurter kept in close contact with Hurst after he joined the law faculty at the University of Wisconsin in the fall of 1937. Often they discussed whether Hurst should accept an offer from a more prestigious law school, but each time Hurst decided against a move. He was convinced that Wisconsin was "just about an ideal 'laboratory' " for developing a new approach to legal education, thanks in large measure to the inspired leadership of its dean, the prominent New Dealer Lloyd K. Garrison.[5] In 1939, when Hurst sent Frankfurter the first fruits of his labors, a set of materials for a new course for first-year law students, his mentor had to agree. "I wish I were in your class in that course," the Supreme Court justice wrote to Hurst. "It strikes me as an admirable demonstration of the way in which the slogan about 'integrating the social sciences' should be carried out within the sensible framework of a law school."[6]

The course, "Law in Society," was part of Garrison's ambitious plans to remake legal education to better prepare students for a career of lawyering beyond the courts. Hurst started work on the course in the latter half of 1938. His first step was to expand a small set of materials Garrison had previously used to introduce law students to the various phases of Wisconsin's legal system. This synchronic view of legal institutions, organized around the problem of injuries in the workplace, became Part One of the "Law in Society" materials. Hurst then compiled, from scratch, a Part Two that studied the law of workplace injury in Wisconsin over time. To provide context for developments in the state, Hurst included selections from the jurisprudential writings of many of the leading legal scholars of his day. The complete materials—two parts in three volumes—were ready for the 1940–41 academic year, when Hurst taught them four days a week to first-semester law students.[7] Hurst insisted that he and Garrison "framed [the course] together," but Garrison, whose obligations during this period included service on the Attorney General's Committee on Administrative Procedure, credited Hurst with the "basic ideas." His principal contribution, Garrison claimed, was "enthusiasm." Beyond that, "I did no more than fill in a few chinks."[8]

"Law in Society" was a New Dealer's idea of a first course in law.[9] In the debates over the nature of law and the desirability of administrative action Hurst came down squarely on the side of New Deal liberals in government and legal academia. First, following the legal realists of the 1920s and 1930s, he described law in positivist terms as "a system of sanctions drawing its authority from sources announced and developed by judges, [law] writers, and legislators." In opposing the New Deal, some elite lawyers had denied that statutes and administrative rulings were part of "the jurisprudence of a nation," for only judicial decisions embodied "a people's conception of justice." Hurst's readings, including a classic passage from Oliver Wendell Holmes, Jr.'s essay, "The Path of the Law," dismissed this view and, in so doing, encouraged his students to consider the rules created by administrative bodies no less a source of "law" than the decisions of the U.S. Supreme Court.[10]

Hurst then directed his readers to ask themselves, "What is the function of law?" His answer, offered as a matter of simple description, embraced many of the values of American liberal thought at mid-century. It was, first, pluralist. "Law," Hurst declared, settled "conflicts between interests (of government, of individuals, and of groups) by extending its protection and aid to particular interests in such a way as to maintain an equilibrium." In part, his notion of "interest" looked back to the early sociological jurisprudence of Roscoe Pound. Thus, a catalogue of "interests" at the end of the first volume included not just the "interests of particular groups" but also the "interests of government" (such as general security, public safety, public health, and natural resources) and "the interests of individuals" (such as personal security, liberty of expression, and publicly provided education).[11] Often, however, Hurst used the word as a synonym for "pressure group," much as realist political scientists did in work he was reading at the time. Political parties had little independent role in the shaping of public policy. As one of Hurst's readings claimed, even Milwaukee's socialists were just "the political organization for the workers whose economic organizations were the trade unions."[12]

Hurst's understanding of the function of law was also evolutionary and progressive to the point of Whiggishness. The equilibrium that law reaches, he wrote, "has been conditioned by the nature of the interests which at any given time have been able . . . to secure the law's recognition and protection." The law has never recognized "all interests of every kind," and so "there has occurred from the beginning a struggle between the different interests to get recognized." This struggle was "much like that of a multitude of people trying to get under the shelter of a small tent in a rain-storm." Every generation had used law to settle the struggle and to determine which interests were to be taken in and which were to be kept out. "In the main," however, "in each generation a wider circle of interests has succeeded in getting under the tent than had ever succeeded before."[13]

To illustrate the expansion of the social interests protected by law, Hurst settled on a single social problem, injury in the workplace. The common law took a narrow view of the interests affected. It regarded only the property of the employers and the employees' "liberty" in contracting for dangerous work, and it placed the cost of injuries exclusively upon the "employee and his dependents." Over time, however, workers and reformers forced the law to recognize harms to other social interests: the decrease in the community's "stock of human productive power," the truncated educations of an injured employee's children, the curtailment of their mother's "function as a homemaker in order to earn outside the home," and the inability of the employee's family to provide for illness and old age. "To allow the loss to lie where, in the first instance it falls," Hurst wrote, "is simply to evade the central problem and to leave the community ultimately to bear the increased costs." Workers' compensation may not be the final stage in the evolution of the law, but it was an unambiguous improvement over what went before.[14]

In defining law in functional terms as the balancing of social interests, the "Law in Society" materials followed a path blazed by the legal realists. Hurst's original contribution lay in attributing the expanding social horizons of law to the increasing sophistication of legislatures and new forms of executive action.[15] Left to themselves, common-law courts could never have supported a tent large enough to shelter the wider interests clamoring for recognition. "Courts exist *primarily to settle controversies*, and for no other purpose," Hurst declared. As a rule, their jurisdiction was too general for them to acquire the specialized expertise that complex social problems demanded. They could not independently commence proceedings, define the issues before them, obtain relevant information, or retain an ongoing oversight of disputes.[16] To remedy these shortcomings, American policy-makers turned to the administrative process. If judges were generalists, administrators were specialists. If judges had to wait until some party presented them with a controversy, administrators could conduct investigations on their own initiative. If judges insisted on formal procedures, administrators could commence work on receipt of a simple letter and disregard the law of evidence. If judges settled discrete cases with final decrees, administrators could continuously review their prior decisions, engage in rule-making, or informally set policy through licensing, contracting, and the selective provision of services.[17]

The Wisconsin Industrial Commission was Hurst's principal illustration of how the administrative process brought new interests under the shelter of the law. Using a case involving an injured carnival worker, Hurst showed how the Commission aggressively took charge of the dispute and ordered compensation, even though the worker's own negligence probably contributed to his death. He also showed how the Commission acted beyond the limits of the individual case by maintaining a system of industrial insurance to raise the funds needed to compensate victims and by promulgating regulations to help prevent similar accidents in the future.

The choice of the Industrial Commission as a model of the administrative process was telling. As the leading exemplar of the "Wisconsin idea" of governance, the Commission took an "associative" approach to state-building. It attempted to coordinate and rationalize the actions of private groups, rather than to develop the capacity to direct the economy or society on its own. Its safety codes and other regulations, for example, were the "best practices" identified by committees of business and labor leaders. As its creator John R. Commons explained, in a passage Hurst reproduced, the results might not have been "ideal," but they were "pragmatic, the best that the nature of the industry would permit." The Industrial Commission was thus part of a long tradition of American reform that sought to rationalize or humanize capitalism without resorting to statist planning.[18]

Hurst, it seems, found the Wisconsin idea quite congenial. In 1938 he wrote to Frankfurter that it was "a bit closer to American roots, and perhaps more hardheaded" than other visions of planning. In 1941 he thought the lesson of Pendleton Herring's *Politics of Democracy* was that public policy should be the collaborative product of "organized private interest groups and the executive and administrative branches of government." Administrators were not to direct economic and social life single-handedly; rather, they were to supply the "broader vision" that private actors might overlook. As Hurst saw it, "the key problem will be whether we can devise interacting schemes, or plot interrelated regions of official and non-official direction of the economy, so as not to overload the official machinery hopelessly beyond the capacity of ordinary human foresight and strength." The prudent administrator followed the "homely principle of learning not to do more than is necessary" and sought "a few points of control whose key location would render unnecessary the occupation of vast expanses of regulation."[19]

In all likelihood, Hurst wrote these words while attempting to translate his ideals for administration into practice in the General Counsel's office of the Board of Economic Warfare. Hurst had not yet finished teaching the "Law in Society" course when news of Pearl Harbor reached Madison. He probably started considering how best to contribute to the war effort as soon as the shock wore off.[20] At the end of December he attended the annual meeting of the Association of American Law Schools in Chicago, where he seems to have met the BEW's General Counsel, Monroe Oppenheimer, who came to the meeting in search of recruits. Willard Wirtz (then a member of Northwestern's law faculty) met Oppenheimer there. Although Wirtz had never heard of the BEW before, he was impressed by the liberal mission Oppenheimer projected and decided to join up.[21] Hurst accepted Oppenheimer's offer sometime in early January, and in early February he was at his desk at the BEW, trying to decide what to make of an agency launched onto the flood tide of wartime Washington with visionary leadership, little authority, an uncertain mission, and the enmity of powerful rivals.[22]

THE BEW AT BAY

Hurst's predicament was all the greater because the case for the Board of Economic Warfare as a matter of administrative or military necessity was embarrassingly weak. Economic warfare—the licensing of exports and the "preclusive" buying of stockpiles to keep strategic materials from falling into enemy hands—was a real enough concern, one pioneered by a British ministry before the United States' entry into the war. The need for a federal agency to coordinate the development and purchase of raw materials on international markets became urgent after Japanese victories cut off access to traditional sources in the Far East. Suddenly Americans looked to the neutral or allied countries of Latin America and West Africa to provide such vital commodities as rubber; chinchona bark for quinine; sisal, abaca, and other fibrous plants for rope and cordage; tungsten, tin, and other metals; and balsa, mahogany, and other forms of lumber.[23]

When the BEW was created in July 1941, however, other federal agencies were already in the field.[24] Since June 1940 the Reconstruction Finance Corporation (RFC), directed by Secretary of Commerce Jesse Jones, had been empowered to acquire "strategic and critical" materials abroad and to engage in preclusive buying. Jones had created several subsidiaries of the RFC to do the work, recruited businessmen to staff them, and directed the recruits to bargain as hard on behalf of government as they had in the private sector.[25] At the State Department, economic warfare had been a concern of Dean Acheson since his appointment as assistant secretary in February 1941. It was entrusted to a new Division of Defense Materials, headed by Thomas K. Finletter, a masterful lawyer recruited from the New York firm of Coudert Brothers.[26] A third potential policy-maker was the Office of the Coordinator on Inter-American Affairs (CIAA), created on the same day as the BEW and charged with (among other things) furthering "the commercial well-being of the Western hemisphere." This was a subject into which the Coordinator, Nelson A. Rockefeller, had considerable insight, thanks to his family's investments in Latin America.[27]

The initial role of the Board of Economic Warfare was simply to advise these agencies. Shrewd political observers, like Dean Acheson, knew that as long as Wallace played by the normal conventions of bureaucratic warfare, his rivals had little to fear. "Cabinet boards and committees were paper tigers," Acheson later observed. "Cabinet officers are too busy and too suspicious of one another to join a raid against a colleague." The BEW's vague mandate, to "consider the broad implications of economic relationships" with foreign countries as identified by Wallace and a staff of a half-dozen advisors, seemed unlikely to lead to concrete proposals requiring the immediate attention of its members. Before May 1942 the BEW met sporadically, without agenda, and often with only the deputies of the cabinet members in attendance.[28]

What the BEW did provide was a job for Henry A. Wallace. As Secretary of Agriculture Wallace had established himself as a liberal paladin with programs targeting rural poverty in the United States, and at the end of his tenure he articulated a vision of economic interdependence and mutual self-interest on a global scale. This new note did nothing to assuage the fears of old-guard Democrats in Congress, to whom Wallace was "a doe-eyed mystic who symbolized all they found objectionable about the hopelessly utopian, market-manipulating, bureaucracy-breeding New Deal," but it was consistent with FDR's increasingly, if guardedly, internationalist views.[29] As the historian John Morton Blum writes, Roosevelt gave Wallace the BEW as a platform from which he could make "bolder proposals for wartime and postwar policy than the President could politically afford to venture himself." Perhaps Wallace's boldest proposal was a speech delivered in May 1942, in which he answered Henry Luce's nationalistic vision of an "American Century" with a globalist call for a "century of the common man."[30]

Wallace was not content with a purely advisory role for the BEW. With the modest funds at his disposal he recruited a vanguard of officials during the fall of 1941. Wallace's selection of Milo Perkins as executive director was a sign to Acheson that the vice president would be no respecter of the normal "rules of bureaucratic warfare." Perkins, a Texas manufacturer who had been one of Wallace's most trusted lieutenants at the U.S. Department of Agriculture (USDA), was an enormously "able, hard-boiled" administrator and "arbitrary, even ruthless," in pursuit of an objective. Under his leadership the BEW could be counted upon to seek a dramatic role for itself.[31]

The choice of the chief of the Office of Imports was a particularly difficult one. Wallace knew the job had to go to a respected figure in the export-import trade, but he had seen his most progressive programs at the USDA frustrated by officials recruited from the ranks of farmers and food processors. In Morris S. Rosenthal, Wallace found an importer who believed in the vice president's "social concepts" and was willing to impose them on the businessmen who served under him.[32] For General Counsel Wallace selected Monroe Oppenheimer, who had come to the USDA in the 1930s as a protégé of one of Yale's legal realists and had overseen the legal affairs of the Resettlement Administration.[33]

The biggest prize Wallace sought during the winter of 1941–42 was control over imports, the most controversial phase of economic warfare. He frequently complained that the "banker's caution" of the RFC was keeping its subsidiaries from building adequate stockpiles of critical materials.[34] He pressed for the right to send staff overseas, even though this threatened the State Department's status as the official representative of the U.S. government abroad.

Although Wallace made little headway, this threat became more substantial when he and Nelson Rockefeller, who, as Coordinator of Inter-American Affairs, had a substantial staff in Latin America, agreed to coordinate their activities. "Being the permanent department of this government charged with the conduct of foreign affairs," a subordinate advised Acheson in December, "the State Department will hesitate to resign to a new and inexperienced organization many of the functions it normally performs." "Great tact" was required, he continued, owing to "the New Deal political and economic outlook of the Board." Acheson, in turn, urged career diplomats in the State Department to accommodate the BEW's requests in order to forestall more serious incursions into their domain. "There seems to be a well-developed tendency at BEW to move toward the establishment of its own representatives in the field," he warned. "I believe that this tendency can be checked or held within reasonable bounds provided the Department works out an efficient and speedy method for furnishing a communication and intelligence service. If this is not done, I believe that the pressure will be irresistible."[35]

For his part, Wallace had no illusions about the State Department. "State plans a balance-of-power game with other agencies," he told FDR in March 1942. Yet he felt he could manage conflicts with its officials without the president's intervention. "Our difficulties with them in connection with raw materials problems have been mostly jurisdictional ones without any reference to principles."

Jesse Jones was a different matter. His appointee at the Export-Import Bank would not provide funds for BEW-directed development projects, and his lieutenants in the RFC subsidiaries ignored the BEW's recommendations that they accelerate their procurement and consider the social consequences of their purchases. "There is a basic conflict of principles between their banker-minded approach and our goods-minded approach," Wallace complained to Roosevelt. Pointing to the RFC's delay in building stockpiles of quinine, opium, and tungsten, he claimed that "it takes weeks to get action that should be gotten in a day or two." He asked Roosevelt to give the Export-Import Bank to the BEW as a "checkbook," to transfer the Division of Defense Materials from State to the BEW, and to permit the BEW to send its own representatives abroad.[36]

Wallace's rivals received an unexpected boon on March 29 when Congressmen Martin Dies, chairman of the special committee on un-American activities, accused thirty-five members of the BEW's staff of prior membership in Communist-front organizations. The press gave greatest coverage to an advocate of nudism, but Dies's list also included Nathaniel Weyl, an economic analyst whose *Reconquest of Mexico* (1939) had taken (in Weyl's words) "a socialist slant" to American investment in Mexico. Wallace and Perkins issued forceful rebuttals, but the affair confirmed congressional conservatives' impression of Wallace as a dangerous visionary who had to be kept on a short leash.[37]

Exasperated with the delays of Jones's staff, but mindful of the need to keep a balky and mistrustful Congress behind the war effort, Roosevelt gave Wallace only part of what he sought. Issued on April 13 without advance notice to the RFC or the State Department, Executive Order 9128 gave the vice president the power to specify the terms of the contracts between the RFC subsidiaries and foreign producers and distributors, to send its own representatives overseas, to create its own government corporations, and to act as Wallace and Perkins directed, without a vote of the full board. The order left the RFC's subsidiaries with the responsibility of executing contracts, disbursing funds, and receiving commodities, and it denied the BEW the Export-Import Bank. It thus made the BEW a significant rival to the RFC and the State Department, but not an overpowering one. Congressional conservatives in particular could be reassured that Jones's agencies would continue to serve as a check on Wallace's endeavors.[38]

At the State Department, the *New York Times* reported, Executive Order 9128 took "the wall off" the building. "There were moments when it seemed that one of the handsomest, and most cultivated entities of government—Assistant Secretary of State Acheson—would never stop vibrating." Undersecretary Sumner Welles quickly protested to FDR and commissioned a review of the BEW's new powers, which concluded that the order had given Wallace "the decisive voice in all operations involving the procurement, production, and financing of supplies procured in foreign countries, and in all dealings with foreign governments concerning these matters." Under the order, the State Department would "*not* be able to shape or control government policy"; it "actually would not be able to work upon them except as a subordinate carrying out the orders of the Board of Economic Warfare." On May 20, FDR issued a "clarification" assigning primary responsibility for "foreign policy and our relations with foreign nations" to State and for "matters of business judgment" to the BEW. Still, as Acheson later confessed, Executive Order 9128 was "a painful, bitter, and humiliating defeat" for the State Department.[39]

The order was an even more humiliating defeat for Jones, as it was widely interpreted as a rebuke for the RFC's failure to finance the production of synthetic rubber to replace output lost with the Japanese capture of plantations in Southeast Asia. Jones resented the charge and was convinced that "Mr. Wallace and his long-haired, incompetent, meddlesome disciples" would only duplicate and delay the efforts of his businesslike staff. Yet he knew that because the RFC subsidiaries continued to hold all records relating to the procurement contracts, they could effectively set the pace of purchases and investment in development projects. When Treasury Secretary Henry Morgenthau, Jr., saw Jones sitting next to Roosevelt at the BEW's first meeting after the April 13 order, he knew how incomplete Wallace's victory actually was. "You don't know what a terrible staller Jesse is," Morgenthau warned Wallace. "He will wear you out with conference after conference and not get anything done." Jones would later admit to having pursued an obstructionist strategy, but he denied that the war effort suffered as a result. "What we actually obstructed," he claimed, were the BEW's "efforts to throw money away to no good purpose."[40]

For all its shortcomings, Executive Order 9128 made the BEW a force to be reckoned with. It energized Hurst and the agency's other lawyers, who descended upon the offices of the RFC subsidiaries like an occupying army. "The whole scene now changed overnight," a BEW lawyer recalled.[41] The agency's staff rapidly grew to almost 2,000 workers in June with recruits from the CIAA, other government agencies, industry, and the universities. By May 1943 more than 4,100 people worked for the BEW in Washington, New York, and Miami, as well as in over twenty foreign countries.[42]

For nine months after its creation in July 1941, the BEW had struggled to justify its existence. With Executive Order 9128, the BEW at last acquired what its leaders could plausibly interpret as a mandate to ensure that a victory for the Allies would also be a victory for the "common man." What they still lacked, as of April 13, 1942, was a strategy for fighting a New Deal war over the continued opposition of bureaucratic rivals and congressional conservatives. The policy Wallace and Perkins ultimately settled on was the insertion of clauses in procurement and development contracts to establish protections for the workers who labored to fulfill them. The policy was narrower than some of the alternatives they had considered, but it better exploited the BEW's authority over the negotiation of procurement contracts. It also was being championed by an extremely able and dedicated member of the General Counsel's staff. "More than anyone else in the Office," wrote the BEW lawyer Robert Mathews in a retrospective report on the labor clauses, "it was Mr. Willard Hurst who painstakingly and persistently worked out the details of the earlier negotiations, secured cooperation of other agencies and introduced the clause in the form that ultimately became basic for the more than 900 procurement contracts that had contained them by the spring of 1945."[43]

Hurst would see his ideals for the administrative state become BEW policy. He would also see that policy fall victim to the politics of bureaucracy and congressional partisanship.

A NEW DEALER AT WAR

Shortly after his arrival at the BEW, Hurst was asked to review an application for a loan from the Export-Import Bank made by the owner of a Haitian plantation owner who wanted to expand his production of sisal, a fibrous plant from which twine was made. When it arrived on Hurst's desk, the application was "exclusively commercial" in its terms. In early March, after consulting a dozen experts at the State Department, the War Production Board, and the Department of Agriculture, Hurst recommended that provisions be added to address the social consequences of the increased production. In particular, reacting to reports that the plantation's workforce was "shot with disease," he called for some "basic labor standards provision regarding minimum wages and conditions of labor."[44]

The provision Hurst circulated on March 17 had two clauses. The first obligated the plantation owner to conduct its operations so "as to maximize production and to minimize those conditions of health, safety, housing and sanitation which may tend to limit productivity." The second obligated the federal government to match any funds the owner furnished for programs that addressed these social needs. As it happened, the owner decided to forego the loan, but he was so eager to have the matching funds that he asked that the same clauses be included in the procurement contract for the sisal. By early April Hurst was looking for other opportunities to use the clauses and had settled on contracts with pharmaceutical companies for cinchona bark collected in Colombia, Guatemala, and Ecuador.[45]

From early April through midsummer, Rosenthal, Hurst, Willard Wirtz, and other BEW lawyers conferred and revised the labor clauses. The most significant change was a refinement of the first clause. In its final form the clause obligated sellers to (1) comply with all local laws on "labor relations, hours of work, wages, unemployment and disability compensation, safety, sanitation, food, shelter, health, education, child labor"; (2) pay wages no less than those paid for "comparable work" in the country in question; (3) adopt "reasonably adequate safeguards against accidents"; (4) provide workers with "adequate and suitable shelter, water, sanitation, medical treatment and protection against diseases"; and (5) "if necessary," assure workers of "the existence of an adequate food supply at a reasonable cost."[46]

Hurst's labor clauses were, in effect, an international version of the Walsh-Healey Act of 1936. Passed after the demise of the National Recovery Administration, that statute forbid federal contractors from employing workers for more than eight hours a day or forty hours a week, from subjecting them to unsanitary or hazardous working conditions, and from paying them less than "the prevailing minimum wages for persons employed on similar work" in their locality. Enforcement of the act was entrusted to lawyers and other administrators in the Division of Public Contracts of the U.S. Department of Labor. Hurst could have learned about the enforcement of the statute from a monograph on the division prepared by the Attorney General's Committee on Administrative Procedure in 1939. He almost certainly discussed the statute in late April when he met with Joseph L. Rauh, Jr., a friend from his student days at the Harvard Law School, who had recently been an assistant general counsel in the department.[47]

Before settling on the labor clauses, Wallace and Perkins had considered other programs for the BEW. The most ambitious was a series of BEW-directed, binational, government corporations that could comprehensively coordinate the disbursement of loans to development projects during the war and beyond. Without some other major financial source, Wallace and Perkins found this avenue blocked by Jones's continued control of the Export-Import Bank, which had binational subsidiaries of its own. Proposals for product-specific corporations, such as the one Hurst developed for the production of fats and oils in Brazil, continued to be mooted at the BEW throughout 1942, but they never proceeded beyond the planning stage, thanks to Jones's looming veto.[48]

In contrast, the BEW could insist on the labor clauses over Jones's objections under the authority it enjoyed by virtue of Executive Order 9128. In the spring and summer of 1942 the labor clauses quickly moved to the top of the BEW's agenda. Perkins first told Jones that the agency was committed to the clauses at a party in May 1942. In June and July, Hurst and his associates wrote the labor clauses in contracts covering the abaca plantations of the United Fruit Company in Guatemala and Honduras. By August 14, when Rosenthal explained the labor clauses at a general staff meeting of the Office of Imports, the clauses were in some eight or nine contracts.[49]

From September on, the BEW insisted on the inclusion of some form of the labor clauses in every contract with a private firm that took a year or more to perform. "The labor clauses should not be negotiated as an isolated item," Hurst had Rosenthal advise his field representatives. "Discussion of them should be introduced naturally and without special emphasis early in the negotiations and should proceed along with discussion of other parts of the deal." They represented "simply a practical method of safeguarding our interest in maximum and uninterrupted production and should not be distorted by being left to the end as the sole remaining point of negotiation."[50] By April 1943, labor clauses had been inserted in about 120 contracts with private concerns in some thirty countries for the production of metals, minerals, plants, and wood products.[51]

Enforcing the clauses throughout Central and South America was a huge task that required far more funds than the BEW had any prospect of obtaining from a suspicious Congress, and so Wallace and Perkins looked to an ally, Nelson Rockefeller, for help. Eager to demonstrate that the CIAA was contributing to the war effort, Rockefeller agreed in principle that the agency would oversee the sellers' compliance with the health and sanitation provisions of the labor clauses where its staff operated. Delighted, Perkins told Oppenheimer that "there has always been the sincerest cooperation between Nelson and me, and I am most anxious that this permeate as far as possible down our staff."[52]

The limits of Rockefeller's cooperation, however, became apparent soon enough. The CIAA refused responsibility for enforcing the clauses with respect to wages, safety, and occupational disease, and it insisted on participating only on a case-by-case basis. Although the CIAA generally approved the BEW's requests, its formal assent rarely translated into action. "I have the feeling that no one person in our Office of Imports 'rides herd' hard enough on Nelson R's office to get sanitation and health work done in areas producing strategic materials," Perkins grumbled in December 1942. In fact, the CIAA only inspected projects located in Bolivia, Colombia, Costa Rica, and Haiti and then only infrequently. The BEW's own enforcement staff was limited to a single safety engineer, recommended by Hurst after a painstaking search. Small wonder, then, that late in the war Mathews found that the financial burden of the clauses on employers had been negligible, because most had paid them "no attention whatever."[53]

The reasons for rejecting an alternative means of enforcement were no less instructive. The BEW's staff included a small and quite progressive contingent of economists who were well aware of European systems of social welfare in which trade unions distributed benefits as representatives of the entire working class. Lincoln Fairley, later a Brain Truster for Harry Bridges's longshoremen's union, urged the BEW to create a similar corporatist scheme to enforce the labor clauses through unions in each country. Only with the "active cooperation of Latin American labor," Fairley argued, would the BEW be spared the overwhelming "problem of specifying labor standards or developing methods of enforcement."[54]

Hurst probably opposed Fairley's proposal on several grounds. First, he may have concluded from his study of the Wisconsin Industrial Commission that trade unions (like other interest groups) were vital sources of information and suggestions but too self-interested to see the needs of entire societies. Only an independent public official could fairly balance all the interests involved. Second, Hurst may have thought that few Latin American unions were strong enough to play the role Fairley envisioned.[55] Finally, Hurst probably thought that giving unions a leading role in the enforcement of the labor clauses would provoke the fierce opposition of congressional conservatives. This was the reason he gave for not including a duty to bargain collectively in the obligations of the labor clauses themselves.[56]

Political calculation also shaped how the BEW justified the labor clauses. Within the agency's confines, Hurst gave three reasons for the clause. First, they would "guarantee conditions essential to maximum output and prevent the interruption of work." Second, they would "counteract Axis propaganda based on alleged 'yankee imperialism.'" Third, they would "promote a more healthy social and economic condition in the countries in which American public investments are now being made."[57]

In public battles with the BEW's rivals in the federal bureaucracy and Congress, however, Wallace and Perkins increasingly emphasized the contribution of the labor clauses to productivity and the prevention of strikes. This strategy did no injustice to the second reason, which seems to have been something of a makeweight. But by defending the labor clauses as a war measure, pure and simple, Wallace and Perkins downplayed the social justification for the clauses to the point of disingenuousness.

Although Hurst and his colleagues at the BEW often claimed that the clauses were simply a "practical method" for advancing "our obvious life and death need of getting out production," they found the connection between standards of health, sanitation, and safety and greater productivity surprisingly difficult to document.[58] Of course even the BEW's severest critics did not maintain that workers suffering from malaria, silicosis, severe malnutrition, or workplace injuries were as efficient as healthy ones. Yet many outsiders suspected the BEW of seeking much more than the minimum standards prevailing in the Latin American countries, and the BEW's own "commodities men" joked about sending " 'gilt-edge' bathtubs" to Bolivian miners and predicted that higher wages would produce absenteeism, dissipation, and "riotous living."[59]

To make the case for the labor clauses, Hurst mounted an exhaustive search for studies that systematically established a causal connection between minimum labor standards and greater productivity. He consulted officials at the Department of Labor, the Bureau of Indian Affairs, the Bureau of Mines, the Public Health Service, and the Pan-American Sanitary Bureau; an officer in the War Department versed in the construction of military bases abroad; and representatives of the United Fruit Company (celebrated for its health and sanitation programs). He also sought the views of university- or foundation-based anthropologists, including the prominent Boasian Melville Herskovits, whose *Economic Life of Primitive Peoples* (1940) had attacked the notion that Third World laborers were "essentially lazy."[60] Yet the results of Hurst's search were disappointingly inconclusive. "At no time, even in later stages of the program," concluded Robert Mathews, "was there an adequate factual basis for the proposition that certain minimum standards do, among primitive native labor, tend to increase efficiency and per capita production. . . . All there was to go on were isolated instances and reminiscences of individuals who had been connected with foreign projects."[61]

Hurst claimed that he and his associates "honestly" believed that the labor clauses would improve productivity and that it was "a real motive" for their actions. This belief was consistent with his own statement in the "Law and Society" materials that industrial accidents and disease "lowered efficiency" and impaired the "stock of human productive power." Yet his failure to establish a causal relationship between improved labor standards and greater productivity did nothing to dissuade critics who charged that the BEW's real motivation was the improvement of conditions among Latin American workers as an end in itself.[62]

The BEW could not publicly acknowledge that goal because of the limits of its jurisdiction. In confidence, Hurst frankly stated that he was trying to give "the social character of the war . . . a tangible boost towards the ideals of a democratic world." The United States was obliged not only to pay for its goods but also to address the dramatic effects its purchases were having on Latin American economies. The difficulty was that FDR's "clarification" of May 20 awarded jurisdiction over matters of "foreign policy and our relations with foreign nations" to the State Department. The BEW was to concern itself only with "matters of business judgment." As Hurst recalled, "we could never come out flatly and make this our co-ordinate argument in favor of the clauses, because then we were in the realm of 'diplomacy,' and not 'economics.' Both sides realized the realities of this, of course, which made the verbal fencing the more ironic."[63]

Presumably at some point Hurst considered the possibility that FDR had his own reasons for fixing the boundary between the State Department and the BEW as he did and that executive officials were obligated to observe that boundary in good faith. After all, the BEW was pursuing a policy that would, in effect, export the New Deal to Latin America just as the political tides were undermining its foundations in the United States.[64] Why was it not enough for Hurst that the president had ordered the BEW to limit its purview to matters of "business judgment" and leave matters of "policy" to others?

In part Hurst's answer was that the procurement and development program would necessarily disrupt the economies of Central and Latin America and that as a result the BEW simply could not do its job without engaging in policy-making. "The scope of the procurement and development program necessary in the war effort throws a corresponding responsibility upon the United States to catch the long run effects of the ways in which those programs are carried out," he told Oppenheimer in June 1942. "A wise judgment upon such long run effects is inextricably interwoven with the planning of the program, in the first instance, the negotiation of agreements thereunder, and the making of inevitable judgments of policy which will be called for in supervising the execution of such programs." If, then, FDR's "clarification" commanded the BEW to leave consideration of the social consequences of contracting to the State Department, it commanded the impossible.[65]

Because policy-making was inevitable, Hurst believed that administrators should use their best judgment on specific issues as they arise and see whether it was countermanded by Congress or the president. Although, like his mentor Felix Frankfurter, Hurst assumed that properly trained bureaucrats would ultimately "remain subject to popular, democratic controls," he believed that the experts could better weigh long-term costs and benefits than popularly elected public officials.[66] In the light of Martin Dies's attack on the BEW, legislative oversight seemed as likely to threaten responsible government as to protect it. "In practice the claims of 'Congress' are typically in fact the claims of a handful of Congressmen, or even of only one or two," Hurst wrote to Raoul Burger after the war. "With the eagerness of the mass media to find news in 'blasts,' 'revelations,' 'exposures' and whatnot, there is some real ground for concern that public interest may suffer if lower-echelon executive officers are put in too much fear of loss of jobs or reputation for the sake of headline-hunting legislators."[67] But whatever the transient concerns of the people, their ultimate wish was to have administrators use their expertise and discretion to strike the balance of power between competing interests that best promoted the general welfare. This was what Hurst believed the labor clauses did.

Of course, Hurst could only have been satisfied with such an answer if his fellow administrators took their jobs as conscientiously as he took his. Yet he knew from his own experience at the BEW that bureaucratic gamesmanship often became an end in itself. "As things unrolled," he later recalled, "I'm afraid . . . the inclusion of a labor clause wherever possible tended to become a symbol of the degree of success being achieved in the contest for power between BEW, State and RFC."[68]

In the latter half of 1942 that contest became extraordinarily fierce, even by the standards of wartime Washington. It would end with the abolition of the BEW in the summer of 1943. In retrospect, Hurst might well have concluded that the most significant lesson of the labor clauses was that even carefully conceived and executed initiatives were subject to the vagaries of bureaucratic in-fighting and party politics. But if *that* was what all "the internal turmoil, palace politics, [and] pressure grouping" of his year at BEW amounted to, how could Hurst reconcile what he once called his "limited experience as a bureaucrat" with the idealized view of administration he had propounded in his law-school classroom?[69]

UNDER FIRE

The conflict over the labor clauses took the form of endemic skirmishing between the BEW and its bureaucratic rivals, punctuated by dramatic congressional hearings in December 1942 and June 1943. The first State Department official to encounter a labor clause recoiled in horror. It was "a complex Frankenstein that will consume us later," he declared. Other diplomats opposed the clause as a likely source of unrest among workers (whose heightened expectations could not possibly be satisfied), a violation of the sovereignty of Latin American nations, and an inexpedient comment upon foreign allies' unwillingness or inability to enforce their own labor laws. After some months the BEW and State arrived at a procedure for clearing the labor clauses, yet frustrating delays in the transmittal of messages and the approval of BEW officials for overseas travel persisted.[70]

Privately BEW officials chafed at being subordinated to "an anachronistic organization which no longer suits the real needs and conditions of modern government." They complained that career diplomats lacked the administrative experience to oversee "the kind of civil service we would need to conform to the new internationalism of the common man." An attache at the American embassy in Peru so exasperated one BEW lawyer that he would later name a mongrel dog after him. Complaints about the unflattering characterizations of American diplomats by BEW officials at Washington cocktail parties forced Perkins to order his staff to be more circumspect.[71]

Relations with the RFC's subsidiaries were another source of irritation for BEW lawyers. Often procurement contracts containing the labor clauses were processed smoothly and cordial relations were maintained. When RFC officials decided that a particular development project was unnecessary, however, the conflict could turn "bloody." According to Wallace, the RFC's staff hampered the BEW's attempt to stockpile chinchona bark by objecting to the tone of its letters, mislaying papers, forgetting offers, and "hand-pick[ing] the 'right kinds of people'" to do business with. Conflict over the need to develop new sources of rubber in Brazil and Peru provoked what was perhaps the most prolonged and heated strife. As Charles F. Luce, a BEW lawyer assigned to the Rubber Division of the Office of Imports, recalled, "It felt like the Axis we were fighting was RFC and State."[72]

For his part, Jesse Jones never accepted Wallace's attempt "to play Santa Claus" in Latin America. He termed the benefits the vice president wanted employers to provide their workers "so 'social' as to be practically eleemosynary." Jones scoffed that the vice president thought that getting Amazonian Indians to eat spinach and string beans would make the world a better place. When Wallace urged that impoverished Bolivian tin miners be given a free hot meal each day, Jones objected that less ore would be mined as a result. As he later declared, "The miners worked only because they had to work to eat."[73]

In December 1942 Jones took his complaints to an executive session of the Senate Banking and Currency Committee. A senator called for an end to the BEW's "untrammeled and whimsical abuse of powers," but Perkins and Wallace stared down the challenge. Perkins denied that the labor clauses were "designed to accomplish some grandiose purpose of revolutionizing social and working conditions"; Wallace protested that they were needed "to get the maximum of materials as fast as possible." As the journalist I. F. Stone dryly observed, "The mere fact that they will enable us to obtain more materials is not enough to down the horrid suspicion that these clauses may also help create a more decent world." Still Stone was pleased that Wallace, "the champion of the common man," had won a round.[74]

It would be the last Wallace would win as chairman of the BEW. In early January 1943 the agency's authority over rubber imports was transferred to an ally of Jones at the War Production Board. Wallace struck back with "Order No. 5," issued while Roosevelt was meeting Winston Churchill in Morocco. Invoking the authority of a general presidential directive against duplication in government, Wallace sought to reduce the RFC subsidiaries to little more than accounting offices. Jones fiercely opposed the gambit, charging that it would require either the transfer of his staff to the BEW or the substitution of "a new, inexperienced staff for an experienced organization."[75] By appealing to sympathetic conservatives in Congress and dangling a never-consummated proposal to transfer a minor RFC subsidiary to BEW, Jones managed to keep Wallace at bay throughout the late winter and spring of 1943.[76]

The controversy came to a head in June before a Congress dominated by a coalition of Republicans and Southern Democrats, which had already dismantled such New Deal agencies as the Civilian Conservation Corps, the Works Progress Administration, the National Youth Administration, and the National Resources Planning Board.[77] Confronted with a request for a 70 percent increase in the BEW's appropriation, Jones's congressional allies subjected Perkins to close questioning about the BEW's salaries, its General Counsel's office, and its labor clauses. When a congressman ventured that the labor clauses were a form of "social uplift," Perkins vigorously denied that the BEW was out to promote some "world vision." "We are as ruthless and as tough and as hard, in terms of getting the maximum inward flow of strategic materials, as any gang of guys ever was," he protested. On June 29 Wallace took the offensive by charging Jones's subordinates with "fighting the war with peacetime red tape, corporate technicalities, and what seems to us to be an unnecessary caution." A White House meeting of the two principals collapsed in an angry exchange, and Jones publicly complained that the BEW's efforts to acquire materials "border[ed] on the hysterical." "Squandering the people's money even in wartime is no proof of patriotism," he declared.[78]

To *Time* magazine the affair was a "Battle of Titans"; to an economist at the BEW, a death struggle between the Four Freedoms and "economic and political fascism at home." In July Perkins made new accusations of obstructionism and told a staff meeting that in speaking out Wallace had done what "any red-blooded American" would have after turning over a rock and spying the "slimy things crawling" beneath. When that remark appeared in the press, FDR promptly abolished the BEW and transferred its duties, together with some duties of the RFC subsidiaries, to a new agency. Wallace and Jones each received reprimands, but, observers agreed, Wallace suffered more. Jones retained his cabinet position, but Wallace was left with only the small staff of the vice president's office, a few inconsequential duties, and every prospect of being dropped from the Democratic ticket in 1944.[79]

RETROSPECT

Hurst viewed the final days of the BEW from the Navy's Bureau of Personnel, where he had been assigned early in January 1943 after being commissioned a lieutenant in the U.S. Naval Reserves. A full reckoning of what Hurst learned during the war would have to account for his experiences within the vast military bureaucracy of the Navy. Still, the BEW episode provides at least a preliminary basis for identifying the lessons Hurst drew from his wartime encounter with the administrative state.[80]

Judging from his postwar writings, Hurst's ideal for the administrative process survived its spectacular collision with the actualities of bureaucratic and party politics at the BEW. Moreover, it was joined by a new ideal that attributed to the legal profession a distinctive function in American statecraft. After the war Hurst would depict lawyers as the professionals most skilled at untangling complicated factual situations, perceiving long-run consequences, and imagining creative solutions to the social problems of the day. Hurst attributed the failure of his efforts at the BEW to the shortsightedness of businessmen and politicians. Had creative, socially conscious lawyers dominated the rest of the federal government as much as they had the BEW, he believed, the result might have been different. Implicit in Hurst's view was a mistrust of popular politics and an ideal of lawyering as a public service, neither of which he ever discarded.[81] "For all its failings," Hurst wrote in 1964, the "legal process served no more distinctive function than to lend leverage to the more farsighted elements in the community, readier than the crowd to postpone present satisfactions for the gains of future growth and stability."[82]

When Hurst's colleague and close friend, Jacob Beuscher, returned to the Wisconsin law faculty after working at the Office of Price Administration (OPA), he professed himself a chastened man. Before the war Beuscher believed that most people thought that lawyers had "a training in social objectivity and in analytical thinking superior to that of ordinary college-trained men." Yet when, at the OPA, Beuscher refused to "draw a fixed line around the 'legal' domain and to stay within it," he encountered the fierce opposition of other administrators. The experience left Beuscher doubting whether "the historic notion of the lawyer's position within American government" was as secure as it once was.[83]

Hurst's experience at the BEW was quite different. As chief of the Office of Imports, Morris Rosenthal insisted on "a genuine partnership" between his "gang" of businessmen and "the legal gang."[84] His top lawyers, he later boasted, were not only some of the ablest in Washington, but "liberals to boot." Their politics was no accident. "Being a liberal myself," Rosenthal explained, "I knew that I would be handicapped" by the "ultraconservatives" among the businessmen on his staff. "It wouldn't be that they would consciously sabotage me, but they had no social knowledge and . . . no political knowledge. They didn't know the problems of the world."[85]

Rosenthal looked to his lawyers to keep the "commodities men" true to "the ideals of Mr. Wallace." He invited lawyers into the inner councils of the Office of Imports and dispersed them throughout the "line" divisions where they served as "an opposite number" to the businessmen in the BEW's dealings with the RFC and State. "My commodity men objected, and some of Washington laughed at me and said the BEW was dominated by lawyers," Rosenthal recalled. "That was okay with me."[86]

After having enjoyed such influence, Hurst had a more favorable impression of the bar's prestige than did Beuscher. Any lawyer who had an "opportunity to see wartime Washington from the inside of a wartime bureaucracy came away with an enhanced feeling of pride," Hurst claimed in 1952. "Responsible administrators" looked to lawyers for "detached, responsible, shrewd judgment." This was especially true for administrators charged with "channeling" production and distribution during the war. In this work the bar certainly "stood well" in comparison to the other professionals and "immensely well in comparison to businessmen."[87]

Before the war, Hurst had not described lawyers as central players in the fashioning of public policy. For example, in the "Law in Society" materials Hurst acknowledged that lawyers had sometimes exercised "creative choice" in their practice, but he seemed to be more impressed by how often "doctrine and professional training" kept them from recognizing the advantages of the administrative process.[88] This dim view of the ability of lawyers to rise to the challenges and opportunities of the new administrative state was consistent with what Hurst later called the "almost purely negative" reaction of the elite bar to the New Deal. It was also consistent with the tales of in-fighting among the members of the attorney general's committee on administrative procedure that Garrison probably recounted as Hurst was assembling the "Law in Society" materials. Under the circumstances, the most Hurst would claim for the bar before Pearl Harbor was skill in deciding which legal agency should determine a particular policy and how that policy should be enforced. Whether government should intervene at all and the substance of the policy to be adopted were matters beyond the professional competence of lawyers.[89]

Already in the spring of 1942 Hurst was changing his views in light of his experiences at the BEW. He still questioned whether lawyers could offer much insight into the shape of public policy from their own expertise. Economists, cultural anthropologists, political scientists, and political historians still seemed to be the primary producers of the relevant knowledge. But lawyers were acquiring a new authority in his thinking—and in his contemporaneous work at the BEW—by becoming "the expert whose skill it is to make social use of the experts in all other fields." The very nature of their profession, which immersed them in many different factual situations, made them "jack[s]-of-all-trades" and prepared them to take the lead in "the coordination and planning of men's interrelated activities." Experts, as Frankfurter had put it in 1930, were to "be on tap, but not on top." Lawyers were to be on top, doing the tapping.[90]

In *The Growth of American Law* (1950), Hurst generalized his experiences at the BEW into a "professional ideal." As he surveyed American legal history, Hurst considered the bar a "law maker" of the same stature as legislatures, courts, constitutional conventions, and executive officials. The legal profession was "one of the great institutions which carried the administrative burden of our society," he wrote. Its members performed the role of "specialist in incisive, accurate, fast appraisal of snarled or complicated situations." They were "makers of institutions, of social tools, of patterns of action." The best combined a "daring readiness to innovate with [a] tough-minded insistence that the need and direction of innovation rest firmly on fact."[91]

According to Hurst, lawyers' influence in industry and government had only grown with the expansion of the administrative state. In the nineteenth century the robber baron Cornelius Vanderbilt could boast, "What do I care about the law. Hain't I got the power?" In the twentieth century, Vanderbilt's gray-flannel successors constantly felt the "pressure of government intervention in the economy" and looked to their lawyers for guidance. The regulators needed their lawyers no less than the regulated. Every major federal agency, Hurst observed, had its general counsel's staff, "directly responsible to, and in continuous contact with, their policy-making heads." Wherever they practiced, lawyers could use the administrative state to claim "a new independence" from clients blinkered by short-term calculations of economic or political advantage. As officers, not just of the courts, but of the state, lawyers could make clients reshape their aims and, "in a measure," at least, take "their values from the law."[92]

Through much of Hurst's postwar corpus, shortsighted businessmen, politicians, and their lawyers triumphed over attempts to use law to preserve public values, much as Jesse Jones and congressional conservatives had triumphed over the BEW. In a review essay published in 1945, Hurst blasted Michigan's territorial legislature for permitting J. J. Astor to strip away the "rich top layer of profits" from the fur trade of the Upper Peninsula and impoverish Native American tribes in the process. (In this respect Astor bore a striking resemblance to Simon Patino and Mauricio Hochschild, absentee owners of Bolivian tin and tungsten mines, whose striking workers prompted an international crisis late in Hurst's tenure at the BEW.)[93] Hurst lamented that the fee simple absolute, a common-law device developed for the transfer of "town lots and peach orchards," had been used to dispose of oil and gas, "an invaluable and irreplaceable resource of the whole population." Creative lawyers might have developed leases to preserve the public interest, but the bar and other lawmakers were "too narrowly focused to promote an economical or humane development" of vital natural resources.[94]

Similar acts of legal inertia and "bastard pragmatism" destroyed Wisconsin's hardwood and white pine forests in Hurst's tragic masterpiece, *Law and Economic Growth* (1964). Thus, in striking down Wisconsin's extensive program of forest reserves, the State Supreme Court Justice Roujet Marshall, formerly lawyer to the Weyerhaeuser lumber interests, displayed both "the practical man's suspicion of ambitious ideas" and "the practical man's sense that public policy was best made by the rough-hewn opportunism of ordinary politics." Yet Hurst also noted that another lawyer, Gabriel Bouck, drafted a statute that gave workers in the industry a lien on lumber for the value of their services. In his notes of an interview conducted for the book, Hurst rendered his informant as stating that Bouck had been motivated by his "public spirit" and his perception of social "need." Hurst agreed. Bouck's statute, he wrote, protected the "dignity and self-respect of the individual" and helped rationalize the "bootstrap finance" of the Wisconsin lumber industry. As an act of social invention by a public-regarding lawyer, Bouck's "log-labor lien" anticipated Hurst's own labor clauses.[95]

Throughout his career Hurst was dismayed by encounters with businessmen "so caught up in a day to day rush of immediate decision making that they have, for years, had no time to try to add up what they're doing." He was still exploring how law and lawyers could protect the "commonwealth and individual values" that eluded the "monetized calculus" of markets in his Curti lectures of 1981 and in his legal history course shortly before his retirement.[96] In the latter, as recorded in 1978, Hurst returned to his days at the BEW to illustrate the limits of the "private bargaining market" as an agency of the social good. "It was early in World War II," Hurst recalled.

The Japanese victories in the Far East had effectively cut off our supplies of raw rubber, which was obviously very critical both for our immediate war effort but also for sustaining the domestic production economy. Jesse Jones, a very able business executive and government administrator, who was largely in charge of the war procurement effort for raw material, came into his office one morning. One of his top lieutenants looked up with a very long face. [Jones asked,] "What's wrong with you?" His lieutenant said, "Well, didn't you see the morning paper and that account of that fire that burned up several thousand tons of raw rubber in the Boston warehouse?" And Jones said in honest astonishment, "What are you so worried about? It was insured wasn't it?"

Hurst explained that recovery of the insured value of the rubber was little comfort in light of the urgent need for the thing itself. Jones only cared about "money-measured" values, and in this he personified a general shortcoming of economic markets. "Monetized values just don't carry you far enough," Hurst warned his students. To protect the broader public interest, the "immediate calculus of those people bargaining in markets" did not suffice.[97]

In the "Law in Society" course, Hurst had attempted to instill in his students a due regard for how the administrative process could supplement markets in securing "the basic conditions of a decent life for the individual" in modern societies.[98] After the war he continued to teach lawyers that administrative action was a social necessity. This lesson became the ultimate message of his historical work. What still requires explanation is why Hurst remained faithful to his ideals after the labor clauses that embodied them had met so spectacular and ignominious a defeat.

THE IDEAL AND THE ACTUAL

One explanation for Hurst's optimism about lawyers and the administrative state notwithstanding the fall of the BEW is straightforward enough: Hurst might have thought the agency too atypical to support any firm conclusions about the administrative process. When compared to the Wisconsin Industrial Commission, for example, the BEW looked like an artifact of party politics. Agencies that responded to broad and deep social trends were another matter altogether, as some of Hurst's BEW colleagues later discovered during distinguished careers of public service.[99] Yet in an interview conducted in 1981 Hurst claimed to have learned "a great deal about bureaucracy in the course of that year in the B.E.W.," with all its "internal turmoil, palace politics, [and] pressure grouping." The lessons, he clearly implied, were general in their application.[100]

One of the lessons, as we have seen, was the need for a legal profession trained to consider the public values often neglected by profit-conscious businessmen and vote-hungry politicians. In drawing this conclusion Hurst surely was not alone. For example, their "fairly consistent experience of finding lawyers doing new and exacting jobs well and imaginatively" during the war convinced the Harvard law professors James Casner and Barton Leach that lawyers would assume "a very large proportion of the national leadership at all levels of authority" during the postwar era.[101] But another lesson Hurst drew from the fall of the BEW was less about legal institutions than about human nature. The salience of the lesson for Hurst may have been as much a matter of his own temperament as an instantiation of a broader cultural trend.

At various times in the late 1940s, Hurst recommended to correspondents two novels by James Gould Cozzens—*The Just and the Unjust* (1942) and *Guard of Honor* (1948)—and a third by the British author Nigel Balchin, *The Small Back Room* (1945). Hurst told Frankfurter that the Cozzens novels were "the best fiction anyone has done about the law in this country" and performed a "penetrating job on law- and bureaucracy-in-action." He commended Balchin's book to Joseph Rauh as "a remarkably acute, novelized picture of bureaucratic in-fighting in wartime England."[102] The protagonists—a young assistant district attorney in *The Just and the Unjust*, a much older judge serving as an inspector in the Army Air Forces in *Guard of Honor*, and a scientist laboring on the staff of an obscure research laboratory in *The Small Back Room*—were all dutiful, intelligent, hardworking men, mindful of their own limitations but also of their abilities, which were superior to those of most of the people around them.[103] Each diligently and intelligently attempted some task—the trial of a felony murder case, the running of an air base in Florida, the sensible employment of Great Britain's scientific resources during the war—only to suffer a major setback at the hands of more frivolous or self-interested characters. Each novel contrasted its hero with the kind of professional politicians and calculating bureaucrats who might have peopled Hurst's own reminiscences of the BEW. In *The Just and the Unjust* a local boss demanded tribute in return for the party's nomination for district attorney; in *Guard of Honor* the protagonist's wife asserted without contradiction that the judge was incapable of the manipulation that a political career entailed; in *The Small Back Room* the scientist sees the chief of his laboratory replaced with a less able but better connected person after cunning bureaucrats engineer the downfall of a minister. Yet in each book the hero perseveres. The foibles and shortcomings of those around them are real enough, but they do not excuse the protagonists from doing their job to the utmost of their abilities.

Perhaps the clearest statement of this stoicism came at the end of *The Just and the Unjust*. In the wake of an unfavorable jury verdict, the young lawyer questioned the wisdom of soldiering on in a conversation with his father. "Don't be cynical," the father replied.

> A cynic is just a man who found out when he was about ten that there wasn't any Santa Claus, and he's still upset. . . . There'll be deaths and disappointments and failures. When they come, you meet them. Nobody promises you a good time or an easy time. . . . There is the present to think of, and as long as you live there always will be. In the present, every day is a miracle. The world gets up in the morning and is fed and goes to work, and in the evening it comes home and is fed again and perhaps has a little amusement and goes to sleep. To make that possible, so much has to be done by so many people that, on the face of it, it is impossible. Well, every day we

do it; and every day, come hell, come high water, we're going to have to go on doing it as well as we can.[104]

Hurst may not have read those words when the novel appeared during his year at the BEW, but they certainly capture the resolve and seriousness of purpose with which he pursued his duties there. In 1978, after enduring the skepticism of Wisconsin's radical students and colleagues, Hurst still looked to Cozzens to explain why one should not give up on the regulatory state. "There are very few disinterested, public-spirited people around guiding affairs," Hurst acknowledged before his students. Yet that fact did not justify a cynical attitude toward government. "A cynic, James Gould Cozzens said years ago, simply is someone who at age eight discovered there was no Santa Claus and never got over it." A realist, in contrast, was "simply one who understands how things go." Yes, government, "although set up to preserve something called the public interest, becomes itself a major target of pride and selfish ambition." But that was no reason to discard a powerful agency for the public good.[105]

At such moments in his teaching and writing Hurst reached toward a goal he set for the field of legal history in 1942: the development in lawyers of "a trained intuition of the affirmative possibilities as well as the limitations of human institutions and the ordinary men who run them and act within their framework." Perhaps if Hurst were a less idealistic person or had been more engaged in battles over legislation and public policy after the war he might have revised his own intuitions about the administrative state in light of the unhappy fate of the labor clauses.[106] He might have attributed the failure of policy-makers not to the inevitable imperfection of all human undertakings but to the partial nature of the particular policy-makers' social vision, the persistence of party politics, and the deep, structural divisions of the governments in which they worked.

Instead, Hurst stuck to his ideals and attributed the setbacks of his own administrative career to what he once called the "limitations of energy, courage, imagination, [and] vitality that adhere in being a human being."[107] In his lectures and writings Hurst showed how those limitations manifested themselves in the past, and he challenged his students and readers to struggle against them in their own lives. Ultimately, younger lawyers with little patience for Niebuhrian cautions about the tragic element in human nature would insist that Hurst's notion of social welfare and social function were particular to his class and time.[108] When they called for participatory democracy, Hurst charged them with "utopianism" and offered examples of lawyers creatively using the liberal state to promote the general social welfare.[109] On such occasions the memory of his own unhappy experience at the BEW was not a source of discouragement. Much like the New York lawyer James Coolidge Carter, confronting the failure of turn-of-the-century America to live up to his quite different standards of conduct, Hurst drew from his experience renewed resolve to lift "up the actual to a nearer approach to the ideal."[110]

NOTES

1. Tocqueville, *Democracy in America,* 1: 273; Root, "Public Service by the Bar," 368–69; Hurst, *Growth of American Law,* 301; Baum, Goldman, and Sarat, "Evolution of Litigation," 300–04, 306–08.

2. Skowronek, *Building a New American State,* 290.

3. Nixon, *Memoirs,* 25–26.

4. Felix Frankfurter to Milo Perkins, January 12, 1942, reel 42, Felix Frankfurter Papers, Library of Congress (hereafter FF-LC). See Ernst, "Hurst and the Administrative State."

5. Hurst to Frankfurter, January 3, 1938, reel 42, FF-LC. See also Frankfurter to Hurst, January 6, 1938, reel 39, part 3, Felix Frankfurter Papers, Harvard Law School Library (hereafter FF-HLS); Hurst to Frankfurter, May 18, 1938, reel 42, FF-LC.

6. Frankfurter to Hurst, February 12, 1940, reel 39, FF-HLS.

7. Eskridge, "Willard Hurst," 1184 n. 10; "Partial Curriculum Committee Report," May 25, 1939, Box 5, Series 11/1/2, University of Wisconsin Archives, Memorial Library, Madison (hereafter Subject Files, WLS-UWA); Hurst, "J. Willard Hurst: An Interview Conducted by Laura L. Smail" (Madison: University Archives Oral History Project, University of Wisconsin-Madison, 1981), 23 (hereafter Hurst, Smail Interview); Hurst, "Content of Courses in Legislation," 291–92. Hurst circulated Part Two in late 1939 as James Willard Hurst, *Developments in the Law of Industrial Accident.* Louis D. Brandeis to Hurst, December 26, 1939, reel 33, series 2, Louis Dembitz Brandeis Papers, Harvard Law School Library. The first edition of the complete materials was Garrison and Hurst, *Law in Society: A Course Designed for Undergraduates and Beginning Law Students* (hereafter *Law in Society,* 1940 ed.). A new edition was used in the Fall 1941 semester: Garrison and Hurst, *Law in Society: A Course Designed for Undergraduates and Beginning Law Students: Cases and Other Materials* (hereafter *Law in Society,* 1941 ed.). The materials remained available only in typescript until Hurst's colleagues published a thorough revision in 1961 as Auerbach, Garrison, Hurst, and Mermin, *The Legal Process.*

8. Hurst, Smail Interview, 20; Garrison to Carl A. Auerbach, April 18, 1960, Box 5, Lloyd Kirkham Garrison Papers, Harvard Law School Library; see also Garrison to David Riesman, Jr., May 26, 1942, Box 54, Series 11/1/1, University of Wisconsin Archives, Memorial Library, Madison (hereafter General Correspondence, WLS-UWA). I believe Hurst was unduly generous in crediting Garrison and that Garrison more accurately captured their relative contributions. Thus I attribute the ideas and expressions in *Law in Society* to Hurst alone in the paragraphs that follow.

9. "Lloyd Garrison made this a lively and liberal law school," Hurst wrote to Joseph L. Rauh, Jr., after the war. Hurst asked Rauh to recommend a "good New Dealer" to join the faculty and help keep Wisconsin that way. Hurst to Rauh, March 19, 1947, May 9, 1947, Box 3, Part 1, Joseph L. Rauh, Jr., Papers, Library of Congress.

10. *Law in Society,* 1941 ed., 1: 223; "Hon. George W. Wickersham Receives the American Bar Association Medal," *American Bar Association Journal* 20 (1934):

624–25; *Law in Society*, 1941 ed., 1: 194–97. Hurst excerpted the work of such legal realists as Thurman Arnold, Albert Kocourek, Jerome Frank, Joseph C. Hutcheson, Jr., and Max Radin. On the relationship between legal realism and the New Deal, see White, *Intervention and Detachment*, 165–66; Duxbury, *Patterns of American Jurisprudence*, 149–58; Shamir, *Managing Legal Uncertainty*, 131–57.

11. *Law in Society*, 1941 ed., 1: 223–24; see Pound, "Theory of Social Interests," 16–45.

12. Hurst, Review of *Politics of Democracy*, 715–17; Pendleton Herring, "Lobby," *Encyclopedia of the Social Sciences* 9 (1931): 565–68, in *Law in Society*, 1940 ed., 3: 495–505; R. M. MacIver, "Interests," *Encyclopedia of the Social Sciences* 8 (1932): 144–48, in *Law in Society*, 1940 ed., 2: 41–45; Gertrude Schmidt, "History of Labor Legislation in Wisconsin" (Ph.D. diss., University of Wisconsin, 1933), in *Law in Society*, 1941 ed., 3: 439.

13. *Law in Society*, 1941 ed., 1: 213.

14. Ibid., 2: i–ii, iii.

15. The legal realist Max Radin noted the similarity between the "Law in Society" course and earlier, "functional" experiments in legal pedagogy. Radin, Review of *Law in Society*, 1085–87; see Kalman, *Legal Realism at Yale*. Hurst thought that *Law in Society* was distinguishable from the realists' casebooks. These were as court-centered as those of the conceptualists, Hurst implied, when what was needed was instruction in "a much broader range of legal agencies." Hurst, Smail Interview, 19–20.

16. *Law in Society*, 1941 ed., 1: 24.

17. *Law in Society*, 1940 ed., 1: 30–31. Hurst dropped this passage in the 1941 edition to make room for an excerpt from the report of the U.S. Attorney General's Committee on Administrative Procedure. *Law in Society*, 1941 ed., 30–94.

18. John R. Commons, *Myself: The Autobiography of John R. Commons* (Madison: University of Wisconsin Press, 1963), in *Law in Society*, 1941 ed., 3: 734–35; see Hawley, "Herbert Hoover," 116–40; Hart, "Herbert Hoover's Last Laugh," 419–44.

19. Hurst, "Research Program," 332. Hurst may have started work on this article before leaving Madison, but internal evidence, such as a new interest in the "legal control of trade with foreign nations" as a means of creating "a better ordered world economy," suggests that he completed it while at the BEW. Ibid., 333. In any event, Garrison had a copy of Hurst's "memorandum on 'Legal History: A Research Program'" in early May. Garrison to Hurst, May 8, 1942, Box 54, General Correspondence, WLS-UWA.

20. At Northwestern, Dean Leon Green convened the faculty and frankly told the younger professors to look for war-related work. Willard Wirtz, conversation with author, Washington, D.C., June 10, 1998. Sources do not permit firm conclusions about the role Hurst's draft status (3A) played in his thinking. Monroe Oppenheimer to Herbert Wechsler, August 7, 1942, Box 1, Entry 101, Records of the Foreign Economic Administration, RG 169, National Archives, College Park, Md.

21. Wirtz, conversation; "Symposium on Lawyers under the United States Civil Service," *American Law School Review* 9 (1942): 1316–17.

22. Lloyd K. Garrison to C. A. Dykstra, January 12, 1942, Box 53, General Correspondence, WLS-UWA. Hurst was still in Madison on February 3, 1942. He filed the first in a regular series of reports on his activities at the BEW on February 19.

Garrison to Charles Bunn, February 3, 1942, Box 53, ibid.; Hurst to Harold W. Starr, February 19, 1942, Box 1189, Entry 240, RG 169.

23. Matson, *Neutrality and Navicerts;* Bidwell, "Our Economic Warfare," 421–37.

24. *Time,* April 27, 1942, 12.

25. Sirevag, *Eclipse of the New Deal,* 101–05.

26. Acheson, *Present at the Creation,* 16–20; *New York Times,* February 28, 1941, 9; *Who Was Who* (Chicago: Marquis's Who's Who, 1981), 7: 194; Wirtz, conversation.

27. Executive Order No. 8840, July 30, 1941, *Federal Register* 6 (1941): 3857–58; U.S. Office of Inter-American Affairs, *History of the Office,* 9; Reich, *Life of Nelson A. Rockefeller.*

28. Acheson, *Present at the Creation,* 40; Sanger, *Administrative History,* 39, 92; *New York Times,* May 22, 1942; Jones and Angley, *Fifty Billion Dollars,* 485–86. The BEW was originally called the Economic Defense Board. It acquired its better-known name shortly after the attack on Pearl Harbor.

29. Kennedy, *Freedom From Fear,* 457.

30. Blum, *V Was for Victory,* 281; Henry A. Wallace, "The Price of World Victory," in Blum, ed., *Price of Vision,* 638.

31. Acheson, *Present at the Creation,* 40–41; "A Job for Mr. Perkins," *Time,* August 25, 1941, 15; J. Ashford Link, "Mr. Perkins Goes to War," *New Republic,* February 9, 1942, 200.

32. Morris S. Rosenthal, interview, September 11, 1943, Box 1, Entry 144, RG 169; Morris Rosenthal to Milo Perkins, October 5, 1941, Box 19, Entry 128, RG 169; "Morris Sigmund Rosenthal," *National Cyclopedia of American Biography* (New York: James T. White, 1961), 43: 33–34.

33. Brown, *Lawyers, Law Schools and the Public Service,* 69–70. After graduating cum laude from the Yale Law School in 1926, Oppenheimer worked as research assistant to the legal realist Wesley Sturges, who occasionally consulted with Jerome Frank at the Agricultural Adjustment Administration. Yale Law School Association, *Yale Law School Alumni Directory, Containing Biographies of Living Alumni* (New Haven, 1949), 366–67.

34. Sirevag, *Eclipse of the New Deal,* 108.

35. Charles W. Yost, "Prospective Functions of the Board of Economic Warfare," December 22, 1941, Box 1, Entry 67, General Records of the Department of State, RG 59, National Archives, College Park, Md.; Dean Acheson to Mr. Shaw, January 16, 1942, ibid.

36. Henry A. Wallace to Franklin Delano Roosevelt, March 4, 20, 1942, in Blum, ed., *Price of Vision,* 56–58.

37. Ogden, *Dies Committee,* 260–64; Weyl, *Reconquest of Mexico;* "Personnel Inquiry D.I. for Nathaniel Weyl," Box 21, Entry 128, RG 169; Buller, "Administrative History of the Board of Economic Warfare," 19; Sanger, *Administrative History,* 79. Weyl may have been the first person to propose writing minimum labor standards into loan applications and procurement contracts as part of his call for the creation of a "labor section" within BEW. Nathaniel Weyl to Rosenthal, February 3, 1942, Box 6, Entry 145, RG 169.

38. Sirevag, *Eclipse of the New Deal,* 109–11; Executive Order 9128, April 13, 1942, *Federal Register* 7 (1942): 2809–10.

39. *New York Times*, April 30, 1942; Sumner Welles to FDR, April 15, 1942, Box 1, Entry 67, RG 59; Anonymous to Dean Acheson, April 18, 1942, ibid.; Acheson, *Present at the Creation*, 41.

40. *New York Times*, April 19, 1942; Wallace Diary, April 23, 1942, in Blum, ed., *Price of Vision*, 69; Jones and Angley, *Fifty Billion Dollars*, 489, 492.

41. Sanger, *Administrative History of the FEA*, 82–86, 124; Rosenthal, interview; Jake Beuscher to Lloyd K. Garrison, April 16, 1942, Box 53, General Correspondence, WLS-UWA; Robert E. Mathews, "The Place of Labor Standards Provisions in the Government's Foreign Procurement Contracts," 9, April 1, 1944, Box 4, Entry 146, RG 169.

42. Joint Committee on Reduction of Nonessential Federal Expenditures, *Reduction of Nonessential Federal Expenditures*, 78th Cong., 1st sess., June 11, 1943, 2342, 2348.

43. Mathews, "Labor Standards," 9a. Esther Brown apparently drew the same conclusion in a study for the Russell Sage Foundation. "One lawyer evolved the idea, made the initial draft, and promoted the desirability of the 'labor clause,' which although much debated was subsequently incorporated in many of the contracts." She did not, however, mention Hurst by name. Brown, *Lawyers, Law Schools and the Public Service*, 88.

44. Mathews, "Labor Standards," 10; Hurst to Oppenheimer, March 3, 1942, Box 2, Entry 101, RG 169.

45. Mathews, "Labor Standards," 10–12, 25–28; Hurst to Creswell Micou, April 1, 1942, Box 483, Entry 1, Records of the Office of Inter-American Affairs, RG 229, National Archives, College Park, Md.; Harold W. Starr to Rosenthal, June 22, 1942, Box 3, Entry 101, RG 169.

46. "Memo of Understanding," n.d., Box 6, Entry 145, RG 169; see Mathews, "Labor Standards," 14, 16.

47. Attorney General's Committee on Administrative Procedure, *The Walsh-Healey Act* (Washington, D.C.: Department of Justice, 1939), 1–3; Hurst to Starr, April 20, 1942, Box 1189, Entry 240, RG 169. Another possible model was the attempt to use procurement contracts to abolish sweatshop conditions in the production of Army uniforms during World War I. Hurst's mentor, Felix Frankfurter, had been involved in these efforts as an official in the War Department and as chairman of the War Labor Policies Board. Hurst could have discussed the labor clauses with the Supreme Court justice during their occasional meetings during the war. In any event, "at an early stage of the war," Hurst borrowed Frankfurter's copy of a "volume of materials regarding labor standards, in connection with the Paris Peace Conference." Parrish, *Frankfurter*, 102–17; Boris, *Home to Work*, 135–47; Frances Hurst, conversation, Madison, Wis., May 12, 1998; Hurst to Frankfurter, May 9, 1946, Reel 42, FF-LC.

48. On the BEW's early interest in development corporations, see Hallett Johnson to Thomas K. Finletter, February 12, 1942, Box 18, Entry 356, RG 59; Hurst to Harold W. Starr, March 25, April 27, 1942, Box 1189, Entry 240, RG 169. In the latter half of December 1942 Hurst prepared a lengthy proposal for a network of government corporations to coordinate the production of fats and oils in Brazil and serve as a "yardstick" for judging the efficiency of private firms. Hurst to Theodore Kreps, n.d., Box 2, Entry 119, RG 169.

49. Mathews, "Labor Standards," 16; Office of Imports, "Staff Meeting Minutes," August 14, 1942, Box 4, Entry 145, RG 169.

50. Rosenthal to All BEW Foreign Field Representatives, Draft, November 15, 1942, Box 6, Entry 145, RG 169. Earlier Hurst had BEW officials instruct field representatives to tell sellers that they would, in effect, be reimbursed for the cost of complying with the labor clauses in the purchase price for their goods. Sidney H. Scheuer to Borgers, Moise, and Sumpter, July 3, 1942, Box 6, Entry 355, RG 59.

51. Almost all the countries were located in Central and South America, although a few contracts dealt with rubber production in West Africa, such as Firestone's plantation in Liberia. Mathews to Rosenthal, April 19, 1943, Box 1, Entry 119, RG 169.

52. Mathews, "Labor Standards," 12; Perkins to Oppenheimer, June 10, 1942, Box 1, Entry 101, RG 169.

53. Mathews, "Labor Standards," 14, 32, 33, 72–73; Hurst to Benedict S. Deinard, September 15, 22, November 10, 1942, Box 1189, Entry 240, RG 169; John C. McLintock to Oppenheimer, July 28, 1942, Box 483, Entry 1, RG 229; Sanger, *Administrative History*, 101–03; Robert E. Mathews to Robert Martin, July 6, 1943, Box 19, Entry 128, RG 169. Perkins's complaint, made to Rosenthal's second-in-command, Arthur Paul, was dated December 8, 1942 and appears in the margins of Rockefeller to Wallace, December 5, 1942, Box 4, Entry 145, RG 169.

Rosenthal believed that BEW was "making progress" in enforcing the labor clauses when the agency was abolished. "Had the BEW lasted throughout the war," he claimed, "there would have been very, very genuine progress made, because each day we were gaining in strength." "The Reminiscences of Morris S. Rosenthal," Columbia Oral History Collection (Columbia University, 1959), 282 (conducted May 1952 to January 1953). Asked whether the BEW lawyers actually thought they would be able to carry off such a massive administrative undertaking, Willard Wirtz replied not only that they did, but that they were surprised that they did not have more success during the life of the agency. Wirtz, conversation.

54. Fairley to Dewey Anderson, September 26, 1942, Box 2, Entry 101, RG 169; Theodore J. Kreps, interview, February 14, 1944, Box 1, Entry 144, ibid.; Fairley to Members of the Interdivisional Manpower Committee, September 5, 1942, Entry 119, ibid. Fairley arranged for Hurst to discuss enforcement with Vincent Toledano, president of Mexico's main labor federation, and Robert Watt of the American Federation of Labor. Hurst to Deinard, December 8, 1942, Box 1189, Entry 240, ibid.; see Fairley to Anderson, November 16, 1942, Box 6, Entry 145, ibid.

55. This was Willard Wirtz's recollection of the BEW lawyers' reasoning in June 1998. In 1942 an overseas representative reported to one of the BEW's economists that Brazil's trade bodies were "strictly company unions" and played "a very insignificant role in accomplishing anything." Bill Sherwood to Theodore J. Kreps, September 30, 1942, Box 1, Entry 119, RG 169. In addition, I cannot rule out the possibility that Hurst objected to the Communist leadership of unions in other Latin American countries. As a member of an AFL-affiliate at the University of Wisconsin in the 1930s, Hurst had spent "many weary hours . . . outsitting the communist sympathizers," who had expected that liberals such as himself would soon "wear out and want to go home and go to bed." Hurst, Smail Interview, 97. That said, I have encountered no document or recollection of Hurst at the BEW that suggests that anti-Communism played a significant part in his thinking.

56. Mathews, "Labor Standards," 15.

57. The quoted language is from a memorandum Hurst prepared, Starr to Rosenthal, June 22, 1942, Box 3, Entry 101, RG 169. See also Oppenheimer to James L. Fly, March 19, 1942, Box 2, Entry 101, RG 169; Mathews, "Labor Standards," 19, 20.

58. The quoted language is from a memorandum Hurst prepared, Rosenthal to All BEW Foreign Field Representatives, Draft, November 5, 1942, Box 6, Entry 145, RG 169.

59. Mathews, "Labor Standards," 16–17, 19–20; John M. Jacobson to Just Lunning, April 20, 1943, Box 1, Entry 145, RG 169.

60. Mathews, "Labor Standards," 16–17; Hurst to Starr, April 14, 1942, Hurst to Deinard, September 29, December 15, 1942, Box 1189, Entry 240, RG 169; Herskovits, *Economic Life of Primitive Peoples*, 76. At Hurst's suggestion, Herskovits addressed a BEW conference on French West Africa and was asked his views on the possible effects of improved working conditions on the efficiency of the Mexican gatherers of a wild shrub under consideration as an alternate source of rubber. Hurst to Deinard, n.d., Box 1189, Entry 240, RG 169 ("Work Report for Week Ending November 21, 1942"); Agenda, Conference on French West Africa and Economic Warfare, December 3, 1942, E. D. Eaton to Herskovits, November 21, 1942, Box 25, Melville J. Herskovits Papers, Northwestern University Library.

61. Mathews, "Labor Standards," 16–17.

62. Hurst quoted in Mathews, "Labor Standards," 22; *Law in Society*, 1941 ed., 2: i, ii.

63. Hurst quoted in Mathews, "Labor Standards," 22.

64. Brinkley, *End of Reform*; Karl, *Uneasy State*, 155–81; Jeffries, "'Third New Deal'?" 387–409.

65. Hurst to Oppenheimer, June 6, 1942, Box 4, Entry 145, RG 169.

66. Parrish, *Frankfurter*, 201. For Hurst's approving account of the rise of "something like an area of prerogative power in administrators subordinate to the chief executive," see Hurst, *Growth of American Law*, 399–400.

67. Hurst to Raoul Burger, November 18, 1963, Box 1, Raoul Burger Papers, Harvard Law School Library. The Dies Committee alarmed Hurst even before he went to Washington. Hurst, "Content of Courses in Legislation," 281.

68. Mathews, "Labor Standards," 22.

69. Hurst, Smail Interview, 39; Hurst to Mark deWolfe Howe, January 1, 1953, Box 3, Mark deWolfe Howe Papers, Harvard Law School Library.

70. Mathews, "Labor Standards," 27, 35–40; Memorandum, "Bolivian Situation; Worcester File," December 24, 1942, Box 1, Entry 101, RG 169; Dean Acheson to Mr. Labouisse, May 14, 1942, Box 1, Entry 67, RG 59; Monroe Oppenheimer to Milo Perkins, November 18, 1942, Box 4, Entry 101, RG 169; Hurst to Deinard, November 30, December 8, 1942, Box 1189, Entry 240, RG 169.

71. Edwin W. Gaumnitz to Milo Perkins, n.d., quoted in Sanger, *Administrative History*, 289, 292; Clark Byse, telephone conversation with author, December 20, 1997; Sirevag, *Eclipse of the New Deal*, 355.

72. *New York Times*, June 30, 1943; Sanger, *Administrative History*, 121–23; Buller, "Administrative History of the Board of Economic Warfare," 1–9 ("Rubber Development"); Wirtz, conversation; Byse, telephone conversation; Charles F. Luce, telephone conversation with author, June 2, 1998.

73. Jones and Angley, *Fifty Billion Dollars*, 425, 491–92.

74. Senate Committee on Banking and Currency, Executive Session, 77th Cong., 2d sess., December 2, 1942, Box 3, Entry 145, RG 169; *New York Times*, December 6, 1942, 35; Senate Committee on Banking and Currency, *To Increase the Borrowing Authority of the Reconstruction Finance Corporation*, 77th Cong., 2d sess., 1942, 65, 87; Stone, *War Years*, 136, 141.

75. Jones to Wallace, February 25, 1943, Box 982, Entry 380, RG 169; see Sirevag, *Eclipse of the New Deal*, 124–26; Sanger, *Administrative History*, 124.

76. Sirevag, *Eclipse of the New Deal*, 124–27; Sanger, *Administrative History*, 124–25; *New York Times*, January 21, February 8, 28, 1943.

77. For the political climate on Capitol Hill, see Blum, *V Was for Victory*, 234–45.

78. House Committee on Appropriations, *National War Agencies Appropriation Bill for 1944*, 78th Cong., 1st sess., June 2, 1943, 388, 394; *New York Times*, June 17, 30, July 1, 6, 1943.

79. "Battle of Titans," *Time*, July 12, 1943, 19; Theodore J. Kreps to Morris S. Rosenthal, July 9, 1943, Box 5, Entry 145, RG 169; Blum, *Price of Vision*, 223 n. 1, 226 n. 1; "Roosevelt's Big Stick Deals Wallace's '44 Prestige a Blow," *Newsweek*, July 26, 1943, 36; Schapsmeier and Schapsmeier, *Prophet in Politics*, 72.

80. Hurst knew he would be joining "BuPers" by the end of December 1942. His reasons for leaving the BEW are as likely to include a desire to join the uniformed services as any dissatisfaction with the agency. Hurst to Secretary of Navy, January 15, 1953, Box 1, James Willard Hurst Papers, University of Wisconsin Archives; Garrison to C. A. Dykstra, December 31, 1942, Box 55, General Correspondence, WLS-UWA. Hurst's work at "BuPers" included compiling the losses suffered by American shipping during the Battle of the Atlantic and directing the preparation of an administrative history of the Bureau. In 1981 Hurst said that the history project taught him how to interview "Annapolis 4–stripers about mistakes that were made in their division" and to direct a research team in "what amounted to a public administration study." The latter experience proved useful as he oversaw the writing of historical monographs on law and policy in Wisconsin by his students and associates during the 1950s and 1960s. Hurst, Smail Interview, 39–40.

81. Hurst to George B. Harris, December 1, 1954, Box 1, Hurst Papers, UWA.

82. Hurst, *Law and Economic Growth*, 584.

83. Beuscher, "Law-Taught Attitudes," 74, 76.

84. Rosenthal to Oppenheimer, April 13, 1943, Box 4, Entry 101, RG 169.

85. Rosenthal, "Reminiscences," 233–34.

86. Rosenthal, interview; Rosenthal, "Reminiscences," 234; "Office of Imports Staff Meeting," July 3, 1942, Box 4, Entry 145, RG 169. In her 1948 study, Esther Brown concluded that "few agencies better illustrate how large a policy-making role lawyers may play" than the BEW. Brown, *Lawyers, Law Schools and the Public Service*, 88.

87. Hurst, "Historian Views the Profession," 80.

88. *Law in Society*, 1941 ed., 2: iii; see also ibid., 1: 218.

89. Hurst, *Growth of American Law*, 355; Hurst, "Content of Courses in Legislation," 284. On the Attorney General's committee, see Shepherd, "Fierce Compromise," 1594–98, 1632–36.

90. Hurst, "Research Program," 323, 327–28; Frankfurter, *Public and Its Government,* 161.

91. Hurst, *Growth of American Law,* 252, 335, 340, 359. As Stanley N. Katz has observed to me, Hurst's own inability to locate a firm factual basis for the labor clauses makes this statement rather ironic.

92. Ibid., 342, 345, 346, 375. For later restatements and elaborations, see Hurst, "Legal Profession," 969–78; Hurst, "Lawyers in American Society," 594–606.

93. Hurst, "Uses of Law," 582, 584. Robert Mathews described some of the BEW lawyers' encounters with the mining barons in Mathews, "Labor Standards," 64–69. In June 1998 Wirtz vividly recalled one of them, Mauricio Hochschild. Hurst was well aware of these confrontations. Hurst to Deinard, December 15, 22, 1942, Box 1189, Entry 240, RG 169.

94. Hurst concluded on an optimistic note, however. The TVA—the model for his own proposal for government corporations at the BEW—suggested that "we may be on the threshold of a new and more fruitful relation of the institutions of social control to the life of the people." Hurst, "Uses of Law," 582–83, 592.

95. Hurst ended the book much as he did the "Law in Society" materials, with the rise of an administrative regime to rationalize the market and promote a "productive future." Hurst, *Law and Economic Growth,* 408, 588, 592, 859 n.97. For Hurst's informant, see "Lumber Industry Legal Problems," Marvin B. Rosenberry Papers (M82–090), State Historical Society of Wisconsin. On the theme of "bastard pragmatism" in Hurst's writings, see McEvoy, "Willard Hurst's Scholarship," 1195; Tushnet, "Lumber and the Legal Process," 114–32.

96. Hurst to Frankfurter, August 2, 1955, reel 42, FF-LC; Hurst, *Law and Markets,* 51, 57.

97. Hurst, *Modern American Legal History,* cassette 34, side 2. On Jones's remark, see Burns, *Roosevelt,* 341.

98. Hurst, "Uses of Law," 577.

99. For example, Charles F. Luce was the administrator of the Bonneville Power Authority and Undersecretary of the Interior in the 1960s, and Willard Wirtz was Secretary of Labor under Presidents Kennedy and Johnson.

100. Hurst, Smail Interview, 39.

101. Casner and Leach, *Cases and Text on Property,* 4. For Leach's war years, see Nostrad, "W. Barton Leach," 726–28.

102. Cozzens, *Just and the Unjust;* Cozzens, *Guard of Honor;* Balchin, *Small Back Room;* Hurst to Frankfurter, January 12, 1949, Reel 42, FF-LC; Hurst to Rauh, March 19, 1947, Box 1, Part 1, Rauh Papers.

103. The critic Elizabeth Janeway once described Cozzens's heroes as "able, responsible men, more burdened by duty than eager for power, learning in maturity that one never really knows enough, stoically bearing the weight of the world." Elizabeth Janeway, review of *The Novels of James Gould Cozzens,* by Frederick Bracher, *New York Times Book Review,* August 9, 1959, 1.

104. Cozzens, *Just and the Unjust,* 434.

105. Hurst, *Modern American Legal History,* cassette 3, side 2; see also Hurst, *Law and Markets,* 134–35, 140.

106. Many friends of Hurst noted and were attracted to his idealism. A specific source is Luce, conversation.

107. Hurst, "Research Program," 324; Hurst in Hartog, "Snakes in Ireland," 375.

108. For Reinhold Niebuhr's influence on Hurst, see Hartog, "Snakes in Ireland," 375; Soifer, "In Retrospect: Willard Hurst," 127.

109. Here see Hurst's letters to Mark V. Tushnet, June 15, 1981, and to John H. Langbein, March 8, 1983, which survive in a collection of correspondence in the possession of Arthur F. McEvoy, the J. Willard Hurst Professor of Law and History at the University of Wisconsin-Madison Law School. I am grateful to Professor McEvoy for permission to examine these papers.

110. Carter, "Ideal and the Actual in the Law," 218.

CHAPTER 7

Reining in the Administrative State: World War II and the Decline of Expert Administration

Reuel E. Schiller

Between 1940 and 1950, administrative law (the rules that govern how agencies operate and the relationship between courts and the administrative state) changed dramatically. During the 1930s, the law allowed administrative agencies to function with a degree of autonomy that would be surprising to us today. By 1950, the judiciary had assumed its familiar role of policing the administrative state. There is a direct link between the United States' involvement in World War II and this metamorphosis. In particular, three aspects of the wartime experience caused changes in American political culture that, in turn, contributed to this transformation of administrative law. First, America's encounter with totalitarianism—both abroad and on the home front—diminished people's trust in the administrative state, which they began to associate with the unchecked power of fascism. Second, the track record of the wartime agencies—particularly the War Production Board and the Office of Price Administration—did little to assure Americans that administrative power could be used in a manner that was both efficient and consistent with democratic principles. Finally, the prosperity the war created caused one-time advocates of the administrative state to question the value of economic planning and to refocus their attention on curing economic maladjustments through Keynesian fiscal policy rather than through administrative control of economic actors. By the end of the war, there were few advocates of extreme administrative autonomy left. Ideological, political, and economic changes dictated that the judiciary be put firmly in control of the administrative state.

AN ERA OF JUDICIAL DEFERENCE

The seventy-five years between the end of the Civil War and the beginning of World War II saw the dramatic growth of the administrative state. By 1940 there were over fifty federal administrative agencies compared to the eleven that existed at the beginning of the Civil War.[1] State administrative agencies multiplied as well. This increase in the size of the administrative state was driven by the perception that the traditional tripartite structure of government was ill-equipped to solve the problems created by a complex, industrial economy. In particular, reformers argued that the allocation of power among the three branches of government was insufficiently flexible for the continuous public policy adjustments necessary to solve these problems. Legislatures had neither the time nor the expertise. Courts were even less well equipped.[2] Guiding a modern economy was too complicated to be left in the hands of inexpert judges who mechanistically followed arcane rules of law instead of crafting appropriate remedies for contemporary problems. As James Landis wrote in his 1938 ode to expert administration, *The Administrative Process*, an obsession with separation of powers or stare decisis limited a court's effectiveness by preventing it from changing laws "as conditions . . . might dictate," pursuing "energetic measures upon the appearance of an emergency," or implementing broad policies through enforcement of individual orders. The solutions to contemporary problems "were determined much less by accepted 'legal principles' than by given political, economic and social considerations."[3] By creating specialized administrative agencies and giving them the power to make laws and adjudicate cases within their areas of expertise, legislators hoped to arrive efficiently at these solutions. A transfer of power from the legislature and the judiciary to agencies was a necessary consequence of doing so.

New Deal-era administrative law reflected these beliefs by allowing administrative agencies an exceptional amount of independence and flexibility. Expert administration was most certainly not "legal," in that it operated in a manner often at odds with traditional assumptions of due process and the division of governmental powers. Agencies blended executive, judicial, and legislative functions. They felt no obligation to follow rules of evidence or to obey their own precedents. Discretion, informed by expertise, was their modus operandi. Getting correct results was more important than the procedures used to achieve them. "For [the administrative process] to be successful in a particular field," wrote Landis, "it is imperative that controversies be decided as 'rightly' as possible. . . . The ultimate test of the administrative is the policy it formulates; not the fairness as between the parties."[4]

Consistent with this derogation of judicial power was the limited control that courts had over the administrative process. New Deal-era administrative law contained a variety of doctrines that prevented courts from hearing appeals from administrative tribunals. The negative order doctrine and the doctrine of implied preclusion each prevented courts from reviewing agency actions at all.[5] The judiciary's commitment to a narrow definition of what an injury was for the purposes of determining standing further limited the access to courts by people who were aggrieved by agency actions.[6] Similarly, the distinction between legally enforceable "rights" and mere "privileges" removed a host of administrative actions from judicial scrutiny.[7]

When the regulated did get their case before a judge they often got a less sympathetic ear than they might have wanted. Before the passage of the Administrative Procedure Act in 1946 there was no unified, legislatively mandated standard for courts to apply when reviewing administrative acts. Instead, each federal or state statute that created an agency provided individual standards for judicial review. Nevertheless, some degree of uniformity developed. Prewar commentators and courts generally divided administrative actions into three types: (1) determinations of fact; (2) determinations of law; and (3) determinations of mixed law and fact (that is, determining whether facts met a legal standard).[8] The standard of review that a court was expected to use differed with the type of action. Review of factual determinations was to be minimal or even nonexistent.[9] Review of legal determinations was supposed to be de novo, while mixed questions of fact and law received some intermediate amount of scrutiny.[10]

Many commentators noted that distinguishing these categories from one another was difficult and that frequently courts applied a relatively lax "reasonableness" or "nonarbitrariness" standard to most administrative actions.[11] Indeed, even before the New Deal, courts repeatedly asserted a presumption that administrative actions were valid.[12] With the advent of the New Deal, they became even more deferential. The Supreme Court repeatedly upheld the factual determinations of agencies without even examining parts of the record that indicated that a decision was incorrect.[13] More remarkable was the Court's tendency to defer to agencies' interpretations of law, traditionally an area where courts were to exercise discretion based on their expertise in legal matters.[14] The New Deal-era judiciary even deferred to agency determinations of constitutional issues.[15]

Courts justified each of these doctrines of judicial deference—implied preclusion, the negative order doctrine, limited due process, narrow standing, and minimal judicial review—with references to expertise and efficiency. Courts had to submit to "the strength due to the judgments of a tribunal appointed by law and informed by experience."[16] A less deferential division of power between the judiciary and agencies would hobble governmental efficiency: "It is not the province of a court to absorb the administrative functions to such an extent that the executive or legislative agencies become mere fact finding bodies deprived of the advantages of prompt and definite action."[17] Such judicial overreaching would also defeat the purpose of creating expert agencies in the first place. An agency "deals with a subject that is highly specialized and so complex as to be the despair of judges. It is relatively better staffed for its task than is the judiciary. Its members not infrequently bring to their task long legislative or administrative experience in their subject."[18] Thus, too much judicial oversight would constitute a judicial usurpation of legislative and executive power, an interference with "fields wisely and happily apportioned by the genius of our polity to the administration of another branch of the Government."[19]

This commitment to expert administration would be tested in the late 1930s and early 1940s. As Americans came face to face with terrifying manifestations of administrative power abroad they began to distrust it. Similarly, the manner in which administrative agencies functioned in the United States during World War II made Americans increasingly skeptical about expertise. By the time administrative law passed through the crucible of World War II, its first principle, that expert administrators were better equipped to make public policy decisions than were courts, had been tested and found wanting. The doctrines of administrative law changed accordingly.

THE TOTALITARIAN SPECTER

During the mid-1930s the true dimensions of European totalitarianism forced themselves into the American consciousness. The bombing of Guernica, the Italian invasion of Ethiopia, Stalin's Show Trials, as well as the trio of Nazi atrocities, the Night of the Long Knives, Kristallnacht, and the passage of the Nuremberg Laws, sent Americans scrambling to differentiate themselves from the European regimes that perpetrated these monstrous acts. Indeed, the successes of European totalitarianism forced American intellectuals to distinguish American politics and culture from the European variants that seemed to act as a seedbed for fascism and Stalinism. Thinkers and manufacturers of popular culture emphasized the importance of the rule of law and the notion that the people were protected from arbitrary state power by a tradition of constitutionalism. These were quickly proffered as attributes of American government that prevented the flourishing of so-called "alien," totalitarian ideologies.[20] Additionally, American democracy was portrayed as pluralist and inclusive. Not only were we tolerant of the great variety of ethnic and racial groups that made up the polity, the nation was made stronger by this diversity. In contrast to fascism, Nazism, and Stalinism, "Americanism" was equated with individualism as well as cultural and political pluralism.[21]

Americans' fears about totalitarianism were not limited to observations about Europe. During the late 1930s and early 1940s many people thought events in America demonstrated frightening tendencies toward totalitarian rule. Of course Roosevelt's right-wing detractors had accused him of having dictatorial ambitions since he came into office in 1933. However, by the middle of the decade a broader spectrum of people had begun to worry about totalitarianism taking hold in the United States. Roosevelt's Court Packing

Plan and his proposed reorganization of the executive branch caused mainstream commentators to worry not only about Roosevelt's ambitions but also about whether economic desperation resulting from the Great Depression might cause the American people to clamor for a dictator.[22]

Ironically, America's entry into the war against fascism in December 1941 intensified, rather than assuaged, this fear. In the years before Pearl Harbor both the popular and elite press portrayed totalitarian governments as demanding militaristic regimentation from their citizens.[23] As the United States geared up to fight, people expressed the fear that the war effort might make similar demands on American citizens. Thus, while isolationists had exploited these worries in the months leading up to Pearl Harbor, by the time America entered the war, even the internationalist allies of the president were warning that "military discipline provides excellent training for citizenship in a totalitarian society."[24] Indeed, the army itself was worried about the effect that mass conscription and military training might have on the citizenry. A 1945 study by two army psychiatrists suggested that many combat veterans would be "angry, regressed, anxiety ridden, dependant men" who would naturally gravitate toward fascist organizations in the United States. The military was so conscious of this problem that it worked assiduously to portray the experience of service and the submission to discipline it required as familiar (like being on a team or obeying your parents) and, even more incredibly, voluntary.[25]

Wrapped up with this general fear of the rise of domestic totalitarianism was the idea that the administrative state would be a vehicle for fostering its growth. Expert administration, with its shabby treatment of separation of powers and its disinclination to follow such legal norms as stare decisis, seemed to many to be the first step on the road to complete executive power. Again, Roosevelt's political enemies had long portrayed the New Deal administrative agencies as the agents of totalitarianism. "Should our present tripartite system of government continue to weaken," wrote O. R. McGuire, chair of the American Bar Association's bitterly anti-New Deal Special Committee on Administrative Law in 1936, "we are faced with the only possible alternatives of anarchy or the introduction of the final phase of Utopianism, a form of government on the Russian, Italian or German models—and let no one tell you the contrary." By the time of the United States' entry into World War II, similar fears were being voiced by less ideological parties. Reviews of *The Administrative Process* accused Landis of promoting "an antique conception of royal power" and of failing to see that expertise alone could not protect people from administrative absolutism.[26] Even a loyal New Dealer, like Louis Jaffe, had become concerned about the autocratic tendencies of the administrative state. Expert administration, Jaffe wrote, was in grave danger of becoming totalitarian. "Value-free concepts" and autonomous "systems of expert justice" simply did not exist. Instead, too much faith in "experts" and "rationalism" could lead to totalitarianism.[27] "Even if we grant . . . the magnificent accomplishments of the New Deal," Jaffe wrote, "we cannot forget that our age has produced elsewhere, and even on occasion in our own country, the most monstrous expressions of administrative power."[28]

The solution to this problem, according to administrative law theorists writing in the 1940s, was to ensure that the judiciary exercised sufficient control over the administrative process. Jaffe condemned the "self-deprecation and abdication" of the New Deal-era judges who, "beguiled by the promise of administrative action . . . were easily persuaded of the irrelevance of the judicial role."[29] Only the courts could protect "the agencies themselves against the temptation of absolutism."[30] "The very subordination of the agency to judicial discretion is intended to proclaim the premise that each agency is to be brought into harmony with the rule of law."[31] Accordingly, Jaffe, as well as other postwar administrative law theorists such as Kenneth Culp Davis, argued that courts should review administrative actions with less deference than they had shown before the war.[32]

By the mid-1940s the belief in a connection between the administrative state and totalitarianism was prevalent among intellectuals across the political spectrum and had even entered mainstream culture. Friedrich von Hayek's *The Road to Serfdom*, which argued that increasing the administrative power of the state inevitably led to totalitarianism, was a best-seller in 1944 and was reissued as a *Reader's Digest* condensed book.[33] In the introduction, Hayek was explicit about where administrative planning would end up: "It is necessary now to state the unpalatable truth that it is Germany whose fate we are in some danger of repeating."[34]

Thinkers with radically different political views from Hayek's echoed his fears. In 1944 Reinhold Niebuhr wrote that "[t]he rise of totalitarianism" suggested that democratic countries should "walk warily" before establishing bureaucracies to solve social problems.[35] "Democratic authority," wrote Robert Lynd in 1942, might be unable to contain the ambitions of bureaucrats. Dwight MacDonald agreed. To him the dropping of the atomic bomb was proof of the American people's inability to control the technological and bureaucratic processes of their government.[36]

THE PROBLEMS OF WARTIME ADMINISTRATION

This growing fear of totalitarianism coincided with one of the most dramatic expansions of federal administrative power in the history of the United States. The consequences of this expansion did little to quiet Americans' worries about the potentially autocratic nature of administrative power. The eruption of World War II in 1939 and the United States' entry two years later resulted in a massive increase in the size of the federal bureaucracy. Twenty-six new agencies were created to manage the enormous undertaking of placing America's economy and society on a wartime footing. Additionally, many existing agencies increased in size to carry out the additional work that the war created. Between 1940 and 1943 the number of civilian federal employees nearly tripled to just under three million.[37] This increase in the size and complexity of the federal bureaucracy was matched by a dramatic increase in the power that the administrative apparatus wielded. Many of the new federal agencies were established to manage the American economy in a manner never before attempted. Two in particular, the War Production Board (WPB) and the Office of Price Administration (OPA), exercised unprecedented power over production and consumption.

Naturally, conservatives who had long been opposed to government involvement in the economy had little stomach for these wartime administrative innovations. As early as April 1941 the National Association of Manufacturers complained to Congress about the expansion of the administrative state caused by the war in Europe.[38] Only weeks after Pearl Harbor the *Wall Street Journal* editorialized that the best way to ensure proper allocation of resources and sufficient production for the war effort was through the free market, not through government control of supply and demand. According to the *Journal*, administrative responses to concerns about wartime preparedness and postwar reconversion were nothing more than a "half-way house to socialism."[39]

The real significance of wartime administration was not that it evoked such reactions from the long-standing enemies of the administrative state. Rather, it is that people's experiences with the WPB and the OPA undermined the faith that many liberals had in expert administration. These agencies also gave a negative image of regulation to many people who might not otherwise have had an opinion about the administrative state.

When the United States entered World War I, Congress had established the War Industries Board (WIB). Under the direction of the financier Bernard Baruch, the WIB was supposed to coordinate the entire American economy so that it would meet the needs of a nation going to war. During and after the conflict, progressives heaped praise on the WIB and touted it as a model for government management and control over the economy in peacetime. The laissez-faire political culture of the 1920s dashed their hopes, but with the advent of the Depression, the motive for widespread economic planning returned. The New Deal's first attempt, the National Recovery Administration, was a colossal failure, but as the United States was drawn into World War II, liberals' hopes for government economic planning returned.[40] Before the United States entered the war, Roosevelt entrusted this project to the Office of Production Management (OPM), created in January 1941. Headed by labor leader Sidney Hillman and former General Motors executive William Knudsen, OPM was supposed to rationalize production by coordinating the distribution of raw materials and labor. In January 1942 OPM's powers were transferred to the War Production Board, directed by Donald Nelson, a former executive at Sears. Nelson was given broad powers—the WPB was supposed to "exercise general responsibility" over the economy—but his leadership left something to be desired. By the end of the war, the WPB had become something of a bete noire to liberals, glaring evidence that the administrative state could be turned against the public interest.

First, the WPB turned out to be a good deal less efficient than its proponents hoped it would be. Far from being a decisive leader, Nelson proved to be incapable of winning (or even participating in) the bureaucratic melees that were necessary to protect an agency's authority within the Roosevelt administration. From the very beginning of the war he was locked in a paralyzing and ultimately unsuccessful battle with the armed services over control of procurement and resource allocation.[41] The ensuing anarchy at the WPB meant that the agency could not fully implement a plan for the distribution of raw materials until the middle of 1943. The result was endemic delay in the fulfillment of war contracts. By the end of 1943 Nelson had essentially lost control of the agency to the WPB's Production Executive Committee, which was chaired by Charles Wilson, the chairman of General Electric, and staffed by the military and executives from several of the largest war contractors.[42]

The agency's inefficiency aside, the character of the Production Executive Committee represented liberals' greatest problem with the WPB and their greatest disillusionment with wartime administration. Far from shaping a coherent wartime production policy by controlling important private economic actors, the WPB seemed to be completely captured by the industries it was supposed to regulate. Liberals as diverse as Harry Truman and I. F. Stone decried the WPB's use of furloughed industry executives in staffing the agency.[43] "Big business," Interior Secretary Harold Ickes wrote in his diary, "is certainly not overlooking any opportunity to entrench itself and is working through its dollar a year men in Washington."[44]

According to liberals, industry capture of the WPB manifested itself in a number of ways. Bruce Catton, one of Nelson's deputies, wrote that over the course of the war the WPB became increasingly secretive about its activities, ultimately turning its press office into a propaganda organ, staffed by advertising executives who attempted "to commit a fraud upon democracy."[45] Others argued that the agency's decision to award contracts on a cost-plus basis rather than through competitive bidding showed that the WPB cared more about industrial profits than winning the war.[46] The most frequently voiced complaint about the WPB was that its capture by large corporations resulted in the exclusion of smaller companies from wartime contracts entirely. Three separate congressional committees repeatedly attacked the agency for failing to spread orders among a wider group of contractors.[47] Agency capture also seemed to dictate the policies of the WPB with respect to reconversion at the war's end. Truman accused the WPB of delaying reconversion because "some selfish business groups . . . want to see their competition kept idle."[48] Indeed, Nelson himself, by then completely marginalized within the agency of which he was the nominal director, made the same accusation. "The powers of the War Production Board," he wrote in July 1944, "should not be used to preserve the competitive pattern of industry, which existed before the war."[49]

Thus the message that liberal policy-makers drew from the WPB's three disastrous years of operation was that effective economic planning by administrative experts was difficult to achieve because agencies were easily captured by the interests they were supposed to regulate.[50] Policy-makers' reaction to the Office of Price Administration was different. Few contemporaries argued that the OPA was a failure, at least until the very end of its existence. Indeed, many Americans—particularly women, African Americans, and those in the working class—saw it as their primary defense against war profiteers and, more generally, believed it to be a method of spreading prosperity.[51] Nevertheless, the OPA's successes came at a cost that left many wondering whether they were worth the price paid.

Roosevelt created the OPA by executive order in April 1941 to head off the inflation predicted to accompany increased production for the war in Europe. In January 1942 Congress gave it the power to fix prices, ration products, and control rents. By April 1942 the prices of nearly 60 percent of food items were controlled by the OPA. By the end of the war OPA rationing affected over 90 percent of consumer goods, including gasoline and clothing. No wartime agency touched the lives of more Americans. The OPA thrust government regulation into domestic transactions and affected such basic matters as the food people could obtain and how they could use their automobiles.[52]

Not surprisingly, an agency with so broad a portfolio ruffled many feathers. To conservatives, the OPA reeked of the worst elements of the New Deal. Staffed by what Republican congressmen referred to as "Leon Henderson and his bunch of draft dodgers," the OPA was leading the country into "regimented chaos."[53] Even after Congress forced Henderson out in late 1942, the OPA was a target of constant criticism. House committees charged that the agency was biased against landlords and businessmen, that its price ceilings and rent controls were arbitrary and unfair, and, worst of all, that its enforcement procedures lacked any of the attributes of due process. Unlawful searches were commonplace, they complained; notice was insufficient, the rules of evidence were ignored, trial examiners were biased, and punishments were unjustifiably severe.[54]

While these congressional attacks were certainly motivated by partisan considerations, less biased contemporary sources noted similar problems. OPA enforcement procedures were occasionally lacking in what most Americans must have considered procedural fairness. Additionally, OPA regulations were frequently obscure and burdened with excessive detail, such as the order, quickly rescinded, prohibiting the sale of sliced bread or the 40,000–word order mandating beef butchering techniques. ("The excess loin (lumbar) and pelvic (sacral) fat shall be trimmed from the inside loin of the full loin by placing the full loin upon a flat surface, with no other support to change its position, meat side down, and removing all the fat which extends above a flat plane parallel with the flat surface supporting the full loin and on a level with the full length of the protruding edge of the lumbar section of the chin bone."[55]) Nor did the OPA improve its image, or the image of the administrative state generally, by directing its inspectors to snoop around baseball stadiums, symphony halls, and nightclubs to confiscate the gas ration coupons of people who had allegedly engaged in prohibited pleasure driving.[56] Similarly, the agency's use of volunteer price-checkers to find and report merchants who violated price ceilings reminded some observers of totalitarian block wardens or "kitchen gestapo." Nosy neighbors, one woman recalled, suddenly felt empowered by the federal government to report people to the ration board for legal but suspicious acts such as a sugar-for-coffee swap between neighbors with differing tastes.[57] As the war drew to a close and organized labor clamored for an extension of the OPA's powers into the postwar period, ration-weary consumers added complaints of capture to their earlier gripes about the agency. "As long as the OLD O.P.A. is being revamped," a 1946 letter to the agency's director, Chester Bowles, read, "why not change the name to the C.I.O-A.F.L. Government Control Association?"[58]

Even some of the OPA's most vociferous defenders recognized that the agency was not without problems. The *New Republic* worried that, after Henderson's ouster, it was falling under the sway of producer-dominated interest groups. In July 1945, the *New Yorker* reported on widespread black marketeering and the demoralization of OPA personnel. As the agency was dismantled in 1946, *Commonweal*'s editors suggested that skepticism was the proper response "when a fanatic begins to talk about OPA law (plus or minus) righting or ruining the American economy and/or the people's welfare."[59] Sympathetic academic critiques—some by former OPA officials—recognized that the agency was overly centralized, that the decentralization it did implement was poorly planned, that it had not satisfactorily coordinated its activities with other agencies, and that it did a poor job of explaining itself to the public.[60]

Indeed, as the war drew to an end academics who were not generally unsympathetic to the administrative state voiced similar critiques of the entire panoply of civilian wartime agencies. The administrative process had become overly bureaucratized and dependent on expertise at the expense of public participation.[61] Individual agencies had become inflexible because they were too centralized, yet coordination between agencies was insufficient. The result was unproductive turf wars between agencies and the unnecessary repetition of tasks by each agency. Agencies were subject to capture and the appearance of capture.[62]

On a broader level, these scholars worried that emergency administrative planning could itself become a danger to democracy. National emergencies could become excuses for delegations of authority to administrative agencies that would not be reclaimed in peacetime. Similarly, the exigencies of wartime planning had resulted in an unhealthy tendency for administrative officials not to pay the proper respect to the wishes of the coordinate branches of the government.[63] The academic defenders of administrative discretion, so easy to find throughout the 1930s, were nowhere to be seen by 1946. Postwar liberals and progressives would never evidence Hayek's hostility toward the administrative state, but the wartime experience had taught them, and the American people generally, that agencies could be inefficient, incompetent, bullying, and perhaps even captured by the interests they were supposed to regulate.

THE PROMISE OF FISCAL POLICY

Americans' reaction to totalitarianism and their experience with wartime administration gave them reason to be more suspicious of the administrative state than they were in the 1930s. In the immediate postwar period, the increasing acceptance of Keynesian solutions to economic problems allowed reformers to act on this suspicion. Fiscal economic policies provided reformers with a method of solving economic dislocations without resorting to the types of administrative apparatus that they now found either troubling or of questionable utility.

Writing in 1972, Richard Polenberg described the way in which World War II affected the policy preferences of the postwar Democratic Party. The economic prosperity that the war brought to the United States seemed to indicate that fiscal policy, both in the form of taxation and government spending, succeeded in bringing the country out of its depression. This phenomenon not only helped the economic well-being of many Americans, it also boosted the reputation of Keynesian economists within the halls of power. The government's ability to achieve high levels of employment and diminish income disparity through public spending had been demonstrated. Keynes was right and World War II had proven it. Now similar economic techniques could be used in peacetime. National defense had been the excuse for government spending during the war. Afterwards, the government could engage in this type of spending without a similar excuse. It could do it simply to promote prosperity.[64]

More recently Alan Brinkley has used Polenberg's observation as part of his description of the transformation of liberalism during World War II. Liberal reformers who, before the war, had been committed to government control of business through regulation and long-term economic planning emerged from World War II converted to Keynesianism. Economic prosperity could be achieved, they argued, by replacing heavy-handed regulation with the lighter touch of fiscal policy. While many New Deal-era regulatory and planning initiatives continued during the postwar period, the new initiatives that liberals clamored for—full employment, the expansion of Social Security, federal spending on education or health, highway programs—were all Keynesian in nature.[65] Keynesianism solved the crucial problem raised by the frightening combination of worldwide depression followed by worldwide war: the former seemed to require a degree of state planning that created the regimes responsible for the latter. Keynesian spending offered a happy solution, a way to end an economic depression without the need to create a potentially oppressive administrative apparatus.

The triumph of fiscal solutions to economic crises thus spurred the "legalization" of the administrative process. Fears of totalitarianism and Americans' experiences with administration during the war had demonstrated the dangers and inefficiencies of expert administration. The postwar validation of Keynesian economic policy removed liberals' last reason for putting up with these problems. Absent a viable alternative to aggressive regulation for preventing economic dislocations, the dangers of expert administration might have to be tolerated. But once an alternative emerged that did not require invasive administration the impulse to rein in the administrative state by placing it under the control of the judiciary seemed essentially cost-free. Conservative opponents of regulation had wanted to do this for a long time. By 1946 liberals and progressives agreed with them.

THE NEW JUDICIAL ASCENDANCY

The contours of postwar administrative law were shaped by the liberals' new perceptions of the administrative state. New laws limited the expertise-driven, judicially-deferential model of the prewar years. Stimulated by fears of totalitarianism and disillusionment with the administrative process caused by the wartime agencies, legislators and judges questioned their faith in expertise. They sought to place the judiciary in charge of the administrative process so that it could protect individuals from arbitrary and liberty-threatening actions of agencies. This phenomena occurred in two ways. First, Congress enacted the Administrative Procedure Act (APA), a statute that established uniform procedures for federal administrative agencies. These procedures "legalized" the administrative process—forcing agencies to conform to judicial norms—and standardized methods of judicial review, thus placing the agencies firmly under the control of the federal judiciary. Second, even without the prompting of Congress, the judiciary itself asserted control over administrative agencies, eliminating the doctrines that had previously insulated administrative agencies from judicial oversight.

The APA has a long and convoluted history.[66] In 1933 the American Bar Association (ABA) created a special committee on administrative law. For the next six years the committee issued scathing attacks on the administrative procedures used in New Deal agencies culminating in its 1938 report. Authored by Roscoe Pound, the dyspeptic, recently retired dean of the Harvard Law School, the report recommended the creation of a code of administrative procedure to limit rule-making and adjudicatory discretion by federal agencies and to subject their actions to stringent judicial review. Early in 1939 congressional Republicans proposed legislation modeled on the ABA's proposal. After contentious hearings and a particularly acrimonious debate in Congress, the measure (known as the Walter-Logan bill) was passed, but not with enough support to override the president's veto.

As Walter-Logan was making its way through Congress, Roosevelt sought to head off criticism of the veto he knew he would exercise by appointing a commission of experts to study the existing procedures governing the federal agencies and to recommend reforms. In early 1941 the so-called "Attorney General's Committee on Administrative Procedure" issued its report. Although the committee's staff had conducted a detailed examination of the inner workings of twenty-nine agencies, the reforms it recommended were minimal. Three of the committee's members issued a minority report, politely entitled "additional views and recommendations," as well as a proposed statute. When Congress turned its attention back to reform of administrative procedure as the war drew to an end, the minority's proposal became the basis for legislation introduced in early 1945 that would become the APA.

The events leading up to the unanimous passage of the APA contrasted dramatically with the tempestuous debate over the Walter-Logan bill. Throughout 1945 Senator Patrick McCarran, the bill's sponsor in the Senate, and the Truman administration hammered out a compromise piece of legislation. Desultory hearings were then held in which agency heads paraded before the House and Senate Judiciary Committees to voice their approval—or at least acceptance—of the bill. After both committees reported favorably on the legislation, the sponsors "debated" the merits of the bill before empty House and Senate chambers. The Senate passed the bill in May 1946, the House followed in June, and President Truman quickly signed it.

Over the course of the six years that Congress was considering administrative law reform the issue went from highly partisan and extremely contentious to bipartisan and susceptible to compromise. This change was in part a symptom of the waning fortunes of the New Deal. Yet it was also the result of the effect of World War II on Americans' beliefs about the administrative state. Throughout the legislative process proponents of reform voiced their fears about the totalitarian nature of administration. When Congress began considering a comprehensive administrative procedure bill for the first time in 1939 the acrimonious debate was riddled with references to totalitarianism. Administrative agencies had to be forced into traditional legal molds (separation of powers, judicial review, rules of evidence, cross-examination) in order to protect liberty. If this was done at the cost of administrative efficiency, so be it. "A noted sage once observed that democracy is like an old scow," Congressman Everett Dirksen declared on the final day of the House debate. "It does not move very fast nor very far at one time, but it never sinks. I prefer these attributes of an old scow with the security it tends to give to democratic processes against the totalitarian superfluous liners of the old world with an impetuous captain giving orders for full speed ahead, no matter what happens."[67]

By 1940 these accusations seemed less like reactionary scare tactics and more like an accurate description of events in Europe. When Congress passed the Walter-Logan bill, many stalwart New Dealers voted for it.[68] Even those who opposed the bill asserted that some type of reform of the administrative process was necessary.[69] Indeed, the Attorney General's Committee considered the tendency of agencies to mix their prosecutorial and judicial functions "plainly undesirable" and incompatible with "Anglo-American tradition." The Committee's minority agreed, highlighting the commitment of "English-speaking peoples"—presumably in contrast to those who spoke German, Russian, or Italian—to separation of powers. The minority also argued that unchecked administrative discretion threatened democracy not only directly but also indirectly by causing people to lose faith in their government. Curbing what was "at least questionable in a democracy" would help "to alleviate the disrespect, distrust, and fear now felt by too large a percentage of citizens."[70]

By 1945, when Congress began considering the legislation that was to become the APA, supporters of increased judicial supervision of the administrative state were able to bolster their arguments with references to the behavior of the wartime agencies. Indeed, the only moments of excitement in the otherwise tepid House and Senate debates occurred when congressmen rose to declare that the wartime agencies were proof positive of the need for the legislation. During Senate hearings Senators Austin and Danaher defended the decision not to exclude the civilian components of the army and navy from the APA all together.[71] On the House floor Emanuel Celler, a liberal New Dealer from New York, questioned the propriety of exempting the OPA and the WPB from certain sections of the act. Congressman Bennet was even more outspoken: "It is against the war agencies that you hear most of the complaints and criticism. It is against the OPA and the CPA [Civilian Production Administration] that you hear most of the criticism." Ultimately the bill's sponsors felt no need to apply the APA to these agencies because the passage of time had mooted the complaints against them. As the House Report noted, "they are rapidly liquidating."[72]

The substance of the APA addressed many of the fears of administrative absolutism and arbitrariness that were plaguing increasing numbers of Americans during the war. First, the act "legalized" the administrative process. It created uniform standards for agency adjudications that made agencies behave more like courts. Officials engaged in fact-finding and prosecution were forbidden from also serving the agency in a judicial capacity. The APA guaranteed the independence of trial examiners by giving them civil service protection and ensuring that their compensation was determined without reference to agency recommendations. It also set out detailed procedures for agency adjudications that included rules of evidence, burdens of proof, a right of cross-examination, and a requirement that decisions be based upon a formal record.[73]

The APA also ensured that the judiciary would exercise substantial control over the administrative process. It established a broad right of judicial review. It also created a uniform standard of review that allowed courts to judge not only formal administrative actions based on some sort of record but all other discretionary actions as well. The APA's requirement that agency actions be based on "substantial evidence" and must not be "arbitrary, capricious, an abuse of discretion, or otherwise not in accordance with law" were ones that courts had arrived at independently and that certain agencies were already statutorily required to use.[74] However, they represented the maximum amount of judicial review that had developed during the 1930s. What had been the ceiling for judicial involvement in the administrative process had become the floor.

With the passage of the APA, a lively debate about the meaning of its provisions commenced. The Truman administration attempted to portray them as little more than a codification of existing administrative procedures, while the American Bar Association and its conservative allies in Congress argued that they were an explicit break from the dangerous New Deal-era tradition of unchecked administrative discretion and judicial passivity.[75] Indeed, the APA's intentional ambiguity was the price paid for its unanimous acceptance. But the members of the federal judiciary, who would resolve these ambiguities, were subject to the same fears as the congressmen who passed the statute. The specter of totalitarianism and wartime maladministration affected those who interpreted the APA just as it did those who voted for it.

Of course the judiciary was unlikely to radically curtail executive authority in the middle of the war. A Supreme Court that would allow such unconscionable exercises of executive power as the internment of Japanese Americans in the name of national security was not about to limit it in other, less controversial areas.[76] Nevertheless, even before the passage of the APA, courts had independently begun to assert their authority over the administrative process. In 1940 and 1941 the Supreme Court began to expand the scope of standing, thereby increasing the number of people who could challenge administrative actions in court.[77] Similarly, in 1943 and 1944, the Court dramatically narrowed the doctrine of implied preclusion.[78] Like the shift in standing doctrine, this made it easier for someone aggrieved by an agency's action to get into court. On the eve of the passage of the APA, the

Court, on its own accord, began to increase the scrutiny it gave to agency actions.[79] That increased scrutiny, arguably mandated by the APA, continued after the war. Reviewing the legislative history of the act, Justice Frankfurter opined that "Congress expressed a mood." That mood was one of dissatisfaction with judicial passivity in the face of administrative action. "Reviewing courts must be influenced by a feeling that they are not to abdicate the conventional judicial function."[80] Indeed, the courts seemed to respond. Judicial reversal of administrative decisions climbed from 19 percent of administrative appeals during the 1941–42 fiscal year to 30 percent during the 1951–52 fiscal year.[81]

The rhetoric of federal judicial decisions evidenced the same fear of a connection between expert administration and totalitarianism as existed in the culture at large. As early as 1940 a Ninth Circuit panel made up entirely of Roosevelt appointees accused the National Labor Relations Board of "the kind of administrative absolutism denounced in democratic assemblies . . . as characteristic of the totalitarianism of the Central European powers." The judges did not believe that Congress intended the National Labor Relations Act to be "a long start on the road to where our civil liberties are regarded as the 'pale phantoms of objective law' which no longer control our deliberations, as the German Chief Justice . . . of the newly constituted court in conquered Poland is reported to have told his colleagues."[82]

The Supreme Court used a selective service case, *Estep v. United States* (1946), to limit drastically the doctrine of implied preclusion of judicial review. Its rationale reflected fears of totalitarian administration. Invoking the idea that totalitarian regimes used racial scapegoating to consolidate their power, Justice Douglas noted that without judicial review, administrative action motivated by prejudice could not be corrected. Justice Murphy's concurrence even more explicitly drew a connection between judicial review and the prevention of the autocratic tendencies of even a liberal democratic nation engaged in total war:

> But the war power is not a blank check to be used in blind disregard of all the individual rights which we have struggled so long to recognize and preserve. . . . All of the mobilization and all of the war efforts will have been in vain if, when it is all finished, we discover that in the process we destroyed the very freedoms for which we fought.[83]

Administrative law cases during the immediate postwar period repeatedly condemned administrative absolutism by invoking the specter of European totalitarianism. The rhetoric was particularly powerful in dissenting opinions. In *Securities and Exchange Commission v. Chenery* (1947), Justices Jackson and Frankfurter dissented from an opinion upholding an SEC decision. "This administrative authoritarianism, this power to decide without law, is what the Court seems to approve in so many words. . . . This decision is an ominous one to those who believe that men should be governed by laws." In *Radio Corporation of America v. United States* (1951), the Court upheld the Federal Communication Commission's decision to certify a particular system of color television broadcasting. Frankfurter issued an opinion, titled "dubitante," in which he belittled administrative expertise and suggested that more judicial supervision of administrative decision-making was necessary. In 1951, as well, Justice Douglas used even more striking language in dissenting from the Court's per curiam affirmance of a decision of the Interstate Commerce Commission. "Unless we make the requirements for administrative action strict and demanding," he warned, "*expertise*, the strength of modern government, can become a monster which rules with no practical limits on its discretion. Absolute discretion, like corruption, marks the beginning of the end of liberty."[84]

These expressions of fear regarding the dangers of administrative expertise, coming from justices like Douglas, Frankfurter, Jackson, and Murphy, each of whom had been a committed New Dealer and proponent of administrative governance, indicate the degree to which the administrative state had fallen out of favor during the 1940s. In 1932 liberals and progressives believed that administrative government was a scientific solution to an economic and social crisis of unparalleled proportions. By 1950 their experiences during World War II had convinced them that it was potentially threatening. The totalitarianism that America fought against had manifested itself through monstrous expressions of administrative power and an active disdain for the rule of law. Too often American wartime agencies had the appearance of incompetent bullies, captured by special interests, acting with an autocratic disregard of due process. Liberals had reversed their opinion of agencies and courts. The institutions that had been established to replace the outdated, conservative, legalistic judiciary were now to be firmly controlled by it.

This shift of power between agencies and courts did not stop the growth of the administrative state. To the contrary, it sanctioned that growth, providing safeguards that were prerequisites for acceptance of the permanent role the bureaucracy would play in American policy-making. "The availability of judicial review," wrote Louis Jaffe in 1965, "is the necessary condition, psychologically, if not logically, of a system of administrative power which purports to be legitimate, or legally valid."[85] The massive administrative state that evolved between World War II and the 1960s drew its legitimacy from the existence of a judiciary that would police the actions of federal and state administrators. Agencies and courts came to be "collaborative instrumentalities of justice," "a 'partnership' in furtherance of the public interest."[86] Yet, as Judge Henry Friendly tartly wrote, "[t]here is little doubt who is considered to be the senior partner."[87] It was America's encounter with totalitarianism during the 1940s that established the terms of this partnership and defined the relative status of the parties to it.

NOTES

1. For a thumbnail sketch of the growth of the administrative state, see Senate, *Administrative Procedure in Government Agencies,* 77th Cong., 1st sess., 1941, 8–11.

2. Several historians have chronicled the tempestuous relationship between courts and the administrative state during the first decades of the twentieth century. See, for example, Horwitz, *Transformation of American Law,* 213–246; Nonet, *Administrative Justice,* 165–243; Skowronek, *Building a New American State,* 259–67.

3. Landis, *Administrative Process,* 23–24, 33.

4. Ibid., 39.

5. See *Shannahan v. United States,* 303 U.S. 596 (1938); *Federal Power Commission v. Metropolitan Edison,* 304 U.S. 375 (1938); *United States v. Corrick,* 298 U.S. 435 (1936); *American Federation of Labor v. NLRB,* 308 U.S. 401 (1940); *Switchman's Union of North America v. National Mediation Board,* 320 U.S. 297 (1944). Though historians tend to argue that judicial passivity in the face of administrative action only came about after Roosevelt appointees came to dominate the federal judiciary, both the negative order doctrine and the doctrine of implied preclusion were used by the Fuller, White, and Taft Courts. See *Proctor & Gamble v. United States,* 225 U.S. 282 (1912); *Illinois Central R.R. v. ICC,* 206 U.S. 441 (1907); *Lehigh Valley R.R. v. United States,* 243 U.S. 412 (1917); *United States v. New River Co.,* 265 U.S. 533 (1924); *Piedmont & Northern Ry. v. United States,* 280 U.S. 469 (1930). For the traditional view, see Pritchett, *Roosevelt Court,* 167; Leuchtenberg, *Supreme Court Reborn,* 227; and Parrish, "Hughes Court," 302–306.

6. *Tennessee Electric Power Co. v. TVA,* 306 U.S. 118 (1939); *Perkins v. Lukens Steel,* 310 U.S. 113 (1940). Once again, there are many pre-New Deal antecedents for these narrow standing decisions. See, for example, *Edward Hines Yellow Pine Trustees v. United States,* 263 U.S. 143 (1923); *Alexander Sprunt & Son, Inc. v. United States.* But see *Chicago Junction Case,* 264 U.S. 258 (1924).

7. *Lynch v. United States,* 292 U.S. 571 (1934). Of course, the rights/privileges distinction was hardly an invention of New Deal-era judges. See *Davis v. Massachusetts*, 167 U.S. 43 (1897). For other pre-New Deal readings of the due process clause that gave administrative agencies wide discretion, see *Bi-Metallic Investment Co. v. State Board of Equalization,* 239 U.S. 441 (1915), and *North American Cold Storage v. Chicago,* 211 U.S. 306 (1908).

8. See, for example, Freund, *Administrative Law,* 705–33; Albertsworth, "Judicial Review," 127–28; Isaacs, "Judicial Review," 781–83.

9. Albertsworth, "Judicial Review," 136–43; Isaacs, "Judicial Review," 781–82; Dobie, "Judicial Review," 557, 559.

10. Albertsworth, "Judicial Review," 143–51; Isaacs, "Judicial Review," 781–82; Dobie, "Judicial Review," 559.

11. Isaacs, "Judicial Review," 789–95; Albertsworth, "Judicial Review," 151–53; Dobie, "Judicial Review," 559–70; Sharfman, *Interstate Commerce Commission,* 385–93; Henderson, *Federal Trade Commission,* 97–98.

12. See, for example, *ICC v. Louisville & Nashville R.R.,* 227 U.S. 83 (1913); *ICC v. Chicago, Rock Island & Pacific Ry.,* 218 U.S. 88 (1910); *Illinois Central Ry. v. ICC,* 206 U.S. 441 (1907).

13. *NLRB v. Waterman Steamship Co.,* 309 U.S. 206 (1940); *NLRB v. Bradford Dyeing,* 310 U.S. 318 (1940); *Swayne & Hoyt v. United States,* 300 U.S. 297 (1937).

14. *Gray v. Powell*, 314 U.S. 402 (1941); *NLRB v. Hearst*, 322 U.S. 111 (1944).

15. *Caughlin v. Chicago Park District*, 4 N.E. 1 (Ill. 1936); *Thayer Amusement Corp. v. Moulton*, 7 A.2d 682 (R.I. 1939); *American Committee on Maternal Welfare v. Mangan*, 14 N.Y.S.2d 39 (1939); *Shoemaker v. Burke*, 92 F.2d 205 (D.C. Cir. 1937); *NLRB v. Federbush*, 121 F.2d 954 (2d. Cir. 1941).

16. *Rochester Tel. Co. v. FCC*, 307 U.S. 125, 138 (1939), quoting *Illinois Central R.R. v. ICC*, 206 U.S. at 454.

17. *Gray v. Powell*, 314 U.S. at 333.

18. *Dobson v. Commissioner of Internal Revenue*, 320 U.S. at 245.

19. *Perkins v. Lukens Steel Co.*, 310 U.S. at 127–28. Several pre-New Deal cases have even stronger language justifying judicial deference with expertise. See, for example, *ICC v. Chicago, Rock Island & Pacific Ry.*, 218 U.S. 88, 110 (1908), which held that only minimal judicial supervision of the administrative process was necessary because expertise itself was a sufficient guard against administrative arbitrariness. "[T]he training that is required, the comprehensive knowledge which is possessed, guards or tends to guard against accidental abuse of its powers or, if the abuse occurs, to correct it," the Court declared.

20. Purcell, *Crisis of Democratic Theory*, 159–78; Purcell, "American Jurisprudence between the Wars," 437–46; White, *Patterns of American Legal Thought*, 136–53; Belz, "Changing Conceptions of Constitutionalism," 640–41, 648–54; Alpers, "Understanding Dictatorship," 154–255.

21. Nelson, *Legalist Reformation*, 121–147; Gerstle, *Working Class Americanism*, 278–309; Nelson, "Changing Meaning of Equality," 19–28; Polenberg, *One Nation Divisible*, 46–85; Alpers, "This is the Army," 143–47; Gleason, "Americans All," 483.

22. Leuchtenberg, *Roosevelt*, 178; Badger, *New Deal*, 285; Alpers, "Understanding Dictatorship," 127–36; Bixby, "Roosevelt Court," 747–52; Cushman, *Rethinking the New Deal Court*, 13–15; Polenberg, *Reorganizing Roosevelt's Government*, 146–61.

23. Alpers, "This is the Army," 132.

24. *Christian Century*, quoted in ibid., 137.

25. Alpers, "This is the Army," 137–38, 140–43, 147–49.

26. McGuire, "Administrative Law and American Democracy," 394; Gardner, Review of *The Administrative Process*, 339; Thurston, Review of *The Administrative Process*, 1018.

27. Quoted in Horwitz, *Transformation of American Law*, 239, 240.

28. Jaffe, *Judicial Control*, 323. Although Jaffe published *Judicial Control* in 1965, much of its contents was taken from articles he wrote in the 1940s and early 1950s. See particularly Jaffe, "Limits of the Administrative Process," 1105; Jaffe, "Judicial Review," 1233; Jaffe, "Justice Frankfurter," 357.

29. Jaffe, *Judicial Control*, 344.

30. Quoted in Horwitz, *Transformation of American Law*, 239.

31. Jaffe, *Judicial Control*, 326–27.

32. Davis, *Administrative Law*, 925–28; Jaffe, *Judicial Control*, chapters 9, 14, and 15.

33. Brinkley, *Liberalism and Its Discontents*, 284; Rosenof, "Freedom, Planning, and Totalitarianism," 149, 150.

34. Quoted in Brinkley, *Liberalism and Its Discontents*, 284.

35. Rosenof, "Freedom, Planning and Totalitarianism," 157–58; Hayek quoted in Brinkley, *Liberalism and Its Discontents*, 86.

36. Lynd and MacDonald quoted in Pells, *Liberal Mind in a Conservative Age*, 18–19, 45–46.

37. Howard and Bone, *Current American Government*, fold out between pp. 46–47, p. 62.

38. Senate Judiciary Committee, *Administrative Procedure*, 77th Cong., 1st sess., 1941, 1218.

39. Blum, *V Was for Victory*, 223–24.

40. Brinkley, *Liberalism and Its Discontents*, 80–81, 82; Brinkley, *End of Reform*, 175–76, 182–85.

41. Koistinen, "Warfare and Power Relations," 96–97; Brinkley, *End of Reform*, 186–89.

42. Lingeman, *Don't You Know There's a War On?*, 112–16; Catton, *War Lords of Washington*, 165–66; Polenberg, *War and Society*, 10–15; Koistinen, "Warfare and Power Relations," 106; Brinkley, *End of Reform*, 237–40.

43. Riddle, *Truman Commission*, 41–43, 65–66; Polenberg, *War and Society*, 90–91; Catton, *War Lords of Washington*, 116–20; Stone, *Business as Usual*, 133–37, 141.

44. Quoted in Waddell, "Economic Mobilization," 190 n. 63.

45. Catton, *War Lords of Washington*, 75–77.

46. Polenberg, *War and Society*, 12–13; Catton, *Warlords of Washington*, 93; Brinkley, *End of Reform*, 186–92.

47. For the Truman Committee's attacks on the WPB, see Blum, *V Was for Victory*, 124–31; Brinkley, *End of Reform*, 192–94. The other two committees that alleged that the WPB discriminated against small business were the Senate Special Committee to Study the Problems of American Small Business (the "Murray Committee") and the House Select Committee Investigating National Defense Migration (the "Tolan Committee"). See Senate Committee, *The Future of Independent Business*, 79th Cong., 2nd sess., 1947, Committee Print # 16, 23–25; and House, *National Defense Migration*, 77th Cong., 2d Sess., 1942, H. Rep. 1879, 17, 19–27.

48. Quoted in Bernstein, "Debate on Industrial Reconversion," 167.

49. Quoted in Brinkley, *End of Reform*, 239; Bernstein, "Debate on Industrial Reconversion," 167–68; Catton, *War Lords of Washington*, 245–55.

50. Brinkley, *End of Reform*, 193, 198–200.

51. Jacobs, " 'How About Some Meat?' " 910.

52. A number of historians have written about the OPA. The most comprehensive treatment, the eighteen-volume series "Historical Reports on War Administration: Office of Price Administration," is summarized in Mansfield, *Short History*. See also Blum, *V Was for Victory*, 91–116; Lingeman, *Don't You Know There's a War On?*, 234–70; Polenberg, *War and Society*, 30–36; Jacobs, " 'How About Some Meat?' "

53. Young, *Congressional Politics*, 100; Jacobs, " 'How About Some Meat?' " 935.

54. The most consistent critic was the House Select Committee to Investigate Executive Agencies, otherwise known as the Smith Committee. The Smith Committee issued three reports, all highly critical of the OPA. House, 78th Cong., 1st sess., 1943, H. Reps. 699, 862, 898.

55. Quoted in Lingeman, *Don't You Know There's a War On?*, 257.

56. Ibid., 240.
57. Jacobs, "'How About Some Meat?'" 925; Satterfield, *Home Front*, 211.
58. Quoted in Jacobs, " 'How About Some Meat?' " 939.
59. A. G. Mezerik, "The OPA Crack-Up," *New Republic* 108 (June 28, 1943): 850; Daniel Lang, "Reporter At Large: Menus, Nylons, Wiping Clothes, and Abdullahs," *New Yorker*, July 14, 1945, 36; "The OPA Complex," *Commonweal* 44 (August 2, 1946): 371.
60. Oppenheimer, "War Price and Rationing Boards," 147; O'Leary, "Wartime Rationing," 1089; Nicholls and Vieg, *Wartime Government*, 67–70.
61. O'Leary, "Wartime Rationing," 1100; Nicholls and Vieg, *Wartime Government*, 54, 69–70, 91–95; Juran, *Bureaucracy*, 38–60.
62. Emmerich, "Some Notes on Wartime Federal Administration," 57–59; Oppenheimer, "War Price and Rationing Boards"; Nicholls and Vieg, *Wartime Government*, 67–70; O'Leary, "Wartime Rationing," 1095.
63. Emmerich, "Some Notes on Wartime Federal Administration," 61; Howard and Bone, *Current American Government*, 44; Nicholls and Vieg, *Wartime Government*, 90, 95.
64. Polenberg, *War and Society*, 94–95.
65. Howard and Bone, *Current American Government*, 332–38.
66. The history of the APA presented in the following paragraphs is taken from Schiller, "Policy Ideals and Judicial Action," 380–424; and Shepherd, "Fierce Compromise," 1557. See also White, *Constitution and the New Deal*, 94–127.
67. *Congressional Record*, 76th Cong., 2d sess., April 18, 1940, 4736. See also ibid., April 15, 1940, 4535.
68. Ibid., April 18, 1940, 4743–44; ibid., November 26, 1940, 13748. Because Francis Walter was a vehement anticommunist, chair of the infamous House Un-American Activities Committee, and coauthor of the racist McCarran-Walter Immigration Act of 1952, he has gotten a reactionary reputation that is only partially deserved. Walter, first elected in 1932, generally supported the social and economic legislation proposed by the Roosevelt, Truman, and Kennedy administrations. He was one of the key Republican supporters of the Marshall Plan. *Dictionary of American Biography* (New York: Scribner's, 1964), supp. 7: 766–67. Such New Deal supporters as Senators Carl Hatch, Henrik Shipstead, and David Walsh voted for Walter-Logan. Indeed, prior to his introduction of the Walter-Logan bill, Senator Logan had been a "reliable supporter" of the New Deal. George Shepherd has noted that 41 percent of Northern Democratic House members and 40 percent of Northern Democratic Senators voted for Walter-Logan. Shepherd, "Fierce Compromise," 1601, 1619, 1622.
69. See House, *Congressman Cellar's Minority Report on Walter-Logan*, 76th Cong., 3rd sess., 1940, H. Rep. 1149.
70. Senate, *Administrative Procedure*, 56, 203, 215.
71. Senate, Judicial Committee Hearings, *Administrative Procedure*, 79th Cong., 1st sess., 1945, 35–51.
72. *Administrative Procedure Act: Legislative History* (Washington, D.C.: U.S. Government Printing Office, 1946), 83, 253, 387. The CPA was the Civilian Production Administration.
73. Public Law 404, 79th Cong., 2nd sess., 1946, §§5, 7, 8, 5(c), 11, 7(b)-(d).

74. Ibid., §10 (a), (e). For a summary of statutory standards before the passage of the APA, see Stason, "'Substantial Evidence' in Administrative Law," 1026–28.

75. Shepherd, "Fierce Compromise," 1662–1675. The Attorney General's Manual is the best example of the Truman administration's position that the APA basically codified existing law. For the opposite view, see McCarran, "Improving 'Administrative Justice,'" 827; Dickenson, "Administrative Procedure Acts," 434.

76. Urofsky, *Division and Discord*, 49–51. Herman Pritchett notes that between 1941 and 1946 agencies received favorable decisions from the Supreme Court in 72 percent of the cases it heard. Pritchett, *Roosevelt Court*, 190. Though Pritchett portrays the Stone Court's reversal rate of 28 percent as indicative of deference, it was, in fact, 7 percent above the average rate at which federal courts of appeals reversed the decisions of administrative agencies during the 1940s. It was almost 10 percent higher than the circuit court reversal rate in the 1941–1942 fiscal year, the first year that statistics of this type were kept. See below, note 81. Furthermore, even if one assumes that the Court was particularly deferential during wartime, there is no reason to believe that its behavior under these extenuating circumstances is indicative of the long-term trend. For example, notwithstanding the Japanese internment cases, the Stone Court decided many cases that gave the judiciary a special role in protecting the rights of minorities.

77. *FCC v. Sanders Brothers*, 309 U.S. 470 (1940); *Scripps-Howard v. FCC*, 316 U.S. 4 (1942).

78. *Reconstruction Finance Corp. v. Bankers Trust*, 318 U.S. 163 (1943); *Stark v. Wickard*, 321 U.S. 288 (1944). See also *Estep v. United States*, 327 U.S. 114 (1946).

79. *Addison v. Holly Hill Farms*, 322 U.S. 607 (1944).

80. *Universal Camera Corp. v. NLRB*, 340 U.S. 474, 487, 490 (1951).

81. Report of the Judicial Conference of the United States, 1942: table 1; ibid., 1952: table B1, p. 112. 1942 was the first year that the Judicial Conference kept statistics on the dispositions of appeals of administrative decisions. The average rate of reversal across decades reveals a less dramatic change. The average reversal rate in the 1940s was about 21 percent. The average rate during the 1950s was 25 percent. Even this more modest change is impressive considering that administrative agencies presumably altered their behavior in response to the doctrinal changes that had occurred.

82. *NLRB v. Sterling Electric Motors*, 112 F.2d 63, 68 (9th Cir. 1940); *Who's Who in America* (Chicago: Marquis Who's Who, 1940–41), 21: 755, 1209, 1713.

83. 327 U.S. at 121–22 (Douglas), 131–32 (Murphy).

84. *SEC v. Chenery*, 332 U.S. 194, 216 (1947); *Radio Corp. America v. United States*, 341 U.S. 412 (1951); *State of New York v. United States*, 342 U.S. 882, 884 (1951).

85. Jaffe, *Judicial Control*, 320.

86. *United States v. Morgan*, 313 U.S. 409, 422 (1941); *Greater Boston Television Corp. v. FCC*, 444 F.2d 841, 851 (D.C. Cir. 1971).

87. Friendly, "Some Kind of Hearing," 1311.

Bibliography

Acheson, Dean. *Present at the Creation: My Years in the State Department*. New York: Norton, 1969.

Ackerman, Bruce A. "Taxation and the Constitution." *Columbia Law Review* 99 (1999): 1–58.

Adams, Michael C. C. *The Best War Ever: America and World War II*. Baltimore: Johns Hopkins University Press, 1994.

———. "The 'Good War' Myth and the Cult of Nostalgia." *Midwest Quarterly* 40 (1998): 59–74.

Albertsworth, E. F. "Judicial Review of Administrative Actions by the Federal Supreme Court." *Harvard Law Review* 35 (1921): 127–53.

Alpers, Benjamin L. "This is the Army: Imagining a Democratic Military in World War II." *Journal of American History* 85 (1998): 129–63.

———. "Understanding Dictatorship and Defining Democracy in American Public Culture, 1930–1945." Ph.D. diss., Princeton University, 1994.

Amenta, Edwin. *Bold Relief: Institutional Politics and the Origins of Modern American Social Policy*. Princeton, N.J.: Princeton University Press, 1998.

Ancheta, Angelo N. *Race, Rights, and the Asian American Experience*. New Brunswick, N.J.: Rutgers University Press, 1998.

Anderson, Karen. *Wartime Women: Sex Roles, Family Relations, and the Status of Women during World War II*. Westport, Conn.: Greenwood Press, 1981.

Anthony, Joseph Garner. *Hawaii under Army Rule*. Honolulu: University Press of Hawaii, 1955.

———. "Martial Law, Military Government and the Writ of Habeas Corpus in Hawaii." *California Law Review* 31 (1943): 477–514.

Aoki, Keith. "No Right to Own?: The Early-Twentieth Century "Alien Land Laws" as a Prelude to Internment." *Boston College Law Review* 40 (1998): 37–72.

Atleson, James B. *Labor and the Wartime State: Labor Relations and Law during World War II*. Urbana: University of Illinois Press, 1998.

Auerbach, Carl A., Lloyd K. Garrison, Willard Hurst, and Samuel Mermin. *The Legal Process: An Introduction to Decision-making by Judicial, Legislative, Executive, and Administrative Agencies*. San Francisco: Chandler Publishing Co., 1961.

Badger, Anthony J. *The New Deal: The Depression Years, 1933–1940*. New York: Noonday, 1989.

Balchin, Nigel. *The Small Back Room*. London: Reprint Society, 1945.

Balogh, Brian. "Reorganizing the Organizational Synthesis: Federal-Professional Relations in Modern America." *Studies in American Political Development* 5 (1991): 119–72.

Baum, Lawrence, Sheldon Goldman, and Austin Sarat. "The Evolution of Litigation in the Federal Courts of Appeals, 1895–1974." *Law and Society Review* 16 (1981–82): 291–309.

Belknap, Michal R. "Frankfurter and the Nazi Saboteurs." *Supreme Court Historical Society Yearbook* 1982: 66–71.

———. "The Supreme Court Goes to War: The Meaning and Implications of the Nazi Saboteur Case." *Military Law Review* 89 (1980): 59–95.

Bell, Derrick. "Xerces and the Affirmative Action Mystique," *George Washington Law Review* 57 (1989): 1595–613.

Belz, Herman. "Changing Conceptions of Constitutionalism in the Era of World War II and the Cold War." *Journal of American History* 59 (1972): 640–69.

Bensel, Richard F. *Sectionalism and Political Development, 1880–1980*. Madison: University of Wisconsin Press, 1984.

Bernstein, Barton J. "The Debate on Industrial Reconversion." *American Journal of Economics and Sociology* 26 (1967): 159–72.

Bernstein, Cyrus. "The Saboteur Trial: A Case History." *George Washington Law Review* 11 (1943): 131–90.

Beuscher, Jacob H. "Law-Taught Attitudes and Consumer Rationing." *Wisconsin Law Review* (1945): 63–76.

Biddle, Francis. *In Brief Authority*. Garden City, N.Y.: Doubleday, 1962.

Bidwell, Percy W. "Our Economic Warfare." *Foreign Affairs* 20 (1942): 421–37.

Bittker, Boris I. "Federal Income Taxation and the Family." *Stanford Law Review* 27 (1975): 1389–463.

———. "The World War II German Saboteurs' Case and Writs of Certiorari before Judgment by the Court of Appeals: A Tale of Nunc Pro Tunc Jurisdiction." *Constitutional Commentary* 14 (1997): 431–51.

Bixby, David M. "The Roosevelt Court, Democratic Ideology and Minority Rights." *Yale Law Journal* 90 (1981): 741–815.

Blum, John Morton. "Unity and Stability during World War II." In *Liberty, Justice, Order*. New York: Norton, 1993.

———. *V Was for Victory: Politics and American Culture during World War II*. New York: Harcourt Brace, 1976.

Blum, John Morton, ed. *From the Morgenthau Diaries*. 3 vols. New York: Harcourt Brace and Co., 1967.

———. *The Price of Vision: The Diary of Henry A. Wallace, 1942–1946*. Boston: Houghton Mifflin, 1973.

Boris, Eileen. *Home to Work: Motherhood and the Politics of Industrial Homework in the United States*. New York: Cambridge University Press, 1994.

Bosworth, Allan R. *America's Concentration Camps*. New York: Norton, 1967.

Brackman, Arnold C. *The Other Nuremberg: The Untold Story of the Tokyo War Crimes Trials*. New York: Morrow, 1987.

Brinkley, Alan. *The End of Reform: New Deal Liberalism in Recession and War*. New York: Knopf, 1995.

———. *Liberalism and Its Discontents*. Cambridge, Mass.: Harvard University Press, 1998.

———. "The Problem of American Conservatism." *American Historical Review* 99 (1994): 409–29.

Brinkley, David. *Washington Goes to War*. New York: Knopf, 1988.

Brokaw, Tom. *The Greatest Generation*. New York: Random House, 1998.

Brooks, Robin. "Domestic Violence and America's Wars: A Historical Interpretation." In *Violence in America: Historical and Comparative Perspectives*. Edited by Hugh Davis Graham and Ted Robert Gurr. New York: Signet Books, 1969.

Brown, Esther Lucile. *Lawyers, Law Schools and the Public Service*. New York: Russell Sage Foundation, 1948.

Brown, Tyrone. "Clerking for the Chief Justice." In *The Warren Court: A Retrospective*. Edited by Bernard Schwartz. New York: Oxford University Press, 1969.

Brownlee, W. Elliot. *Federal Taxation in America: A Short History*. New York: Cambridge University Press, 1996.

———."Reflections on the History of Taxation." In *Funding the Modern American State, 1941–1995*. Edited by W. Elliot Brownlee. New York: Cambridge University Press, 1996.

———. "Tax Regimes, National Crisis and State-Building in America." In *Funding the Modern American State, 1941–1995*. Edited by W. Elliot Brownlee. New York: Cambridge University Press, 1996.

Buller, Lilian L. "Administrative History of the Board of Economic Warfare in the Field of International Economic Relations." Washington, D.C.: U.S. Bureau of the Budget, 1943. *World War II Administrative Histories*. New Haven: Research Publications, 1974.

Burk, Robert F. *The Corporate State and the Broker State: The Du Ponts and American National Politics, 1925–1940*. Cambridge, Mass.: Harvard University Press, 1990.

Burns, James McGregor. *Roosevelt: The Soldier of Freedom*. New York: Harcourt Brace Jovanovich, 1970.

Burt, Robert A. *Two Jewish Justices: Outcasts in the Promised Land*. Berkeley: University of California Press, 1988.

Campbell, D'Ann. *Women at War with America: Private Lives in a Patriotic Era*. Cambridge, Mass.: Harvard University Press, 1984.

Carter, James C., Jr. "The Ideal and the Actual in the Law." *American Bar Association Reports* (1890): 217–45.

Casner, A. James, and W. Barton Leach. *Cases and Text on Property*. Boston: Little, Brown, 1950.

Catton, Bruce. *The War Lords of Washington*. New York: Harcourt, Brace, 1948.

Chan, Sucheng. *Asian Americans: An Interpretive History*. Boston: Twayne, 1991.

Chan, Sucheng, ed. *Entry Denied: Exclusion and the Chinese Community in America, 1882–1943*. Philadelphia: Temple University Press, 1991.

Chapin, Bradley. *The American Law of Treason: Revolutionary and Early National Origins*. Athens: University of Georgia Press, 1964.

Cherry, Robert. "The Culture-of-Poverty Thesis and African-Americans: The Work of Gunnar Myrdal and Other Institutionalists." *Journal of Economic Issues* 29 (1995): 1119–32.

Chirelstein, Marvin. *Federal Income Taxation: A Law Student's Guide to the Leading Cases and Concepts*. 4th ed. Mineola, N.Y.: Foundation Press, 1985.

Cho, Sumi. "Multiple Consciousness and the Diversity Dilemma." *University of Colorado Law Review* 68 (1997): 1035–63.

———. "Redeeming Whiteness in the Shadow of Internment: Earl Warren, Brown, and a Theory of Racial Redemption." *Boston College Law Review* 40 (1998): 73–170; *Boston College Third World Law Review* 19 (1998): 73–170.

Chodorov, Frank. *The Income Tax: The Root of All Evil*. Rev. ed. New York: Devin-Adair, 1959.

———. *One Is a Crowd: Reflections of an Individualist*. New York: Devin-Adair, 1952.

Chuman, Frank F. *The Bamboo People: The Law and Japanese-Americans*. Del Mar, Calif.: Publisher's, 1976.

Clark, Thomas R. "The Limits of State Autonomy: The Medical Cooperatives of the Farm Security Administration, 1935–1946." *Journal of Policy History* 11 (1999): 257–82.

Corwin, Edward S. *Total War and the Constitution*. New York: Knopf, 1947.

Cosgrove, Richard A. *The Rule of Law: Albert Venn Dicey, Victorian Jurist*. Chapel Hill: University of North Carolina Press, 1980.

Cott, Nancy F. *The Grounding of Modern Feminism*. New Haven, Conn.: Yale University Press, 1987.

Cover, Robert M. "Violence and the Word." In *Narrative, Violence, and the Law: The Essays of Robert Cover*. Edited by Martha Minow, Michael Ryan, and Austin Sarat. Ann Arbor: University of Michigan Press, 1992.

Cozzens, James Gould. *Guard of Honor*. New York: Harcourt, Brace, 1946.

———. *The Just and the Unjust*. New York: Harcourt, Brace, 1942.

Cray, Ed. *Chief Justice: A Biography of Earl Warren*. New York: Simon & Schuster, 1997.

Crenshaw, Kimberle Williams. "Race, Reform and Retrenchment: Transformation and Legitimation in Antidiscrimination Law." *Harvard Law Review* 101 (1988): 1331–87.

Currie, David P. *The Constitution in the Supreme Court: The Second Century, 1888–1986*. Chicago: University of Chicago Press, 1990.

Cushman, Barry. *Rethinking the New Deal Court: The Structure of a Constitutional Revolution*. Oxford: Oxford University Press, 1998.

Cushman, Robert E. "The Case of the Nazi Saboteurs." *American Political Science Review* 36 (1942): 1082–91.

Danelski, David J. "The Saboteurs' Case." *Journal of Supreme Court History* (1996): 61.

Daniels, Roger. *Concentration Camps USA: Japanese Americans and World War II*. New York: Holt, Rinehart, and Winston, 1971.

———. *The Politics of Prejudice: The Anti-Japanese Movement in California, and the Struggle for Japanese Exclusion*. Berkeley: University of California Press, 1962.

Danzig, Richard. "Justice Frankfurter's Opinions in the Flag Salute Cases: Blending Logic and Psychologic in Constitutional Decisionmaking." *Stanford Law Review* 36 (1984): 675–723.

Dasch, George. *Eight Spies Against America*. New York: R. M. McBride Co., 1959.

Davis, Kenneth Culp. *Administrative Law*. St. Paul, Minn.: Foundation Press, 1951.

Dembitz, Nanette. "Racial Discrimination and the Military Judgment: The Supreme Court's Korematsu and Endo Decisions." *Columbia Law Review* 45 (1945): 175–239.

Dicey, A. V. *Introduction to the Study of the Law of the Constitution*. 1885. Indianapolis: Liberty Classics, 1982.

Dickenson, John. "Administrative Procedure Acts: Scope and Ground of Broadened Judicial Review." *American Bar Association Journal* 33 (1947): 434–37, 513–19.

Dobie, Armistead M. "Judicial Review of Administrative Actions in Virginia." *Virginia Law Review* 8 (1922): 477–506, 557–588.

Douglas, William O. *The Court Years, 1939–1975: The Autobiography of William O. Douglas*. New York: Random House, 1980.

Dower, John. *War Without Mercy: Race and Power in the Pacific War*. New York: Pantheon Books, 1986.

Dubofsky, Melvyn. *The State and Labor in Modern America*. Chapel Hill: University of North Carolina Press, 1994.

Dudziak, Mary L. *Cold War Civil Rights: Race and the Image of American Democracy*. Princeton, N.J.: Princeton University Press, 2000.

Dunne, Gerald T. *Hugo Black and the Judicial Revolution*. New York: Simon & Schuster, 1977.

Duxbury, Neil. *Patterns of American Jurisprudence*. New York: Oxford University Press, 1995.

Eiler, Keith E. *Mobilizing America: Robert P. Patterson and the War Effort, 1940–1945*. Ithaca, N.Y.: Cornell University Press, 1997.

Emmerich, Herbert. "Some Notes on Wartime Federal Administration." *Public Administration Review* 5 (1945): 55–61.

Erenberg, Lewis A., and Susan E. Hirsch, eds. *The War in American Culture: Society and Consciousness during World War II*. Chicago: University of Chicago Press, 1996.

Ernst, Daniel R. "Willard Hurst and the Administrative State: From Williams to Wisconsin." *Law and History Review* 18 (2000): 1–33.

Eskridge, William N., Jr. "Willard Hurst, Master of the Legal Process." *Wisconsin Law Review* (1997): 1181–89.

Evans, Peyton R. "Federal Corporations: Their Purposes and Functions." *Federal Bar Association Journal* 2 (1936): 319–24, 367.

Fairman, Charles. *The Law of Martial Rule*. 2d ed. Chicago: Callaghan, 1943.

———. "The Law of Martial Rule and the National Emergency." *Harvard Law Review* 55 (1942): 1253–302.

———. *Reconstruction and Reunion 1864–88*. New York: Macmillan, 1971.

Falk, Richard A. *A Global Approach to National Policy*. Cambridge, Mass.: Harvard University Press, 1975.

Fine, Sidney. *Frank Murphy: The Washington Years*. Ann Arbor: University of Michigan Press, 1984.

Finkle, Lee. *Forum for Protest: The Black Press during World War II*. Rutherford, N.J.: Fairleigh Dickinson University Press, 1975.

Fones-Wolf, Elizabeth A. *Selling Free Enterprise: The Business Assault on Labor and Liberalism, 1945–60*. Urbana: University of Illinois Press, 1994.

Fraenkel, Osmond K. "War, Civil Liberties and the Supreme Court, 1941–1946." *Yale Law Journal* 55 (1946): 715–34.

Frank, John P. "Ex parte Milligan v. The Five Companies." *Columbia Law Review* 44 (1944): 639–668.

———. "Hugo L. Black." In *The Justices of the United States Supreme Court, 1789–1987*. Edited by Leon Friedman and Fred L. Israel. New York: Chelsea House, 1980.

———. "Review and Basic Liberties." In *Supreme Court and Supreme Law*. Edited by Edmond Cahn. Bloomington: University of Indiana Press, 1954.

Frankfurter, Felix. *The Public and Its Government*. New Haven: Yale University Press, 1930.

Freedman, Max, ed. *Roosevelt & Frankfurter: Their Correspondence, 1928–1945*. Boston: Little Brown, 1967.

Freund, Ernst. *Cases on Administrative Law*. Saint Paul, Minn.: West, 1928.

Friendly, Henry. "Some Kind of Hearing." *University of Pennsylvania Law Review* 123 (1975): 1267–1317.

Fussell, Paul. *Wartime: Understanding and Behavior during World War II*. New York: Oxford University Press, 1989.

Gardner, George K. Review of *The Administrative Process*, by James M. Landis. *Harvard Law Review* 52 (1938): 336–42.

Garrison, Lloyd K., and Willard Hurst. *Law in Society: A Course Designed for Undergraduates and Beginning Law Students*. Madison, Wisc.: College Typing Co., 1940.

———. *Law in Society: A Course Designed for Undergraduates and Beginning Law Students: Cases and Other Materials*. Rev. ed. Madison, Wisc.: College Typing Co., 1941.

Gerstle, Gary. "Race and the Myth of the Liberal Consensus." *Journal of American History* 82 (1995): 579–86.

———. *Working Class Americanism: The Politics of Labor in a Textile City, 1914–1960*. New York: Cambridge University Press, 1989.

———. "The Working Class Goes to War." In *The War in American Culture: Society and Consciousness during World War II*. Edited by Lewis A. Erenberg and Susan E. Hirsch. Chicago: University of Chicago Press, 1996.

Gilpin, Robert. *War and Change in World Politics*. New York: Cambridge University Press, 1981.

Girdner, Audrie, and Anne Loftus. *The Great Betrayal: The Evacuation of the Japanese-Americans during World War II*. New York: Macmillan, 1969.

Gleason, Philip. "Americans All: World War II and the Shaping of American Politics." *Review of Politics* 43 (1981): 483–518.

Glennon, Robert Jerome. *The Iconoclast as Reformer: Jerome Frank's Impact on American Law*. Ithaca, N.Y.: Cornell University Press, 1985.

Goldfield, Michael. Reply. *American Political Science Review* 84 (1990): 1304–15.

Goluboff, Risa L. "'Won't You Please Help Me Get My Son Home': Peonage, Patronage, and Protest in the World War II Urban South." *Law and Social Inquiry* 24 (1999): 777–806.

Gordon, Robert W. "Hurst Recaptured." *Law and History Review.* 18 (2000): 167–75.

———. "Legal Thought and Legal Practice in the Age of American Enterprise, 1870–1920." In *Professions and Professional Ideologies in America.* Edited by Gerald L. Geison. Chapel Hill: University of North Carolina Press, 1983.

Gott, Gil. "A Tale of New Precedents: Japanese American Internment as Foreign Affairs Law." *Boston College Law Review* 40 (1998): 179–274. *Boston College Third World Law Journal* 19 (1998): 179–274.

Graetz, Michael J. *The Decline (and Fall?) of the Income Tax.* New York: W. W. Norton, 1997.

Grimshaw, Allen D., ed. *Racial Violence in the United States.* Chicago: Aldine Publishing Co., 1969.

Grodzins, Morton. *Americans Betrayed: Politics and Japanese Evacuation.* Chicago: University of Chicago Press, 1949.

Halliday, Terence C., and Lucien Karpik. "Politics Matter: A Comparative Theory of Lawyers in the Making of Political Liberalism." In *Lawyers and the Rise of Western Political Liberalism: Europe and North America from the Eighteenth to Twentieth Centuries.* Edited by Terence C. Halliday and Lucien Karpik. Oxford: Clarendon Press, 1997.

Haney-Lopez, Ian. *White By Law: The Legal Construction of Race.* New York: New York University Press, 1996.

Harris, Cheryl I. "Whiteness as Property." *Harvard Law Review* 106 (1993): 1707–91.

Hart, David M. "Herbert Hoover's Last Laugh: The Enduring Significance of the 'Associative State' in the United States." *Journal of Policy History* 10 (1998): 419–44.

Hartmann, Susan M. *The Home Front and Beyond: American Women in the 1940s.* Boston: Twayne Publishers, 1982.

Hartog, Hendrik. "Snakes in Ireland: A Conversation with Willard Hurst." *Law and History Review* 12 (1994): 370–90.

Hatamiya, Leslie T. *Righting a Wrong: Japanese Americans and the Passage of the Civil Liberties Act of 1988.* Stanford, Calif.: Stanford University Press, 1993.

Hawley, Ellis W. "Herbert Hoover, the Commerce Secretariat, and the Vision of an 'Associative State,' 1921–1928." *Journal of American History* 61 (1974): 116–140.

———. "Social Policy and the Liberal State in Twentieth-Century America." In *Federal Social Policy: The Historical Dimension.* Edited by Donald T. Critchlow and Ellis W. Hawley. University Park: Pennsylvania State University Press, 1988.

Hayek, F. A. *The Road to Serfdom.* 1944. Rev. ed. Chicago: University of Chicago Press, 1994.

Henderson, Gerard Carl. *The Federal Trade Commission: A Study in Administrative Law and Procedure.* New Haven, Conn.: Yale University Press, 1924.

Herring, George C., Jr. *Aid to Russia, 1941–1946.* New York: Columbia University Press, 1973.

Herskovits, Melville J. *The Economic Life of Primitive Peoples.* New York: Knopf, 1940.

Himmelstein, Jerome. *To the Right: The Transformation of American Conservatism.* Berkeley: University of California Press, 1990.

Hines, N. Williams. "Real Property Joint Tenancies: Law, Fact and Fancy." *Iowa Law Review* 51 (1966): 582–624.

Hing, Bill. *Making and Remaking Asian America through Immigration Policy, 1850–1990.* Stanford, Calif.: Stanford University Press, 1993.

Hogan, Michael J. *A Cross of Iron: Harry S. Truman and the Origins of the National Security State, 1945–1954.* New York: Cambridge University Press, 1998.

Holtz, William. *The Ghost in the Little House: A Life of Rose Wilder Lane.* Columbia: University of Missouri Press, 1993.

Honey, Maureen. *Creating Rosie the Riveter: Class, Gender and Propaganda during World War II.* Amherst: University of Massachusetts Press, 1984.

Hooks, Gregory. *Forging the Military-Industrial Complex: World War II's Battle of the Potomac.* Urbana: University of Illinois Press, 1991.

Horwitz, Morton. *The Transformation of American Law, 1870–1960.* Cambridge, Mass.: Harvard University Press, 1992.

———. *The Warren Court and the Pursuit of Justice: A Critical Issue.* New York: Hill and Wang, 1998.

Hosokawa, Bill. *Thirty-Five Years in the Frying Pan.* New York: McGraw-Hill, 1978.

Howard, J. Woodford. "Advocacy in Constitutional Choice: The *Cramer* Treason Case, 1942–1945." *American Bar Foundation Research Journal* (1986): 375–413.

———. "The *Cramer* Treason Case." *Journal of Supreme Court History* vol. 1 (1996): 49–60.

———. *Mr. Justice Murphy: A Political Biography.* Princeton, N.J.: Princeton University Press, 1968.

Howard, L. Vaughn, and Hugh A. Bone. *Current American Government: Wartime Developments.* New York: Appleton-Century, 1943.

Hurst, James Willard. "The Content of Courses in Legislation." *University of Chicago Law Review* 8 (1941): 280–95.

———. *Developments in the Law of Industrial Accident.* Madison, Wisc.: College Typing Co., 1939.

———. *The Growth of American Law: The Law Makers.* Boston: Little, Brown, 1950.

———. "A Historian Views the Profession." In *Conference on the Profession of Law and Legal Education.* Chicago: University of Chicago Law School, 1952.

———. *Law and Economic Growth: The Legal History of the Lumber Industry in Wisconsin, 1836–1915.* Cambridge, Mass.: Harvard University Press, 1964.

———. *Law and Markets in United States History: Different Modes of Bargaining among Interests.* Madison: University of Wisconsin Press, 1982.

———. *The Law of Treason in the United States: Collected Essays.* Westport, Conn.: Greenwood, 1971.

———. "Lawyers in American Society, 1750–1966." *Marquette Law Review* 50 (1967): 594–606.

———. "Legal History: A Research Program." *Wisconsin Law Review* (1942): 323–33.

———. "The Legal Profession." *Wisconsin Law Review* (1966): 969–78.

———. *Modern American Legal History: Forty Classroom Lectures.* Madison: Wisconsin Public Radio, 1978.

———. Review of *The Politics of Democracy*, by Pendleton Herring. *Harvard Law Review* 54 (1941): 714–17.

———. "Treason in the United States." *Harvard Law Review* 58 (1944–45): 226–72, 395–444, 806–57.

———. "The Uses of Law in Four 'Colonial' States of the American Union." *Wisconsin Law Review* (1945): 577–92.

Hyman, Harold M. *A More Perfect Union: The Impact of the Civil War and Reconstruction on the Constitution*. Boston: Houghton Mifflin, 1973.

Ichioka, Yuji. *The Issei: The World of the First Generation Japanese Immigrants, 1885–1924*. New York: Free Press, 1990.

Irons, Peter. "Fancy Dancing in the Marble Palace." *Constitutional Commentary* 3 (1986): 35–60.

———. *Justice at War*. New York: Oxford University Press, 1983.

Isaacs, Nathan. "Judicial Review of Administrative Findings." *Yale Law Journal* 30 (1921): 781–97.

Israel, Fred L. "Military Justice in Hawaii, 1941–1944." *Pacific History Review* 36 (1967): 243–67.

Jackson, Walter A. *Gunnar Myrdal and America's Conscience: Social Engineering and Racial Liberalism, 1938–1987*. Chapel Hill: University of North Carolina Press, 1990.

Jacobs, Meg. "'How About Some Meat?' The Office of Price Administration, Consumption Politics, and State Building from the Bottom Up, 1941–1946." *Journal of American History* 84 (1997): 910–41.

Jaffe, Louis L. "The Effective Limits of the Administrative Process: A Reevaluation." *Harvard Law Review* 67 (1954): 1105–35.

———. *Judicial Control of Administrative Action*. Boston: Little, Brown, 1965.

———. "Judicial Review: 'Substantial Evidence on the Whole Record.'" *Harvard Law Review* 64 (1951): 1233–61.

———. "The Judicial Universe of Mr. Justice Frankfurter." *Harvard Law Review* 65 (1949): 357–412.

James, Scott C. *Presidents, Parties, and the State: A Party System Perspective on Democratic Regulatory Choice, 1884–1936*. New York: Cambridge University Press, 2000.

Janowitz, Morris. "Patterns of Collective Racial Violence." In *Violence in America: Historical and Comparative Perspectives*. Edited by Hugh Davis Graham and Ted Robert Gurr. New York: Signet Books, 1969.

Jeffries, John W. *Testing the Roosevelt Coalition: Connecticut Society and Politics in the Era of World War II*. Knoxville: University of Tennessee Press, 1979.

———. "A 'Third New Deal'? Liberal Policy and the American State, 1937–1945." *Journal of Policy History* 8 (1996): 387–409.

Jensen, Joan. *Passage from India: Asian Indian Immigrants in North America*. New Haven, Conn.: Yale University Press, 1988.

Johnson, James Weldon. *Black Manhattan*. 1930. New York: Da Capo, 1991.

Jones, Carolyn C. "Class Tax to Mass Tax: The Role of Propaganda in the Expansion of the Income Tax during World War II." *Buffalo Law Review* 37 (1989): 685–737.

———. "Split Income and Separate Spheres: Tax Law and Gender Roles in the 1940s." *Law and History Review* 6 (1988): 266–74.

Jones, Jesse, and Edward Angley. *Fifty Billion Dollars: My Thirteen Years with the RFC, 1932–1945*. New York: Macmillan, 1951.

Juran, J. M. *Bureaucracy: A Challenge to Better Management*. New York: Harper & Brothers, 1944.

Kalman, Laura. *Abe Fortas: A Biography*. New Haven, Conn.: Yale University Press, 1990.

———. *Legal Realism at Yale, 1927–1960*. Chapel Hill: University of North Carolina Press, 1986.

Karl, Barry. *The Uneasy State: The United States from 1915 to 1945*. Chicago: University of Chicago Press, 1983.

Katcher, Leo. *Earl Warren: A Political Biography*. New York: McGraw Hill, 1967.

Katznelson, Ira, Kim Geiger, and Daniel Kryder. "Limiting Liberalism: The Southern Veto in Congress, 1933–1950." *Political Science Quarterly* 108 (1993): 283–306.

Katznelson, Ira, and Bruce Pietrykowski. "Rebuilding the American State: Evidence from the 1940s." *Studies in American Political Development* 5 (1991): 301–49.

Kellems, Vivien. *Toil, Taxes and Trouble*. New York: E. P. Dutton, 1952.

Kennedy, David M. *Freedom from Fear: The American People in Depression and War, 1929–1945*. New York: Oxford University Press, 1999.

Kettner, James. *The Development of American Citizenship, 1608–1870*. Chapel Hill: University of North Carolina Press, 1978.

Key, V. O. *Southern Politics in State and Nation*. New York: Knopf, 1949.

Kim, Chin, and Bok Lim Kim. "Asian Immigrants in American Law: A Look at the Past and the Challenge Which Remains." *American University Law Review* 26 (1977): 373–407.

Kim, Hyung-Chan. *A Legal History of Asian Americans, 1790–1990*. Westport, Conn.: Greenwood Press, 1994.

King, Desmond. *Separate and Unequal: Black Americans and the U.S. Federal Government*. New York: Oxford University Press, 1995.

Kluger, Richard. *Simple Justice: The History of Brown v. Board of Education and Black America's Struggle for Equality*. New York: Knopf, 1975.

Koistinen, Paul A. C. "Warfare and Power Relations in America: Mobilizing the World War II Economy." In *The Home Front and War in the Twentieth Century*. Edited by James Titus. Colorado Springs: United States Airforce Academy, Office of Airforce History, 1984.

Kryder, Daniel. "Race Policy, Race Violence, and Race Reform in the U.S. Army during World War II." *Studies in American Political Development* 10 (1996): 130–67.

Kurland, Philip B., and Gerhard Casper, eds. *Landmark Briefs and Arguments of the Supreme Court of the United States: Constitutional Law*. Arlington, Va.: University Publications of America, 1975.

Kutler, Stanley I. *Judicial Power and Reconstruction Politics*. Chicago: University of Chicago Press, 1968.

Lael, Richard L. *The Yamasnıta Precedent: War Crimes and Command Responsibility*. Wilmington, Del.: Scholarly Resources, 1982.

Landis, James. *The Administrative Process*. New Haven, Conn.: Yale University Press, 1938.

Lash, Joseph, ed. *From the Diaries of Felix Frankfurter*. New York: Norton, 1975.
Leff, Mark H. "The Politics of Sacrifice on the American Home Front in World War II." *Journal of American History* 77 (1991): 1296–318.
Leuchtenberg, William E. *Franklin D. Roosevelt and the New Deal, 1932–1940*. New York: Harper & Row, 1963.
———. *The Supreme Court Reborn: The Constitutional Revolution in the Age of Roosevelt*. New York: Oxford University Press, 1995.
Levine, Lawrence W. "Marcus Garvey and the Politics of Revitalization." In *Black Leaders of the Twentieth Century*. Edited by John Hope Franklin and August Meier. Urbana: University of Illinois Press, 1982.
Levy, Eugene. "James Weldon Johnson and the Development of the NAACP." In *Black Leaders of the Twentieth Century*. Edited by John Hope Franklin and August Meier. Urbana: University of Illinois Press, 1982.
Lichtenstein, Nelson. *Labor's War at Home: The CIO in World War II*. New York: Cambridge University Press, 1982.
Lingeman, Richard R. *Don't You Know There's A War On? The American Home Front, 1941–1945*. New York: Putnam, 1970.
Lipsitz, George. *The Possessive Investment in Whiteness: How White People Profit from Identity Politics*. Philadelphia: Temple University Press, 1998.
Logan, Rayford W., ed. *What the Negro Wants*. Chapel Hill: University of North Carolina Press, 1944.
Lurie, Jonathan. *Arming Military Justice*. Vol. 1 of *The Origins of the United States Court of Military Appeals, 1775–1950*. Princeton, N.J.: Princeton University Press, 1992.
MacBride, Roger Lea, ed. *The Lady and the Tycoon: Letters of Rose Wilder Lane and Jasper Crane*. Caldwell, Idaho: Caxton Printers, 1973.
Mansfield, Harvey C. *A Short History of OPA*. Washington, D.C.: U.S. Government Printing Office, 1947.
Manwaring, David. *Render Unto Caesar: The Flag Salute Controversy*. Chicago: University of Chicago Press, 1962.
Mason, Alpheus T. *Harlan Fiske Stone: Pillar of the Law*. New York: Viking, 1956.
———. *Security through Freedom: American Political Thought and Practice*. Ithaca: Cornell University Press, 1955.
Matson, Robert W. *Neutrality and Navicerts: Britain, the United States, and Economic Warfare, 1939–1940*. New York: Garland, 1994.
May, Elaine Tyler. *Homeward Bound: American Families in the Cold War Era*. New York: Basic Books, 1988.
McAdam, Doug. *Political Process and the Development of Black Insurgency, 1930–1970*. Chicago: University of Chicago Press, 1982.
McCaffery, Edward J. *Taxing Women*. Chicago: University of Chicago Press, 1997.
McCarran, Pat. "Improving 'Administrative Justice.'" *American Bar Association Journal* 32 (1946): 827–31, 893–94.
McClain, Charles, Jr. *The Search for Equality: The Chinese Struggle Against Discrimination in Nineteenth Century America*. Berkeley: University of California Press, 1994.
McEvoy, Arthur F. "Willard Hurst's Scholarship: Pragmatism and Morality." *Wisconsin Law Review* (1997): 1191–1203.

McGuire, O. R. "Administrative Law and American Democracy." *American Bar Association Journal* 25 (1939): 393–99, 435.

McWilliams, Carey. *Prejudice. The Japanese Americans: A Symbol of Racial Intolerance.* New York: Public Affairs Committee, 1944.

Meier, August, and Elliot Rudwick. *Black Detroit and the Rise of the UAW.* New York: Oxford University Press, 1979.

Milkman, Ruth. *Gender at Work: The Dynamics of Job Segregation by Sex during World War II.* Chicago: University of Chicago Press, 1987.

Miscamble, Wilson D. "Thurman Arnold Goes to Washington: A Look at Antitrust Policy in the Later New Deal." *Business History Review* 56 (1982): 1–15.

Morison, Samuel Eliot. *The Battle of the Atlantic, September 1939–May 1943.* Vol. 1 of *History of United States Naval Operations in World War II.* Boston: Little, Brown, 1975.

Mowry, George E. *The California Progressives.* Berkeley: University of California Press, 1951.

Munson, F. Granville. "The Arguments in the Saboteur Trial." *University of Pennsylvania Law Review* 91 (1942): 239–52.

Murphy, Bruce Allen. *The Brandeis/Frankfurter Connection.* New York: Oxford University Press, 1982.

Murphy, Paul L. *The Constitution in Crisis Times, 1918–1969.* New York: Harper & Row, 1972.

Myer, Dillon. *Uprooted Americans: The Japanese Americans and the War Relocation Authority during World War II.* Tucson: University of Arizona Press, 1971.

Myrdal, Gunnar. *An American Dilemma: The Negro Problem and Modern Democracy.* New York: Harper & Brothers, 1944.

Nagle, James F. *A History of Government Contracting.* Washington, D.C.: George Washington University, 1992.

Nash, George H. *The Conservative Intellectual Movement in America since 1945.* Wilmington, Del.: Intercollegiate Studies Institute, 1998.

Neely, Mark E. *The Fate of Liberty: Abraham Lincoln and Civil Liberties.* New York: Oxford University Press, 1991.

Nelson, William. "The Changing Meaning of Equality in Twentieth Century Constitutional Law." *Washington and Lee Law Review* 52 (1995): 3–103.

———. *The Legalist Reformation: Law, Politics and Ideology in New York, 1920–1980.* Chapel Hill: University of North Carolina Press, 2001.

Nicholls, William H., and John A. Vieg. *Wartime Government in Operation.* Philadelphia: Blakiston, 1943.

Nixon, Richard M. *The Memoirs of Richard Nixon.* New York: Grosset & Dunlap, 1978.

Nonet, Philippe. *Administrative Justice: Advocacy and Change in a Government Agency.* New York: Russell Sage, 1969.

Nostrad, Lauris. "W. Barton Leach: In His Country's Service." *Harvard Law Review* 85 (1972): 726–28.

Ogden, August Raymond. *The Dies Committee: A Study of the Special House Committee for the Investigation of Un-American Activities, 1938–1944.* 2d ed. Washington, D.C.: Catholic University of America, 1945.

O'Leary, Paul M. "Wartime Rationing and Governmental Organization." *American Political Science Review* 39 (1945): 1089–106.

Oppenheimer, Reuben. "The War Price and Rationing Boards: An Experiment in Decentralization." *Columbia Law Review* 43 (1943): 147–64.

Orren, Karen, and Stephen Skowronek. "Regimes and Regime Building in American Government: A Review of the Literature on the 1940s." *Political Science Quarterly* 113 (1998–99): 689–702.

Paludan, Phillip S. *A Covenant with Death: The Constitution, Law, and Equality in the Civil War Era.* Urbana: University of Illinois Press, 1975.

Parrish, Michael E. *Felix Frankfurter and His Times: The Reform Years.* New York: Free Press, 1982.

———. "The Hughes Court, the Great Depression, and the Historians." *Historian* 40 (1978): 286–308.

———. "Justice Frankfurter and the Supreme Court." In *The Jewish Justices of the Supreme Court Revisited: From Brandeis to Fortas.* Edited by Jennifer Lowe. Washington, D.C.: Supreme Court Historical Society, 1994.

Paul, Randolph E. *Taxation in the United States.* Boston: Little, Brown, 1954.

Pells, Richard. *The Liberal Mind in a Conservative Age: American Intellectuals in the 1940s and 1950s.* New York: Harper & Row, 1985.

Piccigallo, Philip R. *The Japanese on Trial: Allied War Crimes Operations in the East, 1945–1951.* Austin: University of Texas Press, 1979.

Plotke, David. *Building a Democratic Order: Reshaping American Liberalism in the 1930s and 1940s.* New York: Cambridge University Press, 1996.

Polenberg, Richard. "The Decline of the New Deal, 1937–1940." In *The New Deal: The National Level.* Edited by John Braeman, Robert H. Bremner, and David Brody. Columbus: Ohio State University Press, 1975.

———. "The Good War? A Reappraisal of How World War II Affected American Society." *Virginia Magazine of History and Biography* 100 (1992): 295–322.

———. *One Nation Divisible: Class, Race, and Ethnicity in the United States Since 1938.* New York: Penguin, 1980.

———. *Reorganizing Roosevelt's Government: The Controversy over Executive Reorganization, 1936–1939.* Cambridge, Mass.: Harvard University Press, 1966.

———. *War and Society: The United States, 1941–1945.* Philadelphia: Lippincott, 1972.

———. "World War II and the Bill of Rights." In *The Home-Front War: World War II and American Society.* Edited by Kenneth Paul O'Brien and Lynn Hudson Parsons. Westport, Conn.: Greenwood Press, 1995.

Pound, Roscoe. "A Theory of Social Interests." *Publications of the American Sociological Society* 15 (1921): 16–45.

Pressman, Steven. "An American Dilemma: Fifty Years Later." *Journal of Economic Issues* 28 (1994): 577–85.

Pritchett, C. Herman. *The Roosevelt Court: A Study in Judicial Values.* New York: MacMillan, 1948.

Purcell, Edward A., Jr. "American Jurisprudence between the Wars: Legal Realism and the Crisis of Democratic Theory." *American Historical Review* 74 (1969): 424–46.

———. *The Crisis of Democratic Theory: Scientific Naturalism and the Problem of Value.* Louisville: University of Kentucky Press, 1973.

Puttkammer, Ernst W., ed. *War and the Law.* Chicago: University of Chicago Press, 1944.

Quarles, Benjamin. "A. Philip Randolph: Labor Leader at Large." In *Black Leaders of the Twentieth Century*. Edited by John Hope Franklin and August Meier. Urbana: University of Illinois Press, 1982.

Rachlis, Eugene. *They Came to Kill: The Story of Eight Nazi Saboteurs in America*. New York: Popular Library, 1961.

Radford, Gail. "William Gibbs McAdoo, the Emergency Fleet Corporation, and the Origins of the Public-Authority Model of Government Action." *Journal of Policy History* 11 (1999): 59–88.

Radin, Max. Review of *Law in Society*, by Lloyd K. Garrison and Willard Hurst. *Harvard Law Review* 54 (1941): 1082–87.

Randall, James G. *Constitutional Problems under Lincoln*. Urbana: University of Illinois Press, 1951.

Rehnquist, William H. *All the Laws But One: Civil Liberties in Wartime*. New York: Knopf, 1998.

Reich, Cary. *The Life of Nelson A. Rockefeller: Worlds to Conquer, 1908–1958*. New York: Doubleday, 1996.

Riddle, Donald H. *The Truman Commission: A Study in Congressional Responsibility*. New Brunswick, N.J.: Rutgers University Press, 1964.

Ringer, Benjamin. *"We the People" and Others: Duality and America's Treatment of Its Racial Minorities*. New York: Tavistock Publications, 1983.

Root, Elihu. "Public Service by the Bar." *Reports of the American Bar Association* (1916): 355–74.

Rosenof, Theodore. "Freedom, Planning and Totalitarianism: The Reception of F. A. Hayek's *Road to Serfdom*." *Canadian Review of American Studies* 5 (1974): 149–65.

Rossiter, Clinton. *Conservatism in America*. 2d ed. Cambridge, Mass.: Harvard University Press, 1982.

Rostow, Eugene V. "The Japanese-American Cases—A Disaster." *Yale Law Journal* 54 (1945): 489–533.

Rothbard, Murray N. *For a New Liberty: The Libertarian Manifesto*. Rev. ed. New York: Libertarian Review Foundation, 1989.

Rueschemeyer, Dietrich. "Comparing Legal Professions: A State-Centered Approach." *Lawyers in Society: Comparative Theories*. Edited by R. L. Abel and P.S.C. Lewis. Berkeley: University of California Press, 1989.

Rupp, Leila J. *Mobilizing Women for War: German and American Propaganda, 1939–1945*. Princeton, N.J.: Princeton University Press, 1978.

Rupp, Leila J. and Verta Taylor. *Survival in the Doldrums: The American Women's Rights Movement, 1945 to the 1960s*. New York: Oxford University Press, 1987.

Sandler, Stanley. "Homefront Battlefront: Military Racial Disturbances in the Zone of the Interior, 1941–1945." Paper presented at the annual meeting of the American Historical Association, Chicago, Ill., December 1991.

Sanger, Quintin M. *Administrative History of the Foreign Economic Administration and Predecessor Agencies*. Washington, D.C.: Office of the Historian, Foreign Economic Administration, 1946.

Satterfield, Archie. *The Home Front: An Oral History of the War Years in America, 1941–1945*. New York: Playboy Press, 1981.

Schapsmeier, Edward L., and Frederick H. Schapsmeier. *Prophet in Politics: Henry A. Wallace and the War Years, 1940–1965*. Ames: Iowa State University Press, 1970.

Scheiber, Harry N., and Jane L. Scheiber. "Bayonets in Paradise: A Half-Century Retrospect on Martial Law in Hawai'i, 1941–1946." *University of Hawai'i Law Review* 19 (1997): 477–648.

———. "Constitutional Liberty in World War II: Army Rule and Martial Law in Hawaii, 1941–1946." *Western Legal History* 3 (1990): 340–78.

Schiller, Reuel E. "Enlarging the Administrative Polity: Administrative Law and the Changing Definition of Pluralism, 1945–1970." *Vanderbilt Law Review* 53 (2000): 1389–1453.

———. "Policy Ideals and Judicial Action: Expertise, Group Pluralism, and Participatory Democracy in Intellectual Thought and Legal Decision-Making, 1932–1970." Ph.D. diss., University of Virginia, 1997.

Schilling, George T. "Saboteurs and the Jurisdiction of Military Commissions." *Michigan Law Review* 41 (1942): 481–95.

Seidman, Joel. *American Labor From Defense to Reconversion*. Chicago: University of Chicago Press, 1953.

Severn, Bill. *Mr. Chief Justice: Earl Warren*. New York: D. McKay, 1968.

Shamir, Ronen. *Managing Legal Uncertainty: Elite Lawyers in the New Deal*. Durham, N.C.: Duke University Press, 1995.

Sharfman, I. Leo. *The Interstate Commerce Commission: A Study in Administrative Law and Procedure*. 5 vols. New York: Commonwealth Fund, 1931.

Shefter, Martin. *Political Parties and the State: The American Historical Experience*. Princeton, N.J.: Princeton University Press, 1994.

Shepherd, George B. "Fierce Compromise: The Administrative Procedure Act Emerges from New Deal Politics." *Northwestern University Law Review* 90 (1996): 1557–683.

Sherry, Michael S. *In the Shadow of War: The United States since the 1930s*. New Haven, Conn.: Yale University Press, 1995.

Siegel, Reva. "'The Rule of Love': Wife Beating as Prerogative and Privacy." *Yale Law Journal* 105 (1996): 2117–207.

Simon, James F. *The Antagonists: Hugo Black, Felix Frankfurter and Civil Liberties in Modern America*. New York: Simon & Schuster, 1989.

Sirevag, Torborn. *The Eclipse of the New Deal and the Fall of Vice President Wallace, 1944*. New York: Garland, 1985.

Sitkoff, Harvard. "Racial Militancy and Interracial Violence in the Second World War." *Journal of American History* 58 (1971): 661–81.

Skocpol, Theda. *Protecting Soldiers and Mothers: The Political Origins of Social Policy in the United States*. Cambridge, Mass.: Harvard University Press, 1992.

Skocpol, Theda, and Kenneth Finegold. "Explaining New Deal Labor Policy." *American Political Science Review* 84 (1990): 1297–1304.

Skowronek, Stephen. *Building a New American State: The Expansion of National Administrative Capacities, 1877–1920*. New York: Cambridge University Press, 1982.

Slemrod, Joel. "Which Is the Simplest Tax System of Them All?" In *Economic Effects of Fundamental Tax Reform*. Edited by Henry J. Aaron and William G. Gale. Washington, D.C.: Brookings Institution Press, 1996.

Smith, Page. *Democracy on Trial: The Japanese-American Evacuation and Relocation in World War II*. New York: Simon & Schuster, 1995.

Smith, Rogers. *Civic Ideals: Conflicting Visions of Citizenship in U.S. History*. New Haven, Conn.: Yale University Press, 1997.

Soifer, Aviam. "In Retrospect: Willard Hurst, Consensus History, and *The Growth of American Law*." *Reviews in American History* 20 (1992): 124–44.

Southern, David W. *Gunnar Myrdal and Black-White Relations: The Use and Abuse of An American Dilemma, 1944–1969*. Baton Rouge: Louisiana State University Press, 1994.

Sparrow, Bartholomew H. *From the Outside In: World War II and the American State*. Princeton, N.J.: Princeton University Press, 1996.

Stason, E. Blythe. "'Substantial Evidence' in Administrative Law." *University of Pennsylvania Law Review* 89 (1941): 1026–51.

Stone, I. F. *Business as Usual: The First Year of Defense*. New York: Modern Age, 1941.

———. *The War Years, 1939–1945*. Boston: Little, Brown, 1988.

Surrey, Stanley. "Federal Taxation of the Family—The Revenue Act of 1948." *Harvard Law Review* 61 (1948): 1097–164.

Takaki, Ronald. *Strangers from a Different Shore: A History of Asian Americans*. Boston: Little, Brown, 1989.

Taylor, Telford. *Nuremberg and Vietnam: An American Tragedy*. Chicago: Quadrangle Books, 1970.

Tedlow, Richard S. *Keeping the Corporate Image: Public Relations and Business, 1900–1950*. Greenwich, Conn.: JAI Press, 1979.

tenBroek, Jacobus, Edward N. Barnhart, and Floyd W. Matson. *Prejudice, War and the Constitution*. Berkeley: California University Press, 1954.

Thurston, John. Review of *The Administrative Process*, by James M. Landis. *American Political Science Review* 33 (1939): 336–42.

Tocqueville, Alexis de. *Democracy in America*. New York: Knopf, 1951.

Tully, Grace. *F.D.R.: My Boss*. New York: Scribner's, 1949.

Tushnet, Mark V. "Lumber and the Legal Process." *Wisconsin Law Review* (1972): 114–32.

U.S. Bureau of the Census. *Historical Statistics of the United States: Colonial Times to 1970*. Washington, D.C.: U.S. Government Printing Office, 1975.

U.S. Commission on Wartime Relocation and Internment of Civilians. *Personal Justice Denied: Report of the Commission on Wartime Relocation and Internment of Civilians*. Washington, D.C.: Government Printing Office, 1982.

U.S. Office of Inter-American Affairs. *History of the Office of the Coordinator of Inter-American Affairs*. Washington, D.C.: U.S. Government Printing Office, 1947.

Urofsky, Melvin I. "The Court at War and the War at the Court." *Journal of Supreme Court History*. 1996. Vol. 1. Pp. 1–18.

———. *Division and Discord: The Supreme Court under Stone and Vinson, 1941–1953*. Columbia: University of South Carolina Press, 1997.

Vatter, Harold G. *The U.S. Economy in World War II*. New York: Columbia University Press, 1985.

Vickrey, William. *Agenda for Progressive Taxation*. New York: Ronald Press, 1947.

Waddell, Brian. "Corporate Influence and World War II: Resolving the New Deal Political Stalemate." *Journal of Policy History* 11 (1999): 223–56.

———. "Economic Mobilization for World War II and the Transformation of the U.S. State." *Politics and Society* 22 (1994): 165–94.

Walsh, Annmarie Houck. *The Public's Business: The Politics and Practices of Government Corporations.* Cambridge, Mass.: MIT Press, 1978.

Warren, Earl. "The Bill of Rights and the Military." *New York University Law Review* 37 (1962): 181–203.

———. *The Memoirs of Earl Warren.* Garden City, N.Y.: Doubleday, 1977.

Washburn, Patrick S. *A Question of Sedition: The Federal Government's Investigation of the Black Press during World War II.* New York: Oxford University Press, 1986.

Weaver, Robert C. *Negro Labor: A National Problem.* New York: Harcourt, Brace and Company, 1946.

Weglyn, Michi. *Years of Infamy: The Untold Story of America's Concentration Camps.* New York: Morrow, 1976.

Weir, Margaret, Ann Shola Orloff, and Theda Skocpol. *The Politics of Social Policy in the United States.* Princeton, N.J.: Princeton University Press, 1988.

Wesley, Charles H. "The Negro Has Always Wanted the Four Freedoms." *What the Negro Wants.* Edited by Rayford W. Logan. Chapel Hill: University of North Carolina Press, 1944.

Weyl, Nathaniel. *The Reconquest of Mexico.* New York: Oxford University Press, 1939.

White, G. Edward. *The Constitution and the New Deal.* Cambridge, Mass.: Harvard University Press, 2000.

———. *Earl Warren: A Public Life.* New York: Oxford University Press, 1982.

———. *Intervention and Detachment: Essays in Legal History and Jurisprudence.* New York: Oxford University Press, 1994.

———. *Patterns of American Legal Thought.* Indianapolis: Bobbs-Merrill, 1978.

Wilder, Laura Ingalls. *The Long Winter.* 1940. New York: Harper Trophy Book, 1971.

Wildman, Stephanie. *Privilege Revealed: How Invisible Preference Undermines America.* New York: New York University Press, 1996.

Will, George F. "The Cultural Contradictions of Conservatism." *Public Interest* (1996): 40–55.

Witte, John F. *The Politics and Development of the Federal Income Tax.* Madison: University of Wisconsin Press, 1985.

Yamamoto, Eric K. *Interracial Justice: Conflict and Reconciliation in Post-Civil Rights America.* New York: New York University Press, 1999.

Yarbrough, Tinsley E. *Mr. Justice Black and His Critics.* Durham, N.C.: Duke University Press, 1988.

Young, Ronald. *Congressional Politics in the Second World War.* New York: Columbia University Press, 1956.

Index

About the Contributors

DANIEL R. ERNST is Professor of Law at the Georgetown University Law Center. His book, *Lawyers against Labor* (1995), received the Littleton Griswold Prize of the American Historical Association. He is also the author of "Willard Hurst and the Administrative State: From Williams to Wisconsin," *Law and History Review* (2000).

VICTOR JEW is an Assistant Professor of History at Michigan State University. He received his Ph.D. in United States history from the University of Wisconsin, Madison and has taught at the University of Wisconsin, Madison and Cornell University. Specializing in U.S. legal and constitutional history and Asian American history, he is the author of "Exploring Frontiers in Chinese American History: The Anti-Chinese Riot in Milwaukee, 1889," in *The Chinese in America: A History from Gold Mountain to the New Millennium*, ed. Susie Lan Cassel (2002).

SUMI CHO is a Professor of Law at the DePaul College of Law. The holder of a J.D. and a Ph.D. in Ethnic Studies from University of California at Berkeley, she served as coordinator of a symposium issue of the *Boston College Law Review* and *Boston College Third World Law Journal*, published in 1998 and entitled "The Long Shadow of *Korematsu*." The symposium was funded by the U.S. Congress to study the redress of and reparations for the Japanese American internment.

CAROLYN C. JONES is Professor of Law at the University of Connecticut School of Law. She is the author of many articles and book chapters that study the history of taxation and its intersection with American culture, including "Class Tax to Mass Tax: The Role of Propaganda in the Expansion of the Income Tax during World War II," *Buffalo Law Review* (1989), "Split Incomes and Separate Spheres: Tax Law and Gender Roles in the 1940s," *Law and History Review* (1999), and "Hard Shells of Community: Tax Equity Debates within the National Council of Churches after World War II," *Tax Justice* (forthcoming).

DANIEL KRYDER is Visiting Associate Professor of Political Science at Johns Hopkins University. He is the author of *Divided Arsenal: Race and the American State during World War II* (2000). He is currently researching twentieth-century presidents, war, and race policies and the role of history in policy debates and social scientific methods.

REUEL E. SCHILLER is a Professor of Law at the University of California, Hastings College of the Law. He is the author of several articles on the relationship between courts and the administrative state in twentieth-century America, including "Rulemaking's Promise: Administrative Law and Legal Culture in the 1960s and 1970s," *Administrative Law Review* (2001), and "Enlarging the Administrative Polity: Administrative Law and the Changing Definition of Pluralism, 1945–1970," *Vanderbilt Law Review* (2000). He is at work on a book on the same subject.

MELVIN I. UROFSKY is Professor of History and Public Policy at Virginia Commonwealth University and head of the doctoral program in public policy and administration. He is the author or editor of more than forty books, the most recent of which are *Division and Discord: The Supreme Court under Stone and Vinson, 1941–1953* (1997), *Lethal Judgments: Assisted Suicide and American Law* (2000), and *Religious Freedom: Rights and Liberties under the Law* (2002). He also serves as editor of the *Journal of Supreme Court History*.

WILLIAM M. WIECEK is the Congdon Professor of Public Law and Professor of History in the Maxwell School of Syracuse University. He is a constitutional and legal historian who has written on the United States Supreme Court, slavery and its abolition, and the evolution of constitutional doctrines in both professional and political discourse. He has recently completed a history of the Supreme Court from 1941 to 1953 for the "Holmes Devise History of the Supreme Court of the United States" series. He is presently at work on a project involving the private law of slavery.